W9-CZZ-219

A Pocket Guide to Public Speaking

A Pocket Guide to Public Speaking

Getting Started ■ Development ■ Organization ■ Starting, Finishing, and Styling ■ Delivery ■ Presentation Aids ■ Types of Speeches ■ The Classroom and Beyond ■ Citation Guidelines

Dan O'Hair
University of Oklahoma

Hannah Rubenstein

Rob Stewart
Texas Tech University

Bedford / St. Martin's   Boston   ◆   New York

For Bedford / St. Martin's

Developmental Editor: Simon Glick
Editorial Assistant: Alice Mack
Senior Production Editor: Shuli Traub
Senior Production Supervisor: Dennis J. Conroy
Marketing Manager: Richard Cadman
Art Director: Lucy Krikorian
Text Design: Claire Seng-Niemoeller
Copy Editor: Sally Scott
Cover Design: Donna Lee Dennison
Composition: Stratford Publishing Services, Inc.
Printing and Binding: Quebecor World Kingsport

President: Joan E. Feinberg
Editorial Director: Denise B. Wydra
Publisher for Communication: Patricia Rossi
Director of Marketing: Karen Melton Soeltz
Director of Editing, Design, and Production: Marcia Cohen
Managing Editor: Erica T. Appel

Library of Congress Control Number: 2003107545

9 8 7 6 5 4
f e d c b a

For information, write: Bedford / St. Martin's, 75 Arlington
Street, Boston, MA 02116   (617-399-4000)

ISBN: 0-312-40078-0

How to Use This Book

A Pocket Guide to Public Speaking has been designed with today's busy student in mind. Increasingly, speeches and oral presentations are a required part of the curriculum, and you will need concise and accessible guidelines to help you fulfill assignments. *A Pocket Guide to Public Speaking* addresses this need. Whether enrolled in an introductory public speaking class or a course in your major, you will find the tools you need to prepare and deliver a wide range of speeches and presentations.

In Parts 1 through 6 you will find chapters covering all the steps necessary to create a speech — from planning, research, and development, to organization, practice, and delivery. Chapters beginning in Part 7 contain guidelines for creating three of the most commonly assigned types of speeches in public speaking classes: *informative, persuasive,* and *special occasion.* For specific guidelines on speaking in other college classes, in small groups, and on the job, see Part 8.

Finding What You Need

TABLES OF CONTENTS. The brief contents inside the front cover will usually guide you to the information you need. If not, consult the more detailed contents inside the back cover.

INDEX. If you can't locate what you need in either set of contents, consult the index at the back of the book. For example, if you need to prepare a sales presentation for a business course, simply look under "sales presentations," and then go to the designated pages.

CHECKLISTS AND QUICK TIPS. Throughout the book, Checklists summarize key information, while Quick Tips offer practical advice. See pp. 276–77 for a list of these tools and their page references.

SPEAKING BEYOND THE SPEECH CLASSROOM. For help on preparing assignments outside of the public speaking classroom, turn to Part 8, "The Classroom and Beyond." Here you will find detailed directions for speaking in a range of college classes — the social sciences, humanities, education, business, science, and engineering — plus chapters on communicating effectively in groups and on the job.

GLOSSARY.   To locate definitions of terms highlighted in the book, see this helpful study tool beginning on p. 235.

Quick Speech Preparation

If you must prepare a speech quickly (as in giving a first speech early in the semester), try using *A Pocket Guide* as follows:

- Review Chapter 1, "Becoming a Public Speaker," for a brief discussion of key public speaking basics.

- Review Chapter 5, "From A to Z: Overview of a Speech," for a summary of each step in the speechmaking process, from selecting a topic to delivery.

- To help overcome any fears you may have, review Chapter 6, "Managing Speech Anxiety."

- For more on specific types of speeches , consult Chapters 23–25 on informative, persuasive, or special occasion speeches, or the appropriate chapter in Part 8.

Other Useful Tools

CITATION GUIDELINES.   Appendix A (pp. 214–25) contains guidelines for documenting sources in the following styles: *Chicago,* American Psychological Association (APA), Modern Language Association (MLA), Council of Biological Editors (CBE), and Institute of Electrical and Electronic Engineers (IEEE).

TIPS FOR NON-NATIVE SPEAKERS OF ENGLISH.   Appendix D (pp. 229–33) addresses the most common ESL challenges, including difficulty pronouncing words and problems in being understood.

A Pocket Guide to Public Speaking is designed to provide you with a complete overview of the speechmaking process and is a ready resource to be used as the need arises. We wish you much success as you master the indispensable art of public speaking!

A Pocket
Guide to
Public
Speaking

Part 1
Getting Started

1 Becoming a Public Speaker

The ability to speak confidently and convincingly in public is an asset to anyone who wants to take an active role in his or her classroom, workplace, or community. As you master the skills of public speaking, you will find that it is a powerful vehicle for professional and personal growth. In a recent survey of employers, for example, oral communication skills ranked first in such critical areas as interpersonal, analytical, teamwork, and computer skills.

TOP FOUR PERSONAL QUALITIES EMPLOYERS SEEK	
RANK	TYPE OF PREFERRED SKILLS
1	Communication skills
2	Honesty/integrity
3	Teamwork skills
4	Interpersonal skills

Source: Job Outlook 2002, a survey conducted by the National Association of Colleges and Employers, 2002.

Public-speaking training sharpens your ability to reason and think critically. As you study public speaking, you will learn to construct claims and then present evidence and reasoning that logically support them. As you practice organizing and outlining speeches, you will become skilled at structuring ideas and identifying and strengthening the weak links in your thinking.

Whatever you care deeply about, from the environment to lower taxes, public speaking offers a way to express your values and communicate your concerns with others in a civil dialogue.

Public Speaking as a Form of Communication

Public speaking is one of four categories of human communication: dyadic, small group, mass, and public speaking. **Dyadic communication** is a form of communication between two people, as in a conversation. **Small group communication** involves a small number of people who can see and speak directly with one another. **Mass communication** occurs between a speaker and a large audience of unknown people who are usually not present with the speaker, or they are part of such an immense crowd that there can be little or no interaction between speaker and listener.

In **public speaking**, a speaker delivers a message with a specific purpose to an audience of people who are present

Public Speaking Is Linked to Career Success
According to a report titled What Students Must Know to Succeed in the 21st Century, *"Clear communication is critical to success. In the marketplace of ideas, the person who communicates clearly is also the person who is seen as thinking clearly. Oral and written communication are not only job-securing, but job-holding skills."* [1]

during the delivery of the speech. Public speaking always includes a speaker who has a reason for speaking, an audience that gives the speaker its attention, and a message that is meant to accomplish a specific purpose.[2] Public speakers address audiences largely without interruption and take responsibility for the words and ideas being expressed.

Public speaking shares many features of the other forms of communication, but, because the speaker is the focal point of attention in what is usually a formal setting, listeners expect a more systematic presentation than they do in conversation or small groups. As such, public speaking requires more preparation and practice than the other forms of communication.

Elements in the Communication Process

In any communication event, including public speaking, several elements are present. These include the source, the receiver, the message, the channel, and shared meaning (see Figure 1.1).

The **source**, or sender, is the person who creates a message. Creating, organizing, and producing the message is called **encoding**—the process of converting thoughts into words.

The recipient of the source's message is the **receiver**, or audience. The process of interpreting the message is called **decoding**. Audience members decode the meaning of the message selectively, based on their own experiences and attitudes. **Feedback**, the audience's response to a message, can be conveyed both verbally and nonverbally.

The **message** is the content of the communication process: thoughts and ideas put into meaningful expressions, expressed verbally and nonverbally.

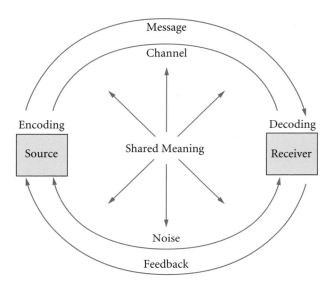

FIGURE 1.1 The Communication Process

The medium through which the speaker sends a message is the **channel**. If a speaker is delivering a message in front of a live audience, the channel is the air through which sound waves travel. Other channels include the telephone, television, computers, and written correspondence. **Noise** is any interference with the message. Noise can disrupt the communication process through physical sounds such as cell phones ringing and people talking, through psychological distractions such as heated emotions, and through environmental interference such as a frigid room or the presence of unexpected people.

Shared meaning is the mutual understanding of a message between speaker and audience. The lowest level of shared meaning exists when the speaker has merely caught the audience's attention. As the message develops, a higher degree of shared meaning is possible. Thus listener and speaker together truly make a speech a speech—they "co-create" its meaning.

Two other factors are critical to consider when preparing and delivering a speech. The **rhetorical situation** includes anything that influences the speaker, the audience, the speech, or occasion. In classroom speeches, it would include (among other things) the speech assignment, the physical setting, the quality of other speakers' presentations, and recent events on campus or in the outside world. Bearing the rhetorical situation in mind ensures that you remain *audience centered*.

A clearly defined *speech purpose* or goal is a prerequisite for an effective speech. What is it that you want the audience to learn or do or believe as a result of your speech? Establishing a speech purpose early in the speechmaking process will help you proceed through speech preparation and delivery with a clear focus in mind.

QUICK TIP

Adopt an Audience Perspective

Speakers who don't know or don't understand their audience (the receivers) are likely to deliver ineffective or inappropriate messages. Whether speaking to an audience of one or one hundred, always adopt an **audience perspective** *— that is, try to determine the needs, attitudes, and values of your audience before drafting your speech.*

The Classical Roots of Public Speaking

Public speaking is a discipline with a long history dating back to before Aristotle (384–322 B.C.E.). Originally the practice of giving speeches was known as **oratory** or **rhetoric**. Ancient public speaking emerged full-force in Greece in the fifth century B.C.E. and became an essential tool in settling civil disputes, determining public policy, and establishing laws. From the beginning, public speakers, notably Aristotle and Cicero (106–43 B.C.E.), divided the process of preparing a speech into five parts, called the **canons of rhetoric**. *Invention* refers to adapting speech information to the audience in order to make your case. *Arrangement* is organizing the speech in ways best suited to the topic and audience. *Style* is the way the speaker uses language to express the speech ideas. *Memory* and *delivery* are the methods of rehearsing and presenting the speech so that you achieve the most effective blend of content, voice, and nonverbal behavior.

Although scholars such as Aristotle and Cicero surely didn't anticipate the omnipresent PowerPoint slideshow that accompanies so many contemporary speeches, the speechmaking structure they bequeathed to us as the canons of rhetoric remain remarkably intact. While often identified by terms other than the original, these canons continue to be taught in current books on public speaking, including this pocket guide.

Learning to Speak in Public

Learning to speak in public can be made less daunting when you realize that you can draw on related skills that you already have.

Draw on Familiar Skills

Planning and delivering a speech is much the same as engaging in a particularly important conversation. When speaking with a friend, you automatically check to make certain that you are understood and then adjust your meaning accordingly. You also tend to discuss issues that are appropriate to the circumstances. When a relative stranger is involved, however, you try to get to know his or her interests and attitudes before revealing any strong opinions. These instinctive adjustments to your audience, topic, and occasion represent critical steps in creating a speech. Although the means of discovery are more involved in public speaking, both the conversationalist and the public speaker try to uncover the audience's interests and needs before speaking.

Preparing a speech also has much in common with writing. For example, as author Robert Perrin notes, both effective speaking and effective writing depend on having a focused sense of who the audience is.[3] Both speaking and writing often require that you research a topic, offer credible evidence, use effective transitions to signal the logical flow of ideas, and use persuasive appeals. Perrin notes that the principles of organizing a speech parallel those of organizing an essay and include offering a compelling introduction, a clear thesis statement, supporting ideas, and a thoughtful conclusion.

Recognize Public Speaking's Unique Requirements

Although public speaking has much in common with everyday conversation and with writing, it is, obviously, "its own thing." More so than writers, successful speakers generally use familiar words, easy-to-follow sentences, and straightforward syntax (subject-verb-object agreement). Oral language is often more interactive and inclusive of the audience than written language. The personal pronouns *we, I,* and *you* occur more frequently in spoken than in written text. Audience members want to know what the speaker thinks and feels and that he or she recognizes them and relates them to the message. Yet because public speaking usually occurs in more formal settings than does everyday conversation, listeners expect a somewhat more formal style of communication from the speaker. When you give a speech, listeners expect you to speak in a clear, recognizable, and organized fashion. Thus, in contrast to conversation, in order to develop an effective oral style you must practice the words you will say and the way you will say them.

Become a Culturally Sensitive Speaker

Every audience member wants to feel that the speaker has his or her particular needs and interests at heart, and everyone wants to feel recognized and included in the speaker's message. To create this sense of inclusion, the public speaker must attempt to understand the audience's beliefs and norms and be culturally sensitive. Culturally sensitive speakers assume differences exist and address them with interest and respect. The flip side of cultural sensitivity is **ethnocentrism,** the belief that the ways of one's own culture are superior to those of other cultures. No matter how passionately they believe in an issue, our most admired public speakers strive to acknowledge and respectfully consider alternative viewpoints.

2   Ethical Public Speaking

Public speakers are in a unique position to influence or persuade others and, at times, move them to act—for better or for worse. With this unique power to affect the minds and hearts of others comes *responsibility*—moral, legal, or mental accountability.[1] Taking responsibility for your message lies at the heart of being an ethical public speaker.

Influence Others Responsibly

As a public speaker, you can establish with audience members a positive sense of what the ancient Greek scholar Aristotle termed **ethos**—and what modern scholars term *character*—by doing the following:

- Ensure that your speech appeals to the greater good and is not just an expression of narrow self-interest.
- Develop your speech with the audience's best interests in mind.
- Treat your listeners with dignity and respect.
- Behave with integrity.

Know the Difference between Legal and Ethical Speech

Codes of ethical speech are built on moral rather than legal principles. Thus the **First Amendment** assures protection both to speakers who treat the truth with respect and to those whose words are inflammatory and offensive. Though often legally protected, racist, sexist, homophobic, pornographic, and other forms of negative speech are clearly *unethical* and should be avoided at all costs. Certain types of speech are actually *illegal,* however:

- Speech that provokes people to violence ("incitement" or "fighting words")
- Speech that can be proved to be **defamatory,** or that potentially harms an individual's reputation at work or in the community
- Certain kinds of speech that invade a person's privacy

How can you tell if your speech contains defamatory language? If you are talking about public figures or matters of public concern, you will not be legally liable unless it can be shown that you spoke with a **reckless disregard for the truth**—that is, if you knew that what you were saying was false but said it anyway. If your comments refer to private persons, it will be easier for them to assert a claim for defamation. You will have the burden of proving that what you said was true.[2]

Respect Audience Values

Our ethical conduct is a reflection of our **values**—our most enduring judgments or standards of what's good and bad in life, of what's important to us. Like human behavior itself, values are not a tidy affair. Clashes of values—within individuals and between groups—are a fact of life in all societies. The more diverse the society, the greater these clashes tend to be. For this reason, it is especially important that you not only recognize but also respect an audience's values—even when they diverge from your own.

Observe Ethical Ground Rules

The qualities of dignity and integrity should infuse every aspect of a speech. **Dignity** refers to "feeling worthy, honored, or respected as a person."[3] **Integrity** refers to incorruptibility—the ability to avoid compromise for the sake of personal expediency.[4] Ethical speaking also requires that we adhere to certain ethical ground rules, or, in the words of ethicist Michael Josephson, "pillars of character."[5] These include being trustworthy, respectful, responsible, and fair in our presentations.

Trustworthiness is a combination of honesty and dependability. It includes revealing your true purpose to your audience—and not sacrificing the truth to it; not using misleading, deceptive, or false information; and properly acknowledging sources.

Respect refers to addressing audience members as unique human beings and refraining from any forms of personal attack. You can demonstrate respect by focusing on issues rather than on personalities and allowing the audience the power of rational choice.

Responsibility refers to: (1) Evaluating the usefulness and appropriateness of the speech topic and purpose; for example, will learning about your topic in some way benefit your listeners? Are your overall speech aims socially constructive? (2) Using sound evidence and reasoning and striving for accuracy in your message and your facts. (3) Using emotional appeals in an ethical manner rather than to shore up otherwise weak arguments.

Fairness refers to making a genuine effort to see all sides of an issue and to be open minded and acknowledging the information listeners need in order to make informed decisions.[6]

Avoid Offensive Speech

As an ethical speaker, it is vital that you avoid expressions of ethnocentrism, stereotypes, or outright prejudice. **Hate**

speech is any offensive communication—verbal or nonverbal—that is directed against people's racial, ethnic, religious, gender, or other characteristics. This kind of speech is never acceptable.

> **CHECKLIST: An Ethical Inventory**
>
> ✓ Have you distorted any information to make your point?
>
> ✓ Have you acknowledged each of your sources?
>
> ✓ Does your speech focus on issues rather than on personalities?
>
> ✓ Have you tried to foster a sense of inclusion?
>
> ✓ Is your topic socially constructive?
>
> ✓ Is the content of your message as accurate as you can make it?
>
> ✓ When appropriate, do you acknowledge alternative and opposing views so that the audience can make informed decisions?

Avoid Plagiarism

Crediting sources is a crucial aspect of any speech. **Plagiarism**—the passing off of another person's information as one's own—is unethical. To plagiarize is to use other people's ideas or words without acknowledging the source. Whether it's done intentionally or not, plagiarism is stealing.

The rule for avoiding plagiarism as a public speaker is straightforward: *Any source that requires credit in written form should be acknowledged in oral form.* These sources include:

- Direct quotations
- Paraphrased information
- Facts and statistics
- Information gathered or reported by someone other than the speaker
- Ideas, opinions, and theories from someone other than the speaker

Your oral presentation need not include the full bibliographic references (names, dates, titles, volume, and page numbers), but you should include complete references on the bibliography page or at the bottom of the speech outline.

Orally Credit Direct Quotations

Direct quotations are statements made verbatim, or word for word, by someone else. Direct quotes should always be acknowledged in a speech. Although it is not a requirement, you can call attention to a source's exact wording with phrases such as "And I quote" or "As (the source) put it" and so forth. For example,

> As my esteemed colleague Dr. Vance Brown told an audience of AIDS researchers at the International AIDS Convention last year, *and I quote,* "The cure may be near or it may be far, but the human suffering is very much in the present."

> *As Shakespeare would say,* "A rose by any other name would smell as sweet."

Orally Credit Paraphrased Information

A **paraphrase** is a restatement of someone else's ideas, opinions, or theories in the speaker's own words.[7] Because paraphrases alter the form but not the substance of another person's ideas, the speaker must acknowledge the original source. After all, they are not the speaker's ideas. For example:

> *According to Professor John Slater of the Cranberry Middle School in New York,* students' increasing reliance on the Internet as a research tool will only result in more cases of plagiarism. *Slater sees* a trend in which students equate cyberspace with "free." Unless we address the issue at the grade-school level, *Slater says,* we risk raising a generation of plagiarizers.

Orally Credit Sources for Facts and Statistics

The source for any data that was not gathered by you should be cited in your speech. You don't have to cite **common knowledge**—information that is likely to be known by many people—but such information must truly be widely disseminated. For example, it is common knowledge that the terrorists flew two planes into the World Trade Center Towers on September 11, 2001. It is not common knowledge that the towers were 1,368 and 1,362 feet high. These facts require acknowledgment of a source, in this case, the Port Authority of New York and New Jersey, the owners of the World Trade

Center Towers.[8] The following three examples illustrate how you can acknowledge and cite facts and statistics in a speech.

> *According to the public information office of the Port Authority of New York and New Jersey, which owned the World Trade Center Towers,* the towers were 1,368 and 1,362 feet high. The Center is actually a complex of seven buildings on 16 acres . . .

> *In a lecture on academic honesty, Grinnell University professor Judy Hunter described* how two-thirds of the cases of plagiarism at the university resulted not because students deliberately sought to deceive their professors but from, *and I quote,* "a mistaken notion of the importance of citation."[9]

> *According to Tiffini Theisen, a reporter for the Orlando Sentinel,* about 4,200 pregnancy-discrimination complaints are filed every year with the U.S. Equal Employment Opportunity Commission and other agencies.

For a printed list of citations, include the following information:

1. Names of author(s) or editor(s) as cited
2. Title of publication
3. Volume or edition number, if applicable
4. Name of publisher
5. Place of publication (city and state); if only published online, give Internet address
6. Date and year of publication
7. Page numbers on which material appears

CHECKLIST: Steps to Avoid Plagiarism

✓ Know how to quote, paraphrase, and summarize sources.

✓ Learn how to keep track of and cite Internet sources.

✓ Keep track of your sources as you collect them.

✓ Create a system for keeping track of your sources, such as using note cards or the footnote feature in Microsoft Word.

3 Listeners and Speakers

Most of us understand that giving a speech involves preparation and practice, but fewer recognize the hard work that listening requires. Rather than being a passive activity that simply "happens" to us, **listening** is the conscious act of recognizing, understanding, and accurately interpreting the messages communicated by others.

Recognize That We Listen Selectively

In any given situation, no two audience members will process the information in exactly the same way. The reason lies in **selective perception** — people pay attention selectively to certain messages and ignore others. Several factors influence what we listen to and what we ignore:

- We pay attention to what we hold to be important.
- We pay attention to information that touches our experiences and backgrounds.
- We sort and filter new information on the basis of what we already know (i.e., we learn by analogy).[1]

With these principles in mind, you should:

- Try to uncover your listeners' interests, needs, values, attitudes, and beliefs.
- Try to touch upon audience members' experiences and backgrounds in order to catch and sustain listeners' attention.
- Use analogies to help listeners learn new ideas.
- Where appropriate, use presentation aids to visually reinforce your message.

Anticipate the Common Obstacles to Listening

Active listening — listening that is focused and purposeful — isn't possible under conditions that distract us.[2] As you listen to speeches, try to identify and overcome some common obstacles.

Minimize External and Internal Distractions

A **listening distraction** is anything that competes for attention that we are trying to give to something else. Distractions can originate outside of us, in the environment (external distractions), or within us, in our thoughts and feelings (internal distractions).

To minimize *external listening distractions,* such as the din of jackhammers or competing conversations, try to anticipate and plan for them. If you have trouble seeing or hearing at a distance, go early and sit in the front. If you have trouble hearing at group meetings, sit near the leader so that most messages will be communicated toward your side of the room.

To minimize *internal listening distractions,* avoid daydreaming, be well rested, monitor yourself for lapses in attention, and consciously focus on listening.

Guard against Scriptwriting and Defensive Listening

Instead of focusing on the speaker, people who engage in *scriptwriting* are thinking about what they, rather than the speaker, will say next.[3] Similarly, people who engage in **defensive listening** decide either that they won't like what the speaker is going to say or that they know better. When you find yourself scriptwriting or listening with a defensive posture, remind yourself that effective listening precedes effective rebuttal.[4] Try waiting for the speaker to finish before devising your own mental arguments.

Beware of Laziness and Overconfidence

Laziness and overconfidence can manifest themselves in several ways: We expect too little from speakers, ignore important information, or display an arrogant attitude. Later, we discover that we missed important information. Never assume that you already know exactly what a speaker will say. You'll very seldom be right.

Work to Overcome Cultural Barriers

Differences in dialects or accents, nonverbal cues, word choice, and even physical appearance can serve as barriers to listening, but they need not if you keep your focus on the message rather than the messenger. Refrain from judging a speaker on the basis of his or her accent, appearance, or demeanor. Focus instead on what is actually being said. Whenever possible, reveal your needs to him or her by asking questions.

> **QUICK TIP**
>
> ### The Responsibilities of Listening
> *As a speaker you have the power of the podium, but as a listener you also have considerable power that you can wield constructively or destructively. As listeners, we are ethically bound to refrain from disruptive and intimidating tactics — such as heckling, name calling, or interrupting — that are meant to silence those with whom we disagree. If we find the arguments of others morally offensive, we are equally bound to speak up appropriately in refutation.*

Practice Active Listening

The following practical steps can help you listen actively:

- Set listening goals and state them in a way that encourages action: "In my colleagues' presentation, I will learn why it took them six months to complete the last phase."
- Seek out main ideas in the speaker's introduction, in his or her use of transitions, and in the speech conclusion.
- Take notes.
- As clues to meaning, take note of body language, eye contact, facial expressions, and gestures.

STEPS IN SETTING LISTENING GOALS

Identify Need: "I must know Suzanne's speech thesis, purpose, main points, and type of organization in order to complete and hand in a written evaluation."

Indicate Performance Standard: "I will get a better grade on the evaluation if I am able to identify and evaluate the major components of Suzanne's speech."

Make Action Statement (Goal): "I will minimize distractions and practice the active listening steps during Suzanne's speech. I will take careful notes during her speech and ask questions about anything I do not understand."

Assess Goal Achievement: "Before I leave the classroom, I will review my notes carefully to make sure that I covered everything."

Listen Critically

As you listen to speeches, use your critical faculties to do the following:

- *Evaluate the speaker's evidence.* Is it accurate? Are the sources credible?

- *Analyze the speaker's assumptions and biases.* What lies behind the speaker's assertions? Does the evidence support or contradict these assertions?

- *Assess the speaker's reasoning.* Does it betray faulty logic? Does the evidence rely on inappropriate causal relationships? Does it rely on fallacies in reasoning?

- *Identify contradictions.* Distinguish significant similarities and differences in opposing views. Make decisions about what you hold to be true based on which evidence best supports a valid conclusion.

- *Consider multiple perspectives.* Is there another way to view the argument? How do other perspectives compare with the speaker's?

- *Summarize and assess the relevant facts and evidence.*

 CHECKLIST: Ensuring Effective Listening

As a speaker:

✓ Recognize the selective nature of listening. Plan your speech accordingly by appealing to audience members' experiences and backgrounds.

As a listener:

✓ Anticipate the common *external obstacles* to listening, such as having trouble hearing or seeing the speaker, and physically position yourself so that you can listen effectively.

✓ Anticipate the common *internal obstacles* to listening, such as fatigue, daydreaming, defensive listening, laziness, and overconfidence, and consciously strive to focus on listening.

✓ Work to overcome *cultural barriers* by focusing on the message and seeking clarification through questioning.

✓ To ensure *active listening,* set listening goals, listen for main ideas, and watch for the speaker's nonverbal cues.

✓ Listen critically by analyzing the speaker's evidence and assumptions, identifying contradictions, and considering multiple perspectives.

Offer Constructive Feedback

Follow these guidelines when evaluating the speeches of others:

- *Be honest and fair in your evaluation.*
- *Adjust to the speaker's style.* Don't judge the content of a speaker's message because of his or her style.
- *Be compassionate in your criticism.* Always start by saying something positive, and focus on the speech, not the speaker.
- *Be selective in your criticism.* Make specific rather than global statements.

4   Types of Speeches

Whether it is delivered in the classroom, the workplace, or in the civic arena, and whether it falls under the label of "research presentation," "sales presentation," or "eulogy," a public speech or presentation can be classified according to three broad types: *informative, persuasive,* and *special occasion.*

The Informative Speech

An **informative speech** provides an audience with new information, new insights, or new ways of thinking about a topic. The goal of the informative speech is to increase the audience's understanding or awareness by imparting knowledge. Informative speeches may be about objects, people, events, processes, concepts, or issues. (For more on informative speeches, see Chapter 23.)

SAMPLE INFORMATIVE SPEECH TOPICS
• Hydrogen-Powered Cars
• Staying Healthy on a Vegetarian Diet
• WikiWikiWebs — Taking Interactive to a New Level
• SuperSlow Exercise
• Top Ten Conspiracy Theories
• Advances in Breast Cancer Treatment

The Persuasive Speech

A **persuasive speech** is speech that is intended to influence the attitudes, beliefs, values, and acts of others. Any issue that would constitute the topic of a persuasive speech represents at least two viewpoints. If the speech is effective, listeners will understand that the alternative presented by the speaker is the "right" choice. Note, however, that by no means do all persuasive speeches explicitly seek a response. Many persuasive speeches focus on "perspective taking"—leading the audience to a perspective that is the speaker's. (For more on persuasive speeches, see Chapter 24.)

SAMPLE TOPICS FOR PERSUASIVE SPEECHES
• Become an Organ Donor
• Adopt a Foster Child
• Take Calcium Supplements for Health
• The NBA Draft Needs Fixing
• Procrastination Hurts
• Spay or Neuter Your Pets
• Treat the Disabled with Dignity, Respect, and Fairness

The Special Occasion Speech

A **special occasion speech** (also called "ceremonial speech") is one that is prepared for a specific occasion and for a purpose dictated by that occasion. Special occasion speeches can be either informative or persuasive or often a mix of both. However, neither of these functions is the main goal; the

CHECKLIST: Identifying Speech Types

✓ Is your goal in speaking primarily to increase the audience's knowledge of a topic or to share your point of view? (Your speech is informative in nature.)

✓ Is it primarily to effect some degree of change in the way your listeners view things? (Your speech is persuasive in nature.)

✓ Is it primarily to entertain, celebrate, commemorate, inspire, or set a social agenda? (Your speech is ceremonial; e.g., a special occasion speech.)

underlying function of a special occasion speech is to enter-tain, celebrate, commemorate, inspire, or set a social agenda. (For more on special occasion speeches, see Chapter 25.)

5 From A to Z: Overview of a Speech

Novice speakers in any circumstances—at school, at work, or in the community—will benefit from preparing and delivering a first short speech. An audience of as few as two other people will suffice to test the waters and help you gain confidence in your ability to "stand up and deliver."

This chapter presents a brief overview of the process of preparing a first speech or presentation. Subsequent chapters expand on these steps.

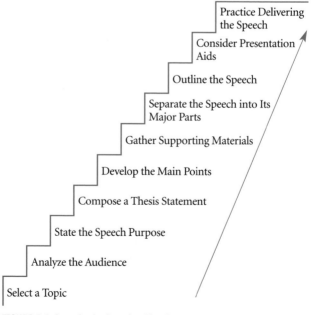

FIGURE 5.1 Steps in the Speechmaking Process

Select a Topic

The first step in creating a speech involves finding something to speak about. Unless the topic is assigned, let your interests — your passions — be your guide. What deeply engages you? What are your areas of expertise? Your hobbies? Beware, however, that even though personal interest is important, it's equally important that your topic be of interest to the audience. Selecting an appropriate topic requires knowledge of who is in the audience and what their interests are.

Analyze the Audience

Much like the individuals composing them, audiences have personalities, interests, and opinions all their own. These factors affect how receptive an audience will be toward a given topic. Thus it is crucial that you learn as much as you can about audience members.

Audience analysis is a highly systematic process of getting to know your listeners. The process involves studying the audience through techniques such as interviews and questionnaires (see Chapter 7). For a brief speech, consider some general variables:

- Begin with some fairly easily identifiable *demographic characteristics:* the ratio of males to females; racial and ethnic differences represented in the group; noticeable age variations; and the proportion of the group that is from out of state or from another country.

- Consider how different people (i.e., older and younger, men and women, international and native-born) might *think or feel differently about your topic.*

State the Speech Purpose

Decide what you wish to convey about your topic — and why. For any given topic, you should direct your speech toward one of three *general purposes* — to *inform,* to *persuade,* or to *mark a special occasion* (see Chapter 8).

Your speech should also have a *specific purpose.* This is an explicit statement, stated as a declarative sentence, of what you expect the speech to accomplish:

— If the general purpose of a speech about a proposed increase in resident student tuition is *to inform,* its specific purpose might be "to identify for the audience the three key points on which students and administrators disagree about increasing resident tuition."

— If the general purpose is *to persuade,* its specific purpose might be "to convince my listeners that the administration does not need to increase resident tuition."

Compose a Thesis Statement

Next, compose a thesis statement that clearly expresses the central idea of your speech. Whereas the specific purpose describes what you want to achieve with the speech, the *thesis statement* concisely identifies, in a single idea, what the speech is about:

GENERAL PURPOSE:	To inform
SPECIFIC PURPOSE:	To inform my audience about the growth of prisons in the United States
THESIS STATEMENT:	The United States built an unprecedented number of prisons during the 1990s.

As with the specific speech purpose, you will use the thesis statement as a guidepost to construct your speech. In the planning stage, always refer to the thesis to make sure that you are developing main points that illustrate or prove the thesis.

Develop the Main Points

Two or three main points are usually sufficient for a short speech—no matter how long the speech, most audiences won't be able to focus on more than seven main points, with between three to five being optimal. These points are your primary pieces of knowledge (in an informative speech) or your key arguments (in a persuasive speech). If you clearly state your specific purpose, the main points will be easily identifiable, if not explicit, in that statement:

SPECIFIC PURPOSE: To convince my listeners that the administration does not need to increase resident tuition

I. Monies from the state surplus should be used to offset the costs of increased enrollments.

II. Twelve other states have diverted funds from their budget surpluses for precisely this purpose.

III. Yet another tuition hike will put the state's institutions of higher education out of reach for too many state residents.

Gather Supporting Materials

Supporting materials illustrate the main points by clarifying, elaborating, and verifying a speaker's ideas. Supporting materials include the entire world of information available to you — from personal experiences to statistics from outside sources. Supporting materials are crucial because they lend credibility to your message by signifying that your ideas are consistent with other people's ideas and actual events (see Chapters 9–11).

Separate the Speech into Its Major Parts

Every speech has three major parts: *introduction, body,* and *conclusion.* As you begin the process of outlining (as described in the next section), separate these parts so that you can give each section the attention it requires.

The *introduction* serves to introduce the topic and the speaker and to alert the audience to your specific speech purpose. A good introduction should catch the audience's attention and interest. Some of the many ways in which speakers

---

MAJOR SPEECH PARTS

Introduction

- Catch the audience's attention with the use of a quote, a short story, an example, or another kind of supporting material.
- Welcome your audience.
- Introduce yourself, your topic, and your speech purpose.

Body

- Introduce the main ideas and illustrate them with supporting materials.
- Organize your ideas and evidence in an appropriate structure.

Conclusion

- Restate the specific speech purpose and reiterate how the main points confirm it.
- Leave your audience with something to think about.
- Thank your listeners for their time.
- Answer questions.

do this include making a startling statement, telling a story, or using humor (see Chapter 15).

Just like the body of a written essay, the speech *body* contains the speech's main points and subpoints, all of which support the speech's thesis. Here you will illustrate or argue each of your main ideas, using supporting material to clarify, elaborate, or substantiate your points.

The *conclusion* restates the speech purpose and reiterates how the main points confirm it. Because the conclusion represents your last opportunity to motivate your listeners, make sure to end on a strong note (see Chapter 15).

Outline the Speech

An outline provides the framework upon which to arrange main points in support of your thesis and subordinate points in support of your main points. Outlines are based on the principle of *coordination and subordination*—the logical placement of ideas relative to their importance to one another. *Coordinate points* are of equal importance and are given parallel alignment. *Subordinate points* are given less weight than the main points they support and are placed to the right of the points they support. (For a full discussion of outlining, see Chapters 12 and 14.)

COORDINATE POINTS

I. Main Point 1
II. Main Point 2

SUBORDINATE POINTS

1. Main Point 1
   A. First level of subordination
      1. Second level of subordination
      2. Second level of subordination
         a. Third level of subordination
         b. Third level of subordination

As your speeches become more involved, you will need to select an appropriate *organizational pattern* (see Chapter 13). You will also need to familiarize yourself with developing both working and speaking outlines (see Chapter 14). *Working outlines* contain points stated in complete sentences, whereas *speaking outlines* (also called "presentation outlines") are far briefer and use either short phrases or key words. Speaking outlines are usually written on 4×6 index cards for use during the speech.

Consider Presentation Aids

Consider whether using visual or auditory aids, or a combination of both, will help your audience understand your points. A *presentation aid* can be as simple as writing the definition of a word on a blackboard or as involved as a multimedia slide show. Presentation aids that summarize and highlight information, such as charts and graphs, can often help the audience to retain ideas and understand difficult concepts. They also can provide dramatic emphasis that listeners will find memorable (see Chapter 20).

Practice Delivering the Speech

The success of any speech depends on how well prepared and practiced you are. So practice your speech — often. It has been suggested that a good speech is practiced at least five times. For a four- to six-minute speech, that's only twenty to thirty minutes (figuring in restarts and pauses) of actual practice time.

Vocal Delivery

Vocal delivery includes speech volume, pitch, rate, variety, pronunciation, and articulation (see Chapter 18). As you rehearse, do the following:

- Pay attention to how loudly or softly you are speaking.
- Pay attention to the rate at which you speak, and aim to speak neither too fast nor too slowly.
- Avoid speaking in a monotone.
- Decide how you want to phrase your statements, and then practice saying them.
- Pronounce words correctly and clearly.

Nonverbal Delivery

Beyond noticing the words of a speech, audiences are also highly attuned to a speaker's nonverbal speech behavior — facial expression, gestures, general body movement, and overall physical appearance. As you rehearse, do the following:

- Practice smiling and otherwise animating your face in ways that feel natural to you. Audiences want to feel that you care about what you are saying, so avoid a deadpan, or blank, expression.
- Practice making eye contact with your listeners. Doing so will make audience members feel that you recognize and respect them.
- Practice gestures that feel natural to you, steering clear of exaggerated movements.

6 Managing Speech Anxiety

For many of us, public speaking tops the list of things we fear. In fact, according to one study, at least 75 percent of students in public-speaking courses approach the course with anxiety.[1] Even accomplished speakers often feel jittery before they give a speech. It turns out that feeling nervous is not only normal but desirable. Channeled properly, nervousness boosts performance. The difference between seasoned public speakers and the rest of us is that the seasoned speakers are more practiced at making their nervousness work for rather than against them. They also use specific techniques that help them cope with and minimize their tension.

Identify What Makes You Anxious

Lack of public-speaking experience, feeling different from members of the audience, and feeling uneasy about being the center of attention—each of these factors can lead to the onset of **public-speaking anxiety**, that is, fear or anxiety associated with either actual or anticipated communication to an audience as a speaker.[2]

Lack of Experience

For those who have had no public-speaking experience, anxiety about what to expect is only natural. And with no experience to fall back on, it's hard to put these anxieties in perspective. It's a bit of a vicious circle. Some people react by deciding to avoid making speeches altogether. Although they avoid the anxiety of speechmaking, they also lose out on the considerable rewards it brings.

Feeling Different

Novice speakers often feel alone—as if they were the only person ever to experience the dread of public speaking. The prospect of getting up in front of an audience makes them extra-sensitive to their personal idiosyncrasies, such as having a less-than-perfect haircut or a slight lisp, or thinking that no one could possibly be interested in anything they have to say.

As novice speakers, we become anxious because we assume that being different somehow means being inferior. Actually, everyone is different from everyone else in many ways. Just as true, nearly everyone experiences nervousness about giving a speech.

Being the Center of Attention

Speakers often comment about how audience members appear to behave toward them during a speech. Listeners might fail to make eye contact with the speaker, converse with one another during a speech, or point. When this occurs, our tendency is to think that we must be doing something inappropriate; then we wonder what's wrong and whether the entire audience has noticed it.

This kind of thinking builds rapidly and, left unchecked, can distract us from the speech itself, with all our attention now focused on "me." As we focus on "me," we become all the more sensitive to things that might be wrong with what we're doing—and that makes us feel even more conspicuous, which increases our anxiety. In actuality (and ironically), an audience notices very little about us that we don't want to reveal, especially if our speeches are well developed and effectively delivered.

QUICK TIP

Your Own Worst Critic
If you find yourself feeling anxious about being the center of attention, remember that you see yourself more critically than an audience does. Audience members notice little about us that we don't want to reveal, so relax and focus on delivering your message.

RECOGNIZING AND OVERCOMING YOUR UNDERLYING FEARS ABOUT PUBLIC SPEAKING	
PROBLEM	SOLUTION
Does a lack of speaking experience intimidate you?	Practice rehearsing your speech several times. Do so in front of at least one other person.
Do you worry about appearing different to others?	Remember that everyone is different from everyone else in many ways. Dress well, be well groomed, and trust that you will make a good impression.
Do you dread being the center of attention?	Focus on the speech instead of yourself. The audience won't notice anything about you that you don't want to reveal, especially if your speech is well planned and rehearsed.

Pinpoint the Onset of Nervousness

Different people become anxious at different times during the speechmaking process. Depending on when it strikes, the consequences of public-speaking anxiety can include everything from procrastination to poor speech performance. By pinpointing the onset of speech anxiety, you can address it promptly with specific anxiety-reducing techniques (see strategies to boost confidence on p. 28).

Pre-Preparation Anxiety

Some people feel anxious the minute they know they will be giving a speech. **Pre-preparation anxiety** at this early stage can have several negative consequences, from reluctance to begin planning for the speech to being so preoccupied with anxiety that you miss vital information necesssary to fulfill the speech assignment.

Preparation Anxiety

For a minority of people, anxiety arises only when they actually begin to prepare for the speech. At that point they might feel overwhelmed at the amount of time and planning that are required. They might hit a roadblock that puts them behind schedule, or they might be unable to locate support for a critical point. These kinds of preparation pressures produce a vicious circle of stress, procrastination, and outright avoidance. All contribute to **preparation anxiety**.

Pre-Performance Anxiety

Some people experience anxiety when they rehearse their speech. At this point, the reality of the situation sets in: Soon they will face an audience of people who will be watching and listening only to them. As they rehearse, they might also realize that their ideas don't sound as focused or as interesting as they should. Knowing that time is short, they begin to get nervous. If this **pre-performance anxiety** is strong enough and is interpreted negatively, they might even decide to stop rehearsing.

Performance Anxiety

For the majority of people, anxiety levels tend to be highest just before they begin speaking.[3] This is true even of actors, who report that their worst stage fright occurs just as they walk on stage to begin their performances. **Performance anxiety** in speechmaking is probably most pronounced during the introduction phase of the speech. This is when the speaker utters the first words of the speech and is most aware of the audience's attention. However, experienced speakers agree that if they control their nervousness during the introduction, the rest of the speech comes relatively easily.

Learn Specific Strategies to Boost Your Confidence

Regardless of when anxiety about a speech strikes, the important thing to remember is to manage your anxiety and not let it manage you. How can you do this? The first step is to have a clear and thorough plan for each speech.

Prepare and Practice

If you are confident that you know your material and have adequately rehearsed your delivery, you're far more likely to feel confident at the podium than otherwise. Thus preparation should begin as soon as possible after a speech is assigned. Once you have prepared the speech, be sure to rehearse it several times.

Modify Thoughts and Attitudes

Negative thoughts increase speech anxiety.[4] Having a positive attitude toward speechmaking, on the other hand, actually results in lowered heart rate and consequent reduced anxiety during the delivery of the speech.[5] Thus, as you prepare for and deliver your speech, it's important to regard it as a valuable, worthwhile, and challenging activity. Remind yourself of all the reasons that public speaking is helpful personally, socially, and professionally. Think positively about public speaking, and remind yourself that it is an opportunity, not a threat.

QUICK TIP

Envision Your Speech as a Conversation
Altering your thinking about public speaking from a "performance" to a "communication" can significantly increase confidence.[6] Try thinking of your speech as an extension of an ordinary conversation. Doing so might help you feel more relaxed about the process, and with each successive speech experience, your attitude toward public speaking will grow more positive.

Visualize Success

Visualization is a highly successful way to reduce nervousness.[7] Following is a script for visualizing success on a public-speaking occasion. The exercise requires you to close your eyes and visualize a series of positive feelings and reactions that will occur on the day of the speech.

> Close your eyes and allow your body to get comfortable in the chair in which you are sitting. Take a deep, comfortable

breath and hold it . . . now slowly release it through your nose. Now take another deep breath and make certain that you are breathing from the diaphragm . . . hold it . . . now slowly release it and note how you feel while doing this. Now one more deep breath . . . hold it . . . and release it slowly . . . and begin your normal breathing pattern.

Now begin to visualize the beginning of a day in which you are going to give an informative speech. See yourself getting up in the morning, full of energy, full of confidence, looking forward to the day's challenges. You are putting on just the right clothes for the task at hand that day. Dressing well makes you look and feel good about yourself, so you have on just what you want to wear, which clearly expresses your sense of inner well-being. As you are driving, riding, or walking to the speech setting, note how clear and confident you feel, and how others around you, as you arrive, comment positively regarding your fine appearance and general de-meanor. You feel thoroughly prepared for the target issue you will be presenting today.

Now you see yourself standing or sitting in the room where you will present your speech, talking very comfortably and confidently with others in the room. The people to whom you will be presenting your speech appear to be quite friendly and are very cordial in their greetings and conversations prior to the presentation. You feel absolutely sure of your material and of your ability to present the information in a forceful, convincing, positive manner.

Now you see yourself approaching the area from which you will present. You are feeling very good about this presentation and see yourself move eagerly forward. All of your audiovisual materials are well organized, well planned, and clearly aid your presentation.[8]

Use Stress-Control Breathing

When you feel stressed, the center of your breathing tends to move from the abdomen to the upper chest, leaving you with a reduced supply of air. The chest and shoulders rise, and you feel out of breath. With *stress-control breathing*,[9] you will feel more movement in the stomach than in the chest. Try stress-control breathing in two stages.

STAGE ONE   Inhale air and let your abdomen go out. Exhale air and let your abdomen go in. Do this for a while until you get into the rhythm of it.

STAGE TWO   As you inhale, use a soothing word such as "calm" or "relax," or use a personal mantra, as follows: "Inhale calm, abdomen out, exhale calm, abdomen in." Go slowly. Each inhalation and exhalation of stress-control breathing takes about three to five seconds.

Start stress-control breathing several days before you're scheduled to speak. Then, once the speaking event arrives, use it while you wait your turn and just before you start your speech.

Practice Natural Gestures

Practice some controlled, natural gestures that might be useful in enhancing your speech, such as holding up your index finger when stating your first main point. Think about what you want to say as you do this, instead of thinking about how you look or feel. (See Chapter 19 for tips on practicing natural gestures.)

Move as You Speak

You don't have to stand perfectly still behind the podium when you deliver a speech. Walk around as you make some of your points. Movement relieves tension, and it helps to hold the audience's attention.

CHECKLIST: Steps in Gaining Confidence

✓ Prepare and practice often.

✓ Modify thoughts and attitudes — think positively.

✓ Accept your nervousness as normal — work with it rather than against it.

✓ Concentrate on your message, not on yourself.

✓ Visualize success.

✓ Breathe deeply.

✓ Use relaxation techniques.

✓ Seek pleasure in the occasion.

Seek Pleasure in the Occasion

Although no one can be forced to enjoy something, most people ultimately find that giving speeches can indeed be fun. It's satisfying and empowering to influence people, and a good speech is a sure way to do that. Think of giving a speech in these terms, and chances are that it will come out that way.

Part 2
Development

7 Analyzing the Audience

Advertisers are astute analysts when it comes to reading people's needs and wants. The best advertisers can closely target both our desires and our fears. To capture an audience's attention and bring them to your point of view, you too must present a topic in ways that are meaningful to your listeners. **Audience analysis** is the process of gathering and analyzing information about your listeners with the explicit aim of adapting your message to the information you uncover. This is the single most critical aspect of preparing for any speech.

Investigate Audience Members' Attitudes, Beliefs, and Values

People tend to evaluate messages in terms of their own — rather than the speaker's — attitudes, beliefs, and values.

Attitudes reflect a predisposition to respond to people, ideas, objects, or events in evaluative ways.[1] To evaluate something is to judge it as relatively good or bad, useful or useless, desirable or undesirable, and so on.

Attitudes are based on **beliefs** — the ways in which people perceive reality.[2] They are our feelings about what is true. The less faith listeners have that something exists — UFOs, for instance — the less open they are to hearing about it.

Both attitudes and beliefs are shaped by **values** — people's most enduring judgments about what's good and bad in life. Values are more enduring than attitudes or beliefs; they are also more resistant to change. Understanding an audience's values points you in the direction of their attitudes and beliefs.

You are far more likely to sustain your listeners' attention if you can uncover audience members' attitudes, beliefs, and values — or, for brevity's sake, *feelings* — toward (1) the topic of your speech; (2) you as the speaker; and (3) the speech occasion. Such **perspective taking** is critical in seeing things from your listeners' point of view.

Gauge Listeners' Feelings toward You as the Speaker

How audience members feel about you will have considerable bearing on their attentiveness and responsiveness to the message. Research on **speaker credibility** reveals that people place their greatest trust in speakers who

- have a sound grasp of the subject
- display sound reasoning skills

- are honest and unmanipulative
- are genuinely interested in the welfare of their listeners[3]

Listeners tend to distrust speakers who deviate even slightly from these qualities. However, merely being an expert is not enough to inspire listeners' trust. We trust only those speakers whom we believe have our best interests in mind.[4]

Gauge Listeners' Feelings toward the Topic

Try to determine what your listeners know about the topic. What is their level of interest? How do they feel about it? Once you have this information, adjust the speech accordingly:

If the topic is *new* to your listeners,

- Start by showing why the topic is relevant to them.
- Relate the topic to familiar issues and ideas.

If your listeners know *relatively little* about your topic,

- Stick to the basics and include background information.

If their attitudes about the topic *differ from yours,*

- Make your points relevant to their attitudes and beliefs rather than to yours.
- Seek a common ground.
- Focus on issues of general social concern.

If your listeners are *negatively disposed* toward your topic,

- Consider modifying or changing your topic if the audience has strong negative attitudes toward it.
- Give them good reasons why their attitudes are unfounded.
- Give them good reasons for changing their attitudes.

QUICK TIP

Appeal to Your Listeners' Concerns
As a general rule, people give more interest and attention to topics toward which they have positive attitudes and that are in keeping with their values and beliefs. The less we know about something, the more indifferent we tend to be. Any speaker seeking a change in attitudes or behavior does well to remember this.

Gauge Listeners' Feelings toward the Occasion

Depending on the speech occasion, people bring different sets of expectations and emotions to it. The speaker who fails to anticipate such attitudes and expectations risks alienating audience members.

Adapt Your Message to Audience Demographics

Demographics are the statistical characteristics of a given population. Six such characteristics are typically considered in the analysis of speech audiences: age, ethnic or cultural background, socioeconomic status (including income, occupation, and education), religion, political affiliation, and gender. Taking demographics into account increases the likelihood that listeners will be receptive to your message.

Age

Each age group brings with it its own concerns and, broadly speaking, psychological drives and motivations. In addition to sharing the concerns associated with a given life stage, people of the same generation often share a familiarity with significant individuals, local and world events, noteworthy popular culture, and so forth. Thus, being aware of the audience's age range allows you to develop points that are relevant to the experiences and interests of the widest possible cross section of your listeners.

Ethnic or Cultural Background

An understanding of and sensitivity to the ethnic and cultural composition of your listeners are key factors in delivering a successful—and ethical—speech. Some audience members may have a great deal in common with you. Others may be fluent in a language other than yours and must struggle to understand you. Some members of the audience may belong to a distinct **co-culture**, or social community, whose perceptions and beliefs differ significantly from yours. (See p. 38, "Adapt to Cultural Differences.")

Socioeconomic Status

Socioeconomic status (SES) includes income, occupation, and education. Knowing roughly where an audience falls in terms of these key variables can be critical in effectively targeting your message.

QUICK TIP

Treat Your Listeners with Dignity
*In any speaking situation, your foremost concern should be to treat your listeners with dignity and to act with integrity. You do this by adhering to certain **ethical ground rules**, or, in the words of ethicist Michael Josephson, "pillars of character."[5] These include being trustworthy, respectful, responsible, and fair in our presentations. (For more on ethics, see Chapter 2.)*

INCOME   *Income* determines people's experiences on many levels. It directly affects how they are housed, clothed, and fed, and it determines what they can afford. Beyond this, income has a ripple effect, influencing many other aspects of life. For example, depending on income, health insurance is either a taken-for-granted budget item or an out-of-reach dream. The same is true for travel and leisure activities. Given how pervasively income affects people's life experiences, insight into this aspect of an audience's makeup can be quite important.

OCCUPATION   In most speech situations, the *occupation* of audience members is an important and easily identifiable demographic characteristic to uncover. The nature of people's work has a lot to do with what interests them. Occupational interests are tied to several other areas of social concern, such as politics, the economy, education, and social reform. Personal attitudes, beliefs, and goals are also closely tied to occupational standing.

EDUCATION   Level of *education* strongly influences people's ideas, perspectives, and range of abilities. If the audience is generally better educated than you are, your speech may need to be quite sophisticated. When speaking to a less-educated audience, you may choose to clarify your points with more examples and illustrations.

Religion

The *Encyclopedia of American Religions* identifies more than 2,300 different religious groups in the United States,[6] from Adventists to Zen Buddhists, so don't assume that everyone in your audience shares a common *religious heritage*. Furthermore, don't assume that all members of the same religious tradition agree on all issues. For example, Catholics disagree on birth control and divorce, Jews disagree on whether to recognize same-sex unions, and so forth.

Political Affiliation

Beware of making unwarranted assumptions about an audience's *political values and beliefs.* Some people like nothing better than a lively debate about public-policy issues. Others avoid anything that smacks of politics. And many people are very serious, and others are very touchy, about their views on political issues. Unless you have prior information about the audience's political values and beliefs, you won't know where your listeners stand.

Gender

Be wary about making generalizations based on gender. This includes avoiding sexist language and other **gender stereotypes**—oversimplified and often distorted ideas about the innate nature of men or women. Strive for language that is inclusive of and respectful toward both sexes.

QUICK TIP

Consider Disability When Analyzing an Audience
One out of every five people in the United States has some sort of physical or mental disability;[7] thus you must ensure that your speech reflects language that accords persons with disability (PWD) dignity, respect, and fairness.

Adapt to Cultural Differences

Audience members hold different cultural perspectives and styles of communicating that may or may not mesh with your own. This becomes instantly apparent when attempts at humor fall flat due to a lack of shared references, but many other dimensions of culture can and do come into play when delivering speeches and presentations. Being alert to differences in values can help you avoid ethnocentrism and deliver your message in a culturally sensitive manner.

One way to prepare for and address potential cultural differences is to consider audience members' likely cultural orientations and evaluate both your content and mode of presentation in light of this information. Geert Hofstede and other researchers have identified four broad cultural orientations that are significant across all cultures in varying degrees,[8] including *individualism-collectivism, uncertainty avoidance, power distance,* and *masculinity-femininity.* These orientations offer insights into the ways in which people may differ in their approach to life:

INDIVIDUALISM VERSUS COLLECTIVISM   *Individualistic cultures* tend to emphasize the needs of the individual rather than those of the group, upholding such values as individual achievement and decision making. In *collectivist cultures,* by contrast, personal identity, needs, and desires are viewed as secondary to those of the larger group. In Hofstede's analysis, the United States, Australia, Great Britain, and Canada rank highest on individualism. Venezuela, Peru, Taiwan, and Pakistan rank highest in collectivist characteristics.

HIGH UNCERTAINTY VERSUS LOW UNCERTAINTY   *Uncertainty avoidance* refers to the extent to which people feel threatened by ambiguity. *High-uncertainty avoidance cultures* tend to structure life more rigidly and formally for its members, while *low-uncertainty avoidance cultures* are more accepting of uncertainty in life and thus allow more variation in individual behavior. Among the nations Hofstede investigated, Portugal, Greece, Peru, Belgium, and Japan rank highest in uncertainty avoidance; Sweden, Denmark, Ireland, Norway, and the United States rank lowest.

HIGH POWER DISTANCE VERSUS LOW POWER DISTANCE   *Power distance* refers to the extent to which a culture values social equality versus tradition and authority. Cultures with *high levels of power distance* tend to be organized along more rigidly hierarchical lines, with greater emphasis placed on honoring authority. Those with *low levels of power distance* place a higher value on social equality. High-power distance countries include India, Brazil, Singapore, Greece, Venezuela, and Mexico. Austria, Finland, Denmark, Norway, New Zealand, and Israel rank lowest on this dimension. The United States ranks somewhat above the midpoint range.

MASCULINE VERSUS FEMININE   The *masculinity* and *femininity dimension* refers to the degree to which a culture values traits that it associates with masculinity and with femininity. Traditional *masculine traits* include ambition, earning power, and overt displays of manliness. *Feminine traits* stress nurturance and cooperation. In Hofstede's analysis, Ireland, the Philippines, Greece, and South Africa ranked highest in masculinity, while Sweden, Norway, Finland, and Denmark ranked highest in femininity. The dominant values in the United States were weighted toward masculinity.

Working from these patterns, you can infer corollary values that your listeners may hold. Note, however, that these patterns reflect the values of the *dominant culture;* they do not necessarily reflect the values of all the groups living within a society. Although individualism characterizes the dominant culture of the United States, for example, various co-cultures, such as Mexican Americans and, to varying degrees, African Americans, have been described as collectivist in nature.[9]

CHECKLIST: Reviewing Your Speech in the Light of Audience Demographics

✓ Does your speech acknowledge potential differences in values and beliefs and address them sensitively?

✓ Have you reviewed your topic in light of the age range and generational identity of your listeners? Do you use examples they will recognize and find relevant?

✓ Have you avoided making judgments based on stereotypes?

✓ Are your explanations and examples at a level that is appropriate to the audience's sophistication and education?

✓ Do you make any unwarranted assumptions about the audience's political or religious values and beliefs?

✓ Does your topic carry religious or political overtones that are likely to stir your listeners' emotions in a negative way?

✓ Is your speech free of generalizations based on gender?

✓ Does your language reflect sensitivity toward people with disabilities?

Seek Information through Surveys, Interviews, and Published Sources

Conducting surveys and interviews of audience members and seeking out published information such as polls and company reports will help you uncover critical demographic and psychological information about members of an audience. Often, it takes just a few questions to get some idea about where audience members stand on each of the demographic factors.

Survey Audience Members

Surveys can be as informal as a telephone poll of two audience members or as formal as the distribution of a written survey, or **questionnaire** — a series of open- and closed-ended questions:

Closed-ended questions elicit a small range of specific answers supplied by the interviewer:

> "Do you or did you ever smoke cigarettes?"

Answers will be either "Yes," "No," or "I smoked for X number of years." Closed-ended questions may be either fixed alternative or scale questions. **Fixed-alternative questions** contain a limited choice of answers, such as "Yes," "No," or "Sometimes." **Scale questions** — also called attitude scales — measure the respondent's level of agreement or disagreement with specific issues:

> "Flag burning should be outlawed":
> Strongly Agree _____   Agree _____   Neutral _____
> Disagree _____   Strongly Disagree _____

Open-ended questions allow respondents to elaborate as much as they wish:

> "How do you feel about using the results of DNA testing to prove innocence or guilt in criminal proceedings?"

By using a mix of open- and closed-ended questions, you can draw a fairly clear picture of the backgrounds and attitudes of the members of your audience. Closed-ended questions are especially helpful in uncovering shared attitudes, experiences, and knowledge of audience members. Open-ended questions are particularly useful for probing beliefs and opinions. They elicit more individual or personal information about the audience members' thoughts and feelings. They are also more time intensive than closed-ended questions.

FORMS OF INTERVIEW/SURVEY QUESTIONS	
QUESTION FORM	DESCRIPTION/PURPOSE IN THE INTERVIEW
Open/Closed	• **Open questions:** Allow the interviewee to elaborate as he or she desires. • **Closed questions:** Permit only "yes," "no," or other limited responses.
Primary/Secondary	• **Primary questions:** Introduce new topics or areas of questioning, e.g., "What made you want to become a veterinarian?" • **Secondary questions:** Expand upon topics introduced in primary questions, e.g., "Did you go to veterinary school right after college?" and "Was it difficult to get student loans?"
Sample Types of Secondary Questions Question Seeking Clarification Question Seeking Elaboration The "Clearinghouse" Question	• **Question seeking clarification:** Designed to clarify the interviewee's statements, e.g., "By 'older mothers,' do you mean over 30, over 40, or over 50?" • **Question seeking elaboration:** Designed to elicit additional information, e.g., "Were there other reasons why you chose your profession?" • **The "clearinghouse" question:** Designed to check that all important information has been discussed, e.g., "Have we covered all the important points?"

Conduct Interviews

An **interview** is a face-to-face communication for the purpose of gathering information. Interviews can be conducted one-on-one or in a group, depending on the time and the feasibility of making such arrangements.

Prepare questions for the interview. Plan the questions you will ask well in advance of the actual interview date.

Word questions carefully. The wording of a question is almost as critical as the information it seeks to uncover:

- Aim to create *neutral questions,* or those that don't lead the interviewee to a forced response.

- Avoid *vague questions,* or those that don't give the person being interviewed enough to go on. He or she must either guess at what you mean or spend time interviewing you for clarification.

- Avoid *leading questions,* or those that encourage, if not force, a certain response and reflect the interviewer's bias (e.g., "Like most intelligent people, are you going to support candidate X?"). Likewise, avoid *loaded questions,* or those that are phrased to reinforce the interviewer's agenda or that have a hostile intent (e.g., "Isn't it true that you've never supported school programs?").

Open the interview carefully. Briefly summarize your topic and informational needs:

- Explain the purpose for which the information will be used.

- State a (reasonable) goal, such as what you would like to accomplish in the interview, and reach agreement on it.

- Acknowledge the interviewee, and express respect for his or her expertise.

- Establish a time limit for the interview and stick to it.

Don't end the interview abruptly. Instead, offer to answer any questions the interviewee may have of you:

- Check that you have covered all the topics (e.g., "Does this cover everything?").

- Briefly offer a positive summary of important things you learned in the interview.

- Offer to send the results of the interview to the interviewee.

- Send a written note of thanks.

Investigate Published Polls and Other Sources

As another source of information about audience members, consider consulting published opinion polls that report on trends in attitudes. Although the polls won't specifically reflect your listeners' responses, they can provide insight into how a representative state, national, or international sample feels about the issue in question. Armed with this knowledge, you can then investigate your specific audience and use this polling data as supporting material for your speeches (see Chapter 9). In addition, organizations of all kinds publish information describing their missions, goals, operations, and achievements. Sources include Web sites and related online articles, print brochures, newspaper and magazine articles, annual reports, industry guides, and agency abstracts.

Assess the Speech Setting

As important as analyzing the audience is assessing and then preparing for the setting in which you will give your speech — size of audience, location, time, seating arrangement, and rhetorical situation:

1. Where will the speech take place?
2. How long am I expected to speak?
3. How many people will attend?
4. Will I need a microphone?
5. How will any projecting equipment I plan to use in my speech, such as an LCD projector, function in the space?
6. Where will I stand or sit in relation to the audience?
7. Will I be able to interact with the listeners?
8. Who else will be speaking?
9. Are there special events or circumstances of concern to my audience that I should acknowledge (e.g., the rhetorical situation)?

8 Selecting a Topic and Purpose

Speechmaking begins with selecting a topic and purpose for speaking, followed by identifying the central idea, or thesis. Topic, purpose, and thesis serve as the blueprint for the public speaker.

Identify the General Purpose of Your Speech

Some of your presentations will have an assigned topic and/or purpose (e.g., "deliver an informative speech" or "speak about topic X"). In others, the choice will be left to you. Even when the topic is specified, you must still refine and adapt the topic to fit the general speech purpose. The **general speech purpose** for any speech answers the question, "Why am I speaking on this topic for this particular audience and occasion?"

— Are you there to inform listeners about your topic? The general purpose of the informative speech is *to increase the audience's understanding or awareness by imparting knowledge.*

— Is your goal to persuade them to accept your views on a topic? The general purpose of the persuasive speech is *to influence the attitudes, beliefs, values, and acts of audience members.*

— Are you there to mark a special occasion? The general purpose of the special occasion speech will be variously *to entertain, celebrate, commemorate, inspire,* or *set a social agenda.*

Choose a Topic That Engages You

Selecting a topic can be approached from a variety of angles. You can begin "at the top" by focusing on broad social issues of national or even global consequence, or you can start closer to the ground by making an inventory of your own interests and life experiences.

Consider Personal Interests

Personal interests run the gamut from favorite activities and hobbies to deeply held goals and values. They provide powerful topics, especially if, by your sharing them, the audience in some way benefits from your experience.

Investigate Grassroots Issues

Most people respond with interest to issues that affect them directly, and, barring war and federal tax hikes, these tend to be of a local nature. Parents want to know about quality day care in the area; town residents need information about upcoming referenda.

Delve into Current Events

People are constantly barraged with newsworthy topics, but few of us have the time to delve into them. What was actually behind the hostage-taking situation in country X? What are the roots of the conflict in the Middle East? Similarly, controversial issues of the day—patenting human genes, prayer in public schools, and so on—usually earn their place in the limelight because they reflect our deepest concerns.

IDENTIFYING TOPICS

FAVORITE HOBBIES	CURRENT EVENTS AND CONTROVERSIAL ISSUES
• Sports	• Pending legislation — crime bills, property taxes, land use
• Volunteering	
• Computers	• Political contests
• Cars	• National security
• Investing	• Creationism vs. evolution
• Fashion	• Violence in the schools
• Books	• Lack of affordable child care
• Home repair	• Welfare to work
• Music	• Environmental issues
• Travel	• Gubernatorial recalls
• Collecting	• Peace in the Middle East
• Cooking	• Congressional redistricting
• Outdoor life	• Future of the Space Program

VALUES AND GOALS	SPECIFIC SUBJECT INTERESTS
• Building a sense of community	• Local history
	• Ancient history
• Working for social justice	• Politics
• Spirituality	• Art
• Being a high-tech entrepreneur	• Religion
	• Science
• Attending law/engineering/ nursing school	• Technology

GRASSROOTS ISSUES	NEW OR UNUSUAL ANGLES
• Land development vs. conservation	• Unsolved crimes
	• Unexplained disappearances
• Local organizations	• Scandals
• School issues	

Try Brainstorming to Generate Ideas

To generate ideas for topics, try **brainstorming** by word association or topic mapping.

To brainstorm by **word association**, write down a single topic that might interest you and your listeners. Next, write down the first thing that comes to mind. Continue this process until you have a list of fifteen to twenty items. Narrow the list to two or three, and then select the final topic:

- health → alternative medicine → naturopathy → fraud in alternative medicine

To brainstorm by **topic mapping**, put a potential topic in the middle of a piece of paper. As related ideas come to you, write them down, as shown in Figure 8.1.

Narrow the Topic

Once you have identified your topic and general speech purpose, you need to narrow your focus. When you narrow a topic, you focus on specific aspects of it to the exclusion of others. As you do so, carefully evaluate the topic in light of audience interests, knowledge, and needs:

- Consider what your listeners are likely to know about the subject.
- Consider what they are likely to want to learn.
- Consider what aspects of the topic are most relevant to the occasion.

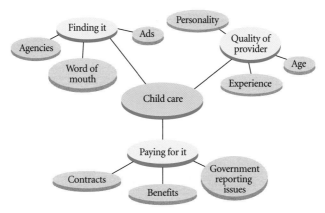

FIGURE 8.1 A Topic Map

Restrict your focus to what you can competently research and then report on in the time you are given to speak:

- Pick a discrete topic category and cover it well.
- Restrict your main points to between two and five.

QUICK TIP

Try Brainstorming by Categories

Just as brainstorming can be used to discover a general topic, it can also be helpful in narrowing one. One way of doing this is to brainstorm by category. Say your general topic is cell phones. One related category is models; another, manufacturers; a third, calling plans. As you brainstorm by category, ask yourself: What questions do I have about the topic? What does my audience know about cell phones? What aspect of cell phones is the audience most likely to want to hear about?

Form a Specific Speech Purpose

The **specific speech purpose** states precisely what the speaker wants the audience to get from the speech. To determine the specific purpose, ask yourself: What do you want the audience to learn/do/reconsider/agree with? Be specific about your aim, and then state this aim in action form, such as "To inform my audience about how the *C. elegans* worms survived the 2003 explosion of the Columbia Space Shuttle."

GENERAL TOPIC:	*C. elegans* worms
NARROWED TOPIC:	The survival of the *C. elegans* worms in the Columbia Space Shuttle explosion
GENERAL PURPOSE:	To inform
SPECIFIC PURPOSE:	To inform my audience about how the *C. elegans* worms survived the 2003 explosion of the Columbia Space Shuttle.

Compose a Thesis Statement

After narrowing your topic and forming your specific purpose, your next step is to formulate a thesis statement. The **thesis statement** (also called "central idea") is the theme or central idea of the speech stated in the form of a single, declarative sentence. The main points, the supporting material, and the conclusion all relate to the thesis.

The thesis statement and the specific purpose are closely linked. Both state the speech topic but in different forms. *The specific purpose describes in action form what you want to achieve with the speech; the thesis statement concisely identifies, in a single idea, what the speech is about.* This can be seen in the specific purpose and thesis statement for a persuasive speech on student internships:

SPECIFIC PURPOSE: To convince my audience that internships are beneficial by linking their academic studies with their future careers.

THESIS STATEMENT: To prepare for a difficult job market and to enhance your résumé, you should get a student internship to help link your academic studies with your future career.

Postpone Development of Main Points

Whether the speech is informative or persuasive, the thesis statement proposes that the statement made is true or is believed. The speech is then developed from this premise; it presents facts and evidence to support the thesis as true. Thus, you should always postpone the development of main points or the consideration of supporting material until you have correctly formulated the purpose and thesis (see Chapter 12).

In a persuasive speech, the thesis statement represents what you are going to prove in the address. All the main points in the speech are arguments that develop the thesis:

GENERAL PURPOSE: To persuade

SPECIFIC PURPOSE: To move the audience to raise money on behalf of the Sierra Club

THESIS: A donation to the Sierra Club is the best charitable gift you can give.

Notice that, after you read the thesis, you find yourself asking "Why?" or saying "Prove it!" This will be accomplished by the main points (see Chapter 12).

In informative speaking, the thesis describes what the audience will learn:

GENERAL PURPOSE: To inform

SPECIFIC PURPOSE: To "set the record straight" on the chronology of World War II

THESIS: Five major events caused the United States to go to war in 1941.

CHECKLIST: Identifying the Speech Topic, Purpose, and Thesis

✓ Have I identified the general speech purpose: to inform, persuade, or mark a special occasion?

✓ Is the topic appropriate to the occasion?

✓ Will the topic appeal to my listeners' interests and needs?

✓ Will I be able to offer a fresh perspective on the topic?

✓ Have I identified what the audience is most likely to know about the subject and what they are most likely to want to learn?

✓ Have I considered how much can I competently research and then report on in the time I am given to speak?

✓ Does my thesis statement sum up in a single declarative sentence what my speech is about?

✓ Is it restricted to a single idea?

✓ Does it make the claim I intend to make about my topic?

✓ Is it stated in a way that is relevant to the audience?

Make the Thesis Statement Relevant and Motivating

Try to express the thesis statement in a way that will motivate the audience to listen. In many cases, creating relevant statements can be accomplished by adding a few key words or phrases to the claim. For example, you can preface an informative thesis statement with a phrase such as "Few of us know" or "Contrary to popular belief" or "Have you ever." Thesis statements for persuasive claims can also be adapted to establish relevance for the audience. Phrases such as "As most of you know" or "As informed members of the community" or "As concerned adults" can help gain audience interest and make listeners see the topic's relevance.

Use information about the audience members to make the topic relevant for them. Consider how the following thesis statement has been adapted for an audience living in a troubled community:

SPECIFIC PURPOSE: To persuade the audience to elect a political candidate

THESIS:	A vote for Politician "X" is a vote for progress.
THESIS WITH RELEVANCE:	Because the time has come for us to deal with the issues in our community, a vote for Politician "X" is a vote for progress.

QUICK TIP

Use the Thesis Statement to Stay Focused

As you develop the speech, use the thesis statement to keep yourself on track. Review your research materials in the light of whether they contribute to the thesis or stray from it. When you actually draft your speech, work your thesis statement into it and restate it where appropriate. Doing so will encourage your audience to understand and accept your message.

---

9 Developing Supporting Material

Good speeches contain accurate, relevant, and interesting **supporting material** in the form of examples, narratives, testimony, facts, and statistics. These "flesh out" the speech — they give substance to the speech's thesis, or central idea.

Examples

Examples illustrate, describe, or represent things. Their purpose is to aid understanding by making ideas, items, or events more concrete. Examples are particularly helpful when they are used to describe or explain things with which the audience may not be familiar. **Brief examples** offer a single illustration of a point. In a speech titled "The Coming Golden Age of Medicine," Richard F. Corlin offers the following brief example to illustrate what American medicine can do:

> We often hear about the problems of the American health care delivery system, but just think what it can do. My 88-year-old father who needed a hip replacement got it — the

week it was discovered that he needed it. That couldn't happen in any other country in the world.[1]

Sometimes it takes more than a brief example to effectively illustrate a point. **Extended examples** offer multifaceted illustrations of the idea, item, or event being described, thereby getting the point across and reiterating it effectively. In a speech titled "Speechwriting Secrets from the Senate," speechwriter Pete Weissman offers the following extended example to illustrate his point that his boss, Senator Patty Murray, is not "an average senator":

> She is not a millionaire. As a teenager, her dad was disabled by multiple sclerosis. Her mom went to school, held down a job, cared for her dad, and raised seven kids. For a while, her family relied on food stamps to get through some tough months. Clearly, she doesn't come from a wealthy background like many of her Senate colleagues.[2]

In some speeches you may need to make a point about something that could happen in the future if certain events occurred. Since it hasn't happened yet, you'll need a **hypothetical example** of what you believe the outcome will be. Republican Representative Vernon Ehlers of Michigan offered the following hypothetical example when he spoke at a congressional hearing in support of a bill to ban human cloning:

> What if in the cloning process you produce someone with two heads and three arms? Are you simply going to euthanize and dispose of that person? The answer is no. We're talking about human life.[3]

Narratives

One of the most powerful means of conveying a message is through a **narrative**, or **story**. Narratives tell tales, both real and imaginary, about practically anything under the sun. Common to all narratives are the essential storytelling elements of a plot, characters, setting, and some sort of timeline.

Narratives can be brief and simple descriptions of short incidents worked into the speech, or relatively drawn-out accounts that constitute most of the presentation. In either event, a successful story will strike a chord with the audience.

In the following example, Bonnie Campbell, director of

the Violence Against Women Office of the U.S. Department of Justice, used a brief real-life story to introduce her speech, titled "Breaking the Silence on Domestic Violence":

> Last November 26, Christopher Bailey of St. Albans, West Virginia, finished the argument by beating his wife, Sonya, until she collapsed. Then he put her in the trunk of their compact car and drove for five days through West Virginia and Kentucky before taking her to an emergency room. Sonya Bailey suffered irreversible brain damage and remains in a permanent vegetative state — becoming another domestic violence statistic.[4]

Many speakers, whether they're ministers at the Sunday morning pulpit or high-tech entrepreneurs rallying the troops, liberally sprinkle their speeches with **anecdotes** — brief stories of interesting, humorous, or real-life incidents. In a speech about the need to preserve our national parks, Brock Evans, the director of the Endangered Species Coalition, does this artfully:

> One of the leaders of the fight was a fifth-generation rancher, Carroll Noble. . . . [H]e had a spread over near Pinedale. I'll never forget how he loved this Wyoming land, and how he expressed his feelings about it. One day, we were having dinner at his place. He had a big picture window there, framing that whole magnificent vista of the Wind River Range, its snow-capped jagged peaks, and the great tumbling mass of green forest spilling down its flank to the lake. At one point, he gestured out there, and turned to me with the greatest sadness: "You see that?" he said. "If they start cutting that, I'll never look out that window again."[5]

QUICK TIP

The Power of a Story

The power of a good story lies in its ability to capture audience interest or to encourage identification on the part of the listener. To determine whether your story is likely to engage the audience effectively, analyze your audience. Who are they? What do they need and want from your speech? What are their concerns and past experiences? What stories or anecdotes are appropriate to the occasion?

Testimony

When looking for supporting material, consider quoting or paraphrasing people who have an intimate knowledge of your topic. **Testimony** is firsthand findings, eyewitness accounts, and people's opinions. **Expert testimony** includes findings, eyewitness accounts, or opinions from professionals trained to evaluate a given topic. **Lay testimony**, or testimony by nonexperts such as eyewitnesses, can reveal compelling firsthand information that may be unavailable to others.

When citing testimony, make sure that you supply the name and qualifications of the person whose testimony you use. When referring to testimony, use such terms as "according to," "as stated by," or "in a conversation with . . . she stated." Also, tell your listeners when and where the testimony was offered. It isn't necessary to cite the exact date (though do keep a written record of this); in the oral presentation, terms such as "recently," "last year," and so forth are fine. The following is an example:

> In testimony before the U.S. House Committee on the Judiciary last week, victims' rights advocate Ellen Greenlee of the National Legal Aid and Defender Association said, "The proposals for a victims' rights constitutional amendment threaten to bring the American criminal justice system — in all its incarnations, federal, state, local, tribal, military, juvenile — to its knees."[6]

Facts and Statistics

Research has demonstrated that most people require some type of evidence, usually in the form of facts and statistics, before they will accept someone else's claims or position.[7]

Facts represent documented occurrences, including actual events, dates, times, people, and places.

Statistics are summarized data that measure the size or magnitude of something, demonstrate trends, or show relationships. *Descriptive statistics* describe things (e.g., there are this many number of this). Here, a speaker uses descriptive statistics to substantiate the claim that more needs to be done to protect the U.S. worker on the job:

> But, our work is far from done. Every year, work-related accidents and illnesses cost an estimated 56,000 American

CHECKLIST: Evaluating Your Research Needs

Do you need . . .

✓ Examples to illustrate, describe, or represent your ideas?

✓ A story or anecdote to drive your point home?

✓ Firsthand findings, in the form of testimony, to illustrate your points or strengthen your argument?

✓ Relevant facts, or documented occurrences, to substantiate your statements?

✓ Statistics to demonstrate relationships?

lives—more than the total American lives lost in battle during the entire 9-year Vietnam War.[8]

Inferential statistics are data collected from a sample or representative group and then generalized to a larger population. Poll and survey results are based on inferential statistics:

A 2002 survey by Chargemore Insurance Co. found that four out of ten employees (40%) feel their jobs are "very" or "extremely stressful."

Using this type of statistic requires that the data or information come from a representative sample. This means that your data must come from the same sample source (people, raw numbers) as the one you are inferring or comparing.

Rather than statements of truth, statistics are merely reports of data and thus must be used with care. Before using statistics in your speech, assess their reliability and validity. Consider whether the data was collected scientifically and interpreted objectively:

• What was the sampling size?

• Are the results statistically significant?

• Was the experiment well designed?

If you are reporting on a poll, ask yourself the following questions before presenting the results to your audience:

• Who did the poll? Who paid for it and why?

• How many people were interviewed? How were they chosen?

- What area (nation, state, or region) and what group(s) (teachers, lawyers, Democratic voters, etc.) were these people chosen from? Should others have been chosen?
- When was the poll done?
- What is the sampling error for the poll results?
- What other kinds of factors could have skewed the poll results?[9]

10 Locating Supporting Material

Finding the right mix of supporting material (e.g., examples, facts, statistics, opinions, stories, and testimony) for your speech requires that you conduct primary research, secondary research, or a combination of both. **Primary research** is original or firsthand research such as interviews and surveys conducted by you, the speaker (see Chapter 7). **Secondary research**, the focus here, includes all information recorded by individuals other than actual participants in an event or study.

Locate Secondary Sources

The most likely sources of secondary research include books, newspapers, periodicals, government publications, and reference works such as encyclopedias, almanacs, books of quotations, and atlases.

QUICK TIP

Essential Reference Sources
*Consider beginning your library research by consulting two essential resources — the reference librarian and the card or online catalog. (See Chapter 11 on using virtual libraries on the World Wide Web.) **Reference librarians** are information specialists who are trained to help you in your search. Online or card catalogs list what a library owns. Both are searchable by author, title, and subject.*

Books

Books explore topics in depth. A well-written book provides detail and perspective and can serve as an excellent source of supporting examples, stories, facts, and statistics. To locate a book in your library's holdings, refer to the library's card or online catalog. To search the titles of all books currently in print in the United States, refer to *Books in Print* in print or online at <www.booksinprint.com>. Alternatively, log onto Amazon.com (<www.amazon.com>), Barnes&Noble.com (<www.barnesandnoble.com>), or another major online bookseller and key in your topic.

Newspapers and Periodicals

In addition to reports on the major issues and events of the day, many newspaper stories include detailed background or historic information. Three comprehensive sources for searching newspaper articles can be accessed online: *Lexus Nexus Academic Universe News service, InfoTrac Newspaper Collection,* and *Newspaper Abstracts.* Many newspapers also offer online versions with searchable archives.

A **periodical** is a regularly published magazine or journal. Periodicals are excellent sources because they usually include all types of supporting material discussed in Chapter 9. They include general-interest magazines such as *Time* and *Newsweek,* as well as the thousands of specialized academic, business, and technical magazines, newsletters, and journals. Most popular magazines are indexed in the *Wilson Periodical Abstracts.* Many libraries offer access to the online databases such as *InfoTrac Online, Expanded Academic ASAP,* and *EBSCO Academic Search Elite.* There are also many periodical databases that are devoted to special topics such as business, health, education, and sociology.

Government Publications

Finding and using government documents can be daunting, but it's worth the effort, given that nearly all the information comes from primary sources. The *Guide to U.S. Government Publications,* available in print, microfiche, and online (<www.access.gpo.gov>), offers a step-by-step guide to researching government publications. FirstGov.gov is the official U.S. gateway to all government information and services, from the federal government, local, and tribal governments to nations around the world. The University of Michigan's Documents Center (<www.lib.umich.edu /govdocs/>) is another excellent starting point.

Reference Works

Reference works include, but are not limited to, encyclopedias, almanacs, biographical resources, books of quotations, poetry collections, and atlases.

ENCYCLOPEDIAS   **Encyclopedias** summarize knowledge that is found in original form elsewhere. Their usefulness lies in providing an overview of subjects. *General encyclopedias* attempt to cover all important subject areas of knowledge. *Specialized encyclopedias* delve deeply into one subject area such as religion, science, art, sports, or engineering. The most comprehensive of the general encyclopedias is the *Encyclopedia Britannica,* available in print form, on CD-ROM and DVD, and online.

For a more in-depth look at a topic, specialized encyclopedias of all types range from the *McGraw-Hill Encyclopedia of Science and Technology* to the *Encyclopedia of Religion* and the *Encyclopedia of Physical Education, Fitness, and Sports.*

ALMANACS   **Almanacs** and **fact books** contain facts and statistics and are published annually. As with encyclopedias, there are both general and specialized almanacs. In the general category, two of the most comprehensive sources are the *World Almanac* and *Book of Facts.* Other helpful almanacs include *The Guinness Book of World Records, The Information Please Almanac,* and *The People's Almanac.*

BIOGRAPHICAL RESOURCES   For information about famous or noteworthy people, the *Biography Index* is an excellent starting point. Available in print, CD-ROM, and online, and published quarterly, this comprehensive resource indexes biographical material from periodicals, books, and newspapers. For analyses and criticism of the published works of individuals you may be speaking about, see *The Essay and General Literature Index, Dictionary of American Biography, Dictionary of World Biography,* and *Current Biography.*

BOOKS OF QUOTATIONS   Quotations are often used in speech introductions and conclusions; they are also liberally sprinkled throughout examples, narratives, and testimony. *Bartlett's Familiar Quotations* contains passages, phrases, and proverbs traced to their sources. Many collections are targeted directly at public speakers, including *Quotations for Public Speakers: A Historical, Literary, and Political Anthology,* by Robert G. Torricelli,[1] and *Nelson's Complete Book of Stories, Illustrations, and Quotes: The Ultimate Contemporary Resource for Speakers,* by Robert J. Morgan.[2]

POETRY COLLECTIONS   Speakers often use lines of poetry or entire poems both to introduce and conclude speeches and to illustrate points in the speech body. Every library has a collection of poetry anthologies as well as the collected works of individual poets. Updated yearly, the *Columbia Granger's Index to Poetry* indexes poems by author, title, and first line. Online, search for poetry on the Bartleby site (<www.bartleby.com/>).

ATLASES   An **atlas** is a collection of maps, text, and accompanying charts and tables. Atlases provide geographic, statistical, and demographic information about particular regions, countries, states, or cities. Two excellent print atlases are the *National Geographic Atlas of the World* and the *Rand McNally Commercial Atlas and Guide.* Online, access maps on the National Geographic Web site (<www.nationalgeographic.com/maps/index.html>).

Multicultural Reference Works

Until fairly recently, standard reference works such as encyclopedias and almanacs claimed to be comprehensive but generally paid little attention to the culture and accomplishments of the many minority groups that make up the United States. Today, publishers are addressing this long-standing need.

The Gale Encyclopedia of Multicultural America contains 152 original essays on specific minority and ethnic groups in the United States, from Arab Americans to the Yupiat.[3] Gale also publishes a wide range of multivolume biographical sets and almanacs containing portraits, quotes, interviews, and articles about prominent men and women of specific minority groups and focusing on major aspects of group culture.

Critically Evaluate Your Sources

Whether you are reviewing a book, a newspaper article, or any other source, consider the following:

- What is the author's background — experience, training, and reputation — in the field of study?

- How credible is the publication? Who is the publisher? Is the person or organization reputable? What other publications has the author or organization published?

- How reliable is the data, especially the statistical information? Generally, statistics drawn from government documents and scientific and academic journals are more reliable than those reported in the popular press (e.g., general-interest magazines).

- How recent is the reference? As a rule, it is best to be familiar with the most recent source you can find, even when the topic is historical. (See Chapter 2, p. 11, for directions on how to orally credit sources in your speech.)

QUICK TIP

Save Sources Systematically

Keep track of your sources as you collect them, and create a system for keeping track of them, such as using the footnote feature on Microsoft Word. Take extra care when tracking and citing Internet sources, saving URLs as you go.

---

11 Doing Effective Internet Research

As with conducting research in a library, the key to a productive search in cyberspace lies in a well-thought-out research strategy, an understanding of the kinds of information available on the Internet, and a basic grasp of how to use Internet search tools.

Critically Evaluate Each Internet Source You Use

When searching on the Internet for supporting materials for your speech, time pressures may lead you to rely on information sources that are immediately available and accessible but not necessarily the best. Look for the following:

CREDIBLE PRIMARY SOURCES For example, if your topic is on organ donation, look for sites sponsored by the U.S. government first (or the government of another country). Government-sponsored sites are free of commercial taint and are likely to contain highly credible primary materials.

AUTHORSHIP If an individual operates the site, look for relevant biographical information, such as links to a résumé or a listing of the author's credentials. For an institutional or organizational site, look for a mission or "About Us" statement. For all sites, look for contact information. A source that doesn't want to be found is generally not a good source to cite.

DOCUMENTATION Does the site credit sources? If so, does the site provide links to them? Follow these links, and evaluate the sources as well.

TYPE Examine the **domain** in the Web address—the suffixes at the end of the address that tell you the nature of the site: educational (".edu"), government (".gov"), military (".mil"), nonprofit organization (".org"), business/commercial (".com"), and network (".net"). A *tilde* (~) in the address usually indicates that it is a personal page rather than part of an institutional Web site.

CURRENCY Does the page indicate when it was created or updated? Web sites that do not have this information may contain outdated or inaccurate material.

Learn to Distinguish Information from Propaganda, Misinformation, and Disinformation

Elizabeth Kirk of the Johns Hopkins University's Sheridan Library offers important distinctions among *information, propaganda, misinformation,* and *disinformation.* Bearing in mind these distinctions when evaluating both print and

Internet sources can help you critically assess their credibility.[1] Meaningful speeches are based on sound information rather than propaganda, misinformation, or disinformation.

- **Information** is data set in a context for relevance. Information tells us something that is understandable and has the potential to become knowledge when we view it critically and add it to what we already know.

- **Propaganda** is information represented in such a way as to provoke a desired response. The purpose of propaganda is to instill a particular attitude: to encourage you to think a particular way.

- **Misinformation** always refers to something that is not true. One common form of misinformation on the Internet is the *urban legend* — a fabricated story passed along by unsuspecting people.

- **Disinformation** is the deliberate falsification of information. For example, the Enron Corporation's falsified profit-and-loss statements are a good example of disinformation in action.

QUICK TIP

Corroborate Internet Sources
Always try to verify information you find on the Internet with at least two other reputable sources. Research the credibility of the author or organization responsible for the information by "Googling it" (keying the source's name into the Google search engine) or by using your local library. Beware that the existence of multiple Internet citations for a given piece of information does not in any way guarantee its reliability: Like viruses, propaganda, misinformation, and disinformation spread with lightning speed.

Use Internet Search Tools Efficiently

To locate information on the Internet efficiently, familiarize yourself with the function of search engines, human directories, library gateways, and specialized databases ("vortals").

Distinguish among Different Kinds of Search Engines

Search engines index the contents of the Web. **Crawler-based search engines** (also called "automated search engines"; see

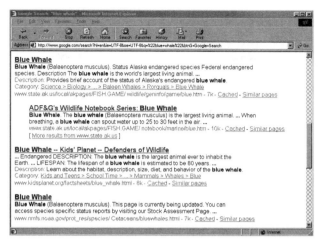

FIGURE 11.1 List of Hits from a Crawler-Based Search Engine

Figure 11.1) use powerful software to scan millions of documents for keywords and phrases you command them to search. A program then creates a huge index from the pages that have been read, compares it to your search request, and returns matching results. Results are generally ranked from most relevant to least relevant, though criteria for relevance can vary. Examples include Google (<www.google.com>), Alta Vista (<www.altavista.com>), AlltheWeb (<www.alltheweb .com>), and Teoma (<www.teoma.com>).

Pay for placement search engines such as Overture allow advertisers to bid on popular search terms that are relevant to their site, with the top position going to the highest bidder. They are generally not reliable for researching your speech.

Meta-Search Engines

Individual search engines such as those just listed compile their own databases of Web pages. **Meta-search engines**, on the other hand, scan a variety of individual search engines simultaneously and can be useful for conducting preliminary searches to determine the types of resources available online. Examples include:

- *Dogpile:* Searches eleven individual search engines (<www.dogpile.com>)

- *Vivisimo:* Categorizes results into topic-based hierarchical folders (<www.vivisimo.com>)

- *MetaCrawler:* Simultaneously queries AltaVista, Look-Smart, About, and others (<www.metacrawler.com>)
- *Ask Jeeves:* Searches its own database of questions and answers compiled by human editors; also delivers metasearch results (<www.ask.com>)

Specialized Search Engines

Consider using a **specialized search engine** that is devoted entirely to your topic. Easy Searcher 2 (<www.easysearcher.com/>) is a compilation of some 300 engines, both commercial and those focused on specific topics.

Human Directories

A **human directory** (also called a **subject directory**) is a searchable database of Web sites that have been submitted to that directory and then assigned by a human editor to an appropriate category or categories, such as "Reference," "Science," or "Arts and Humanities." Editors of directories such as Yahoo! and the Open Directory Project (see Figure 11.2) analyze and often rate the information accepted into their databases. Compared to search engines, human directories are consistently likely to yield higher-quality information (if retrieving far fewer links) because human editors vet and index the sites. Examples include Yahoo! (<www.yahoo.com>), About.com (<www.about.com>), Open Directory Project (<www.dmoz.org>), and LookSmart (<www.looksmart.org>).

Hybrid Search Engines: Range plus Relevance

The trend today is toward **hybrid search engines**—those that combine crawler-based search engine results with results from a human directory.[2] For example, the human directory Yahoo! now complements its listings with search results from Google, a crawler-based engine. Similarly, Google uses Open Directory Project's human directory to enhance its automatically generated listings.[3]

Library Gateways

A **library gateway** is an entry point into a large collection of research and reference material that has been selected and reviewed by librarians. Most universities and local libraries offer library gateways in the form of their library's home

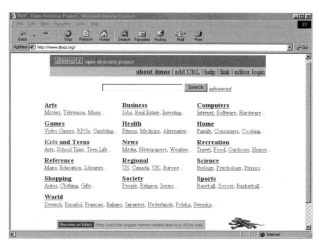

FIGURE 11.2 List of Categories from Open Directory Project

page. Here you will find information on its periodicals holdings and recent acquisitions, along with an online library catalog plus outside links reviewed by librarians for quality. The page may also contain links to the online databases to which the library subscribes. With password in hand, you can search for and retrieve abstracts and articles electronically.

Virtual libraries such as the *Librarians' Index to the Internet* and the *Internet Public Library* that exist only on the Internet are excellent gateways that offer links to an extraordinary array of resources for the public speaker. **Subject-specific databases** ("**vortals**") are gateways in which subject specialists point to specialized databases created by professors, researchers, experts, governmental agencies, business interests, or other specialists and individuals who have a deep interest in a particular field and have accumulated and compiled Web links to it.[4] Because much of this information is not accessible to general search engines and human directories, gateways are sometimes considered part of the **invisible web** — the portion of the Web that includes pass-protected sites, documents behind firewalls, and the contents of proprietary databases.[5] Library gateways and specialty search engines are good sources of direct links to such information.[6] Examples of virtual libraries include:

- The Librarians' Index to the Internet (<http://lii.org /search>)
- Living Web Virtual Library (<www.livingweb.com/>)

- PINAKES (<www.hw.ac.uk/libWWW/irn/pinakes/pinakes.html>)
- Internet Public Library (IPL) (<www.ipl.org/>)
- refdesk.com (<www.refdesk.com/>)
- WWW Virtual Library (<http://vlib.org/>)
- Academic Info (<www.academicinfo.net/>)
- Digital Librarian (<www.digital-librarian.com/>)
- Infomine (<http://infomine.ucr.edu/>)

Create an Online Search Strategy

As you begin researching your topic, take some time to consider your goal. Is it to brainstorm or narrow a topic? To find a scholarly article? To locate a specific quotation, fact, or figure? To locate everything you can on a topic?

To maximize the odds of finding the materials you need, familiarize yourself with the search commands of the search tools you select. In most search tools, you can go to the Help command located near the search window.

Most search tools are programmed to respond to the following basic commands:

- Quotations marks (" ") to find exact phrases (e.g., "white wine"). Without the quotations, search tools will list all relevant sites with the word "white" as well as those with the word "wine."
- Boolean operators, or words placed between the keywords in a search, that specify how the keywords are related:[7]
  - AND narrows your search by indicating words that must appear in a document: apple AND fruit. With some search engines, you will need to use a plus sign: apple +fruit.
  - OR expands your search by permitting results that contain any of the terms: preschool OR "nursery school".
  - NOT restricts your search by excluding specific terms: "bed and breakfast" NOT motel. With some search engines, you will need to use a minus sign: "bed and breakfast" –motel.
  - An asterisk stands in for letters that could vary: "public speak*"

Bookmark Sources
When you find a useful Web site, immediately add it to your browser's bookmark list — a pull-down menu that saves direct links to Web sites so that you can return to the site with ease.

Cite and Record Internet Sources

As with all research sources, you should document your Internet sources as you prepare and draft your speech. Styles of documenting Internet sources vary according to discipline. Three of the most widely used formats include the American Psychological Association (APA) style, the Modern Language Association (MLA) style, and Chicago style (see Appendix A). Each style varies in the precise format of information, but all generally require that you provide as much of the following information as possible:

- Name of the author, editor, or site maintainer (if applicable)
- Publication information of any print version, year, volume number, and page number
- Date of electronic publication or last revision
- Title of the page or a description, such as "home page"
- Retrieval date statement (e.g., "Retrieved on May 12, 2001" or "Accessed on June 12, 2003")
- URL[8]

Part 3
Organization

12 Organizing Main and Supporting Points

A speech structure is simple, composed of just three general parts: an introduction, a body, and a conclusion. The **introduction** establishes the purpose of the speech and shows its relevance to the audience. The **body** of the speech presents main points that are intended to fulfill the speech purpose. Main points are developed with various kinds of supporting material to fulfill this purpose. The **conclusion** brings closure to the speech by restating the purpose, summarizing main points, and reiterating why the thesis is relevant to the audience. In essence, the introduction of a speech tells listeners where they are going, the body takes them there, and the conclusion lets them know they have arrived.

Chapter 15 focuses on how to create effective introductions and conclusions. In this chapter we explore the body of the speech. It consists of three elements: *main points, supporting points,* and *transitions.*

Use Main Points to Make Your Claims

Main points express the key ideas and major themes of the speech. Their function is to represent each of the main elements or claims being made in support of the speech topic.

To create main points, identify the central ideas and themes of the speech. What are the most important ideas you want to convey? What key ideas emerge from your research? What ideas can you substantiate with supporting material? Each of these ideas or claims should be expressed as a main point.

Use the Purpose and Thesis Statements as Guides

Main points should flow directly from the specific purpose and thesis statements, as seen in the following example:

SPECIFIC PURPOSE STATEMENT:	(the goal of the speech): To show my audience, through a series of easy steps, how to perform meditation.
THESIS STATEMENT:	(the central idea of the speech): When performed correctly, meditation is an effective and easy way to reduce stress.
MAIN POINTS:	I. The first step of meditation is the "Positioning."
	II. The second step of meditation is "Breathing."
	III. The third step of meditation is "Relaxation."

Restrict the Number of Main Points

Research has shown that audiences can comfortably take in only between two and seven main points.[1] For most speeches, between two and five main points should be sufficient.

QUICK TIP

Key Points as Bookends for Your Speech
Listeners have a better recall of points made at the beginning and the end of a speech than of those made in between. If it is especially important that listeners remember certain ideas, introduce the points near the beginning of the speech and reiterate them at the conclusion.

Restrict Each Main Point to a Single Idea

A main point should not introduce more than one idea. If it does, it should be split into two (or more) main points:

INCORRECT: I.   West Texas has its own Grand Canyon, and South Texas has its own desert.

CORRECT: I.   West Texas boasts its own Grand Canyon.

              II. South Texas boasts its own desert.

Express each main point as a *declarative sentence* (e.g., one that makes a statement or assertion). This emphasizes the point and makes it stand out. For example, if one of your main points is that poor children are suffering because of changes in welfare laws, you should clearly state, "Today, poor children are suffering because of changes in the welfare laws." As shown in the example about West Texas and South Texas, when possible state your main points in *parallel form*, that is, in similar grammatical form and style (see Chapter 16). This helps listeners understand and retain the points, and it lends power and elegance to your words.

Use Supporting Points to Prove Your Claims

Supporting points represent the supporting material or evidence you have gathered to justify the main points (see Chapter 9). Use them to substantiate or prove your thesis with the material you've gathered in your research—examples, narratives, testimony, facts, and statistics.

Use Indentation to Arrange Supporting Points

In an outline, supporting points are indented to appear in a subordinate position to main points. As with main points, supporting points should be arranged in order of their importance or relevance to the main point. The most common format is the **Roman numeral outline**. Main points are enumerated with uppercase Roman numerals (I, II, III . . .), while supporting points are enumerated with capital letters (A, B, C . . .), Arabic numerals (1, 2, 3 . . .), and lowercase letters (a, b, c . . .), as seen in the following:

I. Main point
    A. Supporting point
        1. Sub-supporting point
            a. Sub-sub-supporting point

Here is an example from a speech about children's negative attitudes toward school:

I. The increase in study drill sessions in preparation for standardized tests, from one hour to three hours daily, is causing students anxiety about attending school.
    A. Teachers report that students' reactions to the lengthened study drills have been negative.
        1. Teachers report a noticeable rise in acting-out behaviors.
        2. Teachers report a tenfold increase in class-time requests to visit the nurse.
    B. During the past two months, 600 parents have lodged complaints with the principal about the extended study drill session.
        1. The majority (85 percent) said that their children cried at night about the lengthy study sessions.
        2. A minority (15 percent) reported that their children had to be forced to go to school.
II. The elimination of the art and science classes in favor of longer drill sessions has only increased students' negative feelings toward school.
    A. Art classes have long been a favorite of school-age children.
    B. Student reaction to the elimination of science classes has been strongly negative.

1. Students staged a sit-down strike in the cafeteria to protest the elimination of science classes.
2. Several students transferred to other schools in order to take science classes.

Principles of Organizing Main and Supporting Points

A well-organized speech is characterized by unity, coherence, and balance. Try to adhere to these principles as you arrange your speech points.

Unity

A speech exhibits *unity* when it contains only those points implied by the purpose and thesis statements. Each main point supports the thesis, and each supporting point provides evidence for the main points. Each sub-supporting point supports each supporting point. Finally, each point should focus on a single idea.

Coherence

A speech exhibits *coherence* when it is organized clearly and logically. The speech body should follow logically from the introduction, and the conclusion should follow logically from the body. Within the body of the speech itself, main points should follow logically from the thesis statement, and supporting points should follow logically from the main points. Transitions (see p. 73) serve as logical bridges that help establish coherence.[2]

To ensure coherence, adhere to the principle of **coordination and subordination** — the logical placement of ideas relative to their importance to one another. Ideas that are coordinate are given equal weight. An idea that is subordinate to another is given relatively less weight. In outlines, **coordinate points** are indicated by their parallel alignment, and **subordinate points** are indicated by their indentation below the more important points. For an example, see the outline shown earlier on students' negative attitudes toward school: Coordinate points are aligned with one another, while subordinate points are indented below the points that they substantiate. Thus Main Point II is coordinate with Main Point I, Subpoint A is subordinate to Main Point I, Subpoint B is coordinate with Subpoint A, and so forth.

Balance

The principle of *balance* suggests that appropriate emphasis or weight be given to each part of the speech relative to the other parts and to the theme. The body of a speech should always be the longest part, and the introduction and conclusion should be of roughly the same length. Stating the main points in parallel form is one aspect of balance. Assigning each main point at least two supporting points is another.

QUICK TIP

Create at Least Two Subpoints . . . or None
If you have only one subpoint, consider how you might incorporate it into the superior point. Think of a main point as a body and supporting points as legs; without at least two legs, the body cannot stand.

Use Transitions to Give Direction to the Speech

Transitions are words, phrases, or sentences that tie the speech ideas together and enable the speaker to move smoothly from one point to the next. Transitions can be considered the "neurosystem" of speeches: They provide consistency of movement from one point to the next and cue the audience that a new point will be made. Transitions can take the form of full sentences, phrases, or single words.

Use Transitions between Main Points

When moving from one main point to another, **full-sentence transitions** are especially effective. For example, to move from Main Point I in a speech about sales contests (*Top management should sponsor sales contests to halt the decline in sales over the past two years*) to Main Point II (*Sales contests will lead to better sales presentations*), the speaker might use the following transition:

Next, let's look at exactly what sales contests can do for us.

Use Transitions between Supporting Points

Transitions between supporting points can also be handled with full sentences. For example, the transition from Supporting Point A (*Sales personnel will be motivated by competition*) to

Supporting Point B (*Contests are relatively inexpensive*) could be made by the following transition:

> Another way that sales competitions will benefit us is by their relative cost effectiveness.

Conjunctions or phrases (sometimes called **signposts**) such as the following can be just as effective:

> Next . . .
>
> First . . . (second, third, and so forth)
>
> We now turn . . .
>
> Finally, let's consider . . .
>
> If you think that's shocking . . .
>
> Similarly . . .

TRANSITIONAL WORDS AND PHRASES
To show comparisons: Similarly; In the same way; Likewise; Just as
To illustrate cause and effect: As a result; Hence; Because; Thus; Consequently
To illustrate sequence: First, second, third . . . ; Following this; Later; Earlier; At present; In the past
To contrast ideas: On the other hand; And yet; At the same time; In spite of
To summarize: In conclusion; In summary; Finally; Let me conclude by saying

Sample Techniques for Posing Transitions

Transitions are often posed in **restate-forecast form,** restating the point just covered and previewing the point to be covered next:

> Now that we've established a need for sales contests (*restatement*), let's look at what sales contests can do for us (*forecast*).

Transitions can also be stated as **rhetorical questions**, or questions that do not invite actual responses. Instead, they stimulate listeners to anticipate probable answers, alerting them to the forthcoming point (see Chapter 15).

> Will contests be too expensive? Well, actually . . .
>
> How do the costs of contests stack up against the expense of training new people?

Use Previews and Summaries as Transitions

Previews are transitions that tell the audience what to expect next. In speech introductions a *preview statement* describes what will be covered in the body of the speech (see Chapter 15). Within the body itself, **internal previews** can be used to alert audience members to ensuing main points:

> Victoria Woodhull was a pioneer in many respects. Not only was she the first woman to run her own brokerage firm; she was also the first to run for the presidency of the United States, though few people know this. Let's see how she accomplished these feats.

Similar to the internal preview, the **internal summary** draws together important ideas before the speaker proceeds to another speech point. Internal summaries are often used

---

CHECKLIST: Reviewing Your Speech Organization

✓ Do your main points follow logically from your thesis statement?

✓ Is each main point substantiated by at least two supporting points?

✓ Do you spend roughly the same amount of time on each main point?

✓ Do your supporting points follow logically from the main points?

✓ Do your supporting points offer sufficient evidence in support of the main points?

✓ Do your supporting points reflect a variety of supporting materials: narratives, testimony, facts, and statistics?

✓ Does each main point and supporting point focus on a single idea?

✓ Are your main and supporting points stated in parallel form?

✓ Do you use transitions between the introduction and the body and between the body and the conclusion?

✓ Do you use transitions to move from one main point to another and one subpoint to the next?

in speech conclusions; within the body of the speech, they can help listeners review and evaluate the thread of the theme thus far:

> It should be clear that the kind of violence we've witnessed in the schools and in our communities has a deeper root cause than the availability of handguns. Our young children are crying out for a sense of community, of relatedness and meaning, that they just aren't finding in the institutions that are meant to serve them.

See Chapter 14, "Using Outline Formats," to learn how to include transitions in the outline of your speech.

13 Selecting an Organizational Pattern

Once you have selected the main points for your speech, you must decide on the type of arrangement or combination of arrangements for them. You can then proceed to flesh out the main points with subordinate ideas.

Public speeches make use of at least a dozen different organizational arrangements of main and supporting points. Here we look at seven commonly used patterns for all forms of speeches: chronological, spatial, causal (cause-effect), problem-solution, topical, narrative, and circle. These patterns offer an organized way to link points together to maximum effect. In Chapter 24, you will find three additional patterns of organization designed specifically for persuasive speeches.

QUICK TIP

Mix and Match

The pattern of organization for your subpoints need not always follow the pattern you select for your main points. For instance, for a speech about the history of tattooing in the United States, you may choose a chronological pattern to organize the main points but switch to a cause-effect arrangement for some of your subpoints regarding why tattooing is on the rise today. Organization, whether of main points or subpoints, should be driven by what's most effective for the particular rhetorical situation.

Arranging Speech Points Chronologically

Some speech topics lend themselves well to the arrangement of main points according to their occurrence in time relative to each other. A **chronological pattern of arrangement** (also called *temporal pattern*) follows the natural sequential order of the main points and is appropriate for any topic that involves a series of sequential steps. A scientist might describe the steps in a research project on fruit flies, for example, or a cook might explain the steps in a recipe. A speech describing the development of the World Wide Web, for example, calls for a chronological, or time-ordered, sequence of main points:

THESIS STATEMENT:	The Internet evolved from a small network designed for military and academic scientists into a vast array of networks used by billions of people around the globe.
MAIN POINTS:	I. The Internet was first conceived in 1962 as the ARPANET to promote the sharing of research among scientists in the United States.
	II. In the 1980s, a team created TCP/IP, a language that could link networks, and the Internet as we know it was born.
	III. At the end of the Cold War, the ARPANET was decommissioned, and the World Wide Web comprised the bulk of Internet traffic.[1]

Arranging Speech Points Using a Spatial Pattern

When the purpose of your speech is to describe or explain the physical arrangement of a place, a scene, or an object, logic suggests that the main points can be arranged in order of their physical proximity or direction relative to each other. This calls for a **spatial pattern of arrangement**. For example, you can select a spatial arrangement when your speech provides the audience with a "tour" of a particular place:

THESIS STATEMENT:	El Morro National Monument in New Mexico is captivating for its variety of natural and historical landmarks.
MAIN POINTS:	I. Visitors first encounter an abundant variety of plant life native to the high-country desert.

    II.   Soon visitors come upon an age-old watering hole that has receded beneath the 200-foot cliffs.

    III. Beyond are the famous cliff carvings made by hundreds of travelers over several centuries of exploration in the Southwest.

In a speech describing a computer company's market growth across regions of the country, a speaker might use the spatial arrangement as follows:

THESIS STATEMENT:	Sales of Digi-Tel Computers have grown in every region of the country.
MAIN POINTS:	I. Sales are strongest in the Eastern Zone.
	II. Sales are growing at a rate of 10 percent quarterly in the Central Zone.
	III. Sales are up slightly in the Mountain Zone.

Arranging Speech Points Using a Causal (Cause-Effect) Pattern

Some speech topics represent cause-effect relationships. Examples might include (1) Events Leading to Higher Interest Rates, (2) Reasons Students Drop Out of College, and (3) Causes of Spousal Abuse. The main points in a **causal (cause-effect) pattern of arrangement** usually take the following form:

I. Cause

II. Effect

Sometimes a topic can be discussed in terms of multiple causes for a single effect, or a single cause for multiple effects, as shown below:

MULTIPLE CAUSES FOR A SINGLE EFFECT: REASONS LEADING STUDENTS TO DROP OUT OF COLLEGE	**SINGLE CAUSE FOR MULTIPLE EFFECTS: RESULTS OF DROPPING OUT OF COLLEGE**
I. Cause 1 (lack of funds)	I. Cause (lack of funds)
II. Cause 2 (unsatisfactory social life)	II. Effect 1 (lowered lifetime earnings)

MULTIPLE CAUSES FOR A SINGLE EFFECT: REASONS LEADING STUDENTS TO DROP OUT OF COLLEGE	**SINGLE CAUSE FOR MULTIPLE EFFECTS: RESULTS OF DROPPING OUT OF COLLEGE**
III. Cause 3 (unsatisfactory academic performance)	III. Effect 2 (decreased overall job satisfaction)
IV. Effect (drop out of college)	IV. Effect 3 (increased stress level)

Some topics are best understood by presenting listeners with the effect(s) first and the cause or causes subsequently. For example, in an informative speech on the 1988 explosion of Pan Am Flight 103 over Lockerbie, Scotland, a student speaker arranged his main points as follows:

THESIS STATEMENT: The explosion of Pan Am Flight 103 over Lockerbie, Scotland, killed 270 people and resulted in the longest-running aviation investigation in history.

MAIN POINTS:
I.   (Effect) Two-hundred and fifty-nine passengers and crew members died; an additional eleven people on the ground perished.

II.   (Effect) Longest-running aviation investigation in history.

III.   (Cause) Court found cause of explosion was a terrorist act, bomb planted by Libyan citizen Al Megrahi.

IV.   (Cause) Many people believe that Megrahi did not act alone, if he acted at all.

Arranging Speech Points Using a Problem-Solution Pattern

In a **problem-solution pattern of arrangement**, the main points are organized to demonstrate the nature and significance of a problem and then to provide justification for a proposed solution. This type of arrangement can be as general as two main points:

I. Problem (define what it is)

II. Solution (offer a way to overcome the problem)

But many problem-solution speeches require more than two points to adequately explain the problem and to substantiate the recommended solution:

I.   The nature of the problem (identify its causes, incidence, etc.)

II.   Effects of the problem (explain why it's a problem, for whom, etc.)

III. Unsatisfactory solutions (discuss those that have not worked)

IV.   Proposed solution (explain why it's expected to work)

The following is a partial outline of a persuasive speech about teen pregnancy arranged in a problem-solution format. (For more on using the problem-solution pattern for persuasive speeches, see Chapter 24.)

THESIS STATEMENT: Once you realize the nature and probable causes of the problem of teen pregnancy, it should be clear that current solutions remain unsuccessful and an alternative solution—peer counseling—should be considered.

MAIN POINTS: I.   Early unwed pregnancies

    A. Average age of teen mothers

    B. National and local incidence

II.   Probable causes of teen pregnancy

    A. Dysfunctional family structure

    B. Dysfunctional social relationships

    C. Early sexual activity

III. Unsuccessful solutions

    A. School-based sex education

    B. Mass-media campaigns encouraging abstinence

IV.   Peer counseling as a possible solution

    A. How peer counseling works

    B. Coupled with school-based sexuality curriculum

Arranging Speech Points Topically

When each of the main points of a topic is of relatively equal importance, and when these points can be presented in any order relative to the other main points, consider a **topical pattern of arrangement** (also called *categorical pattern*). In this arrangement main points are organized logically by ideas or categories. Consider an informative speech about choosing Chicago as a place to establish a career. The speaker plans to emphasize three reasons for choosing Chicago: the strong economic climate of the city, its cultural variety, and its accessible public transportation. These three points can be arranged categorically and in any order without affecting each other or the speech purpose negatively. For example:

I.   Accessible transportation

II. Cultural variety

III. Economic stability

This is not to say that, when using a topical arrangement, you should arrange the main points without careful consideration. You may decide to arrange the points in the order of the audience's most immediate needs and interests:

I.   Economic stability

II. Cultural variety

III. Accessible transportation

QUICK TIP

The Freedoms of the Topical Pattern

Topical arrangements give you the greatest freedom to structure main points according to how you wish to present your topic. You can approach a topic by dividing it into two or more categories, for example. You can lead with your strongest evidence or leave the heavy artillery until you near the conclusion. If your topic does not call out for one of the other patterns described in this chapter, be sure to experiment with the topical pattern.

Alternate Patterns of Organization

Storytelling is often a natural and effective way to get your message across. In the **narrative organizational pattern**, the speech consists of a story or series of short stories, replete with character, settings, and plot. This type of pattern can be especially powerful when the stories are striking or compelling.

At a political convention in Los Angeles, except for the introduction and conclusion, actress Susan Sarandon's speech consisted entirely of stories about four people whom she believed were unfairly sentenced under the Three Strikes law:

> There are over 3,000 people serving life sentences under the Three Strikes law for minor offenses. These are just a few of those cases. . . .
>
> Shane Reams started using cocaine at age fifteen while delivering drugs for his biological father. He ran away from home. . . . Shane committed residential burglaries from his family and neighbors. . . . He never received any treatment. . . .[2]

CHECKLIST: Choosing an Organizational Pattern

Does your speech . . .

✓ Describe a series of developments in time or a set of actions that occurs sequentially? Use the *chronological pattern of organization*.

✓ Describe or explain the physical arrangement of a place, a scene, or an object? Use the *spatial pattern of organization*.

✓ Explain or demonstrate a topic in terms of its underlying causes or effects? Use the *causal (cause-effect) pattern of organization*.

✓ Demonstrate the nature and significance of a problem and justify a proposed solution? Use the *problem-solution pattern of arrangement*.

✓ Stress natural divisions in a topic, in which points can be moved to emphasize audience needs and interests? Use a *topical pattern of arrangement*.

✓ Convey ideas through a story, using character, plot, and settings? Use a *narrative pattern of arrangement*.

✓ Demonstrate how one idea leads to another and then another, eventually leading back to the speech thesis? Use a *circle pattern of arrangement*.

Sarandon's speech concludes with a brief call for action, encouraging the audience to vote for a proposition that would roll back the law.

In the **circle organizational pattern**, the speaker develops one idea, which leads to another, which leads to a third, and so forth, until he or she arrives back at the speech thesis.[3] In a speech on the role friendship plays in physical and mental well being, a student speaker showed how acts of consideration and kindness lead to more friendships, which in turn lead to more social support, which then results in improved mental and physical health. Each main point leads directly into another main point, with the final main point leading back to the thesis.

14 Using Outline Formats

Once you've selected a pattern for organizing your main points, the next step is to outline the speech. Outlines are critical to organizing a speech, providing a visual representation of its basic structure and revealing any weaknesses in the logical ordering of points. Equally important, outlines are key to the successful *delivery* of a speech. The degree to which listeners understand your speech and find you credible will be directly linked to how well you've organized it.[1]

Most speakers create two outlines: a working outline (also called *preparation* or *rough outline*), and a speaking, or delivery, outline. Speeches can be outlined in *complete sentences, phrases,* or *key words*. Figure 14.1 provides an overview of the steps involved in organizing and outlining a speech.

Begin with a Working Outline

The purpose of the **working outline** is to establish and organize main points and develop supporting points to substantiate them. "Working" outlines are meant to be changed as you work through the mass of information and ideas you've collected for your speech. A completed working outline should contain prompts for everything you plan to do in your speech, including detailed directions for use of presentation aids.

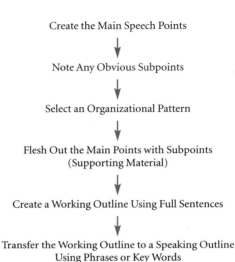

Create the Main Speech Points

Note Any Obvious Subpoints

Select an Organizational Pattern

Flesh Out the Main Points with Subpoints
(Supporting Material)

Create a Working Outline Using Full Sentences

Transfer the Working Outline to a Speaking Outline
Using Phrases or Key Words

FIGURE 14.1 Steps in Organizing and Outlining the Speech

Use Full Sentences in the Working Outline

Many experts recommend using full sentences in the working outline. Sentence outlines represent the full "script," or text, of the speech. In a **sentence outline**, each main and supporting point is stated as a full declarative sentence. So too are the introduction, conclusion, and transition statements. Often, these sentences are stated in precisely the way the speaker wants to express the idea.

Following is an excerpt in full-sentence format from the introduction of a speech by Thomas Donahue about the trucking industry:[2]

I. Let's look at each of the elements and touch briefly on areas where trucking has made a difference in safety and where we've prepared to do more.

    A. The trucking industry supported and helped build the Interstate Highway System.

    B. We have done a great deal for truck safety, and the results speak for themselves.

    C. Truck drivers are at the heart of our industry, and they are obviously central to the safety equation.

CHECKLIST: Steps in Creating a Working Outline

✓ State your topic, general purpose, specific speech purpose, and thesis.

✓ Label each speech part (e.g., "Introduction," "Body," and "Conclusion").

✓ Establish your main points (optimally two to five).

✓ Write out everything you wish to state in your speech exactly as you plan to phrase it.

✓ Write out each speech point in a full sentence.

✓ Label and write out transitions in full sentences.

✓ Note briefly any sources you will reference in your speech in parentheses.

✓ Prepare a complete bibliography, and append it to the outline.

Transfer Your Ideas to a Speaking Outline

Once you've completed the working outline, you must transfer its ideas to a **speaking outline** (also called a *delivery outline*) — the one you will use when practicing and actually presenting the speech. Speaking outlines are much briefer than working outlines and contain phrases or key words — the latter being preferred by many — rather than full sentences. Using a full-sentence outline for actual delivery of the speech is not recommended, because it restricts eye contact and forces the speaker to focus more on the outline than on the process of giving the speech. The less you rely on your outline notes, the more eye contact you can have with the audience. With sufficient practice, phrases or key words will jog your memory so that you can deliver your ideas naturally.

A **phrase outline** uses a partial construction of the sentence form of each point. The idea is that the speaker is so familiar with the points of the speech that a glance at a few words associated with each point will serve as a reminder of exactly what to say, as in the following outline for the speech about the trucking industry:

I. Elements where trucking has made a difference

   A. Industry helped build Interstate Highway System

   B. Truck safety results speak for themselves

   C. Drivers are heart of industry and central to safety

The **key-word outline** uses the smallest possible units of understanding to outline the main and supporting points. Compared to other formats, key-word outlines permit more eye contact, greater freedom of movement, and better control of your thoughts and actions.

I. Elements

   A. Interstate Highway System

   B. Safety

   C. Drivers

Your speaking outline should contain brief parenthetical notes indicating transitions—such as "(PREVIEW)." It should also include, in parentheses, any sources that you plan to cite. Include prompts for any presentation aids you plan to use, again in parentheses. You might want to use a highlighter pen to further differentiate these cues from the rest of the outline (see Figure 14.2).

For purposes of outlining, the introduction and conclusion are *not* among the main points, either in the working outline or in the speaking outline. Introductions and conclu-

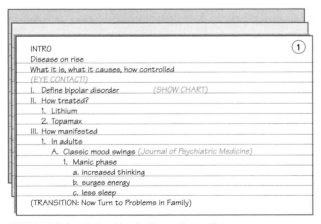

INTRO   (1)
Disease on rise
What it is, what it causes, how controlled
(EYE CONTACT!)
I. Define bipolar disorder   (SHOW CHART)
II. How treated?
    1. Lithium
    2. Topamax
III. How manifested
    1. In adults
       A. Classic mood swings (Journal of Psychiatric Medicine)
          1. Manic phase
             a. increased thinking
             b. surges energy
             c. less sleep
(TRANSITION: Now Turn to Problems in Family)

FIGURE 14.2 Sample Speaking Outline on Notecards

sions are so important in making a lasting impression that speakers often write out phrasing for them word for word in speaking outlines or spend extra time memorizing such phrasing.

The key to the successful delivery of any speech is practice. The more you rehearse your speech, the more comfortable you will become when you speak from the key-word outline. For additional information on practicing with a speaking outline, see Chapter 17, "Choosing a Method of Delivery."

QUICK TIP

Sometimes Only Exact Wording Will Do

When exact wording is critical to an accurate representation of your speech material (as in presenting highly technical material or conveying quotations or facts verbatim), you may want to write it out in full sentences, even when using a phrase or key-word outline.

 CHECKLIST: Steps in Creating a Speaking Outline

✓ Select 4 × 6 notecards or small sheets of paper that you can easily handle without distraction.

✓ Use a large-size print that can be comfortably read at a glance. If it's handwritten, use easy-to-read ink and large letters.

✓ Identify each main and subpoint with a key word or phrase that is likely to jog your memory accurately.

✓ Write out any quotations, difficult-to-remember or difficult-to-pronounce names, statistical information, and other material that must be stated precisely.

✓ Include prompts for important transitions.

✓ Include prompts for sources that you plan to cite.

✓ Include prompts for displaying presentation aids.

✓ Practice the speech five times, using the speaking outline.

Part 4
Starting, Finishing, and Styling

15 Developing the Introduction and Conclusion

Although introductions and conclusions are not more important than the body of the speech, they are critical to its overall success. Introductions prepare the audience to hear the speech. A good opening previews what's to come in a way that invites listeners to stay the course. Conclusions ensure that the audience remembers the speech and reacts in a way that the speaker intends.

Any kind of supporting material — examples, stories, testimony, facts, or statistics — can be used to open and conclude a speech as long as it accomplishes these objectives (see Chapter 9 on supporting material).

Preparing the Introduction

The choices you make about the introduction can affect the outcome of the entire speech. In the first several minutes (one speaker pegs it at ninety seconds[1]), audience members will decide whether they are interested in the topic of your speech, whether they will believe what you say, and whether they will give you their full attention.

CHECKLIST: Guidelines for Preparing the Introduction

✓ Prepare the introduction after you've completed the speech body. This way, when you turn to the introduction, you will know exactly what you need to preview.

✓ Keep the introduction brief — as a rule, no more than 10 to 15 percent of the body of the speech. Nothing will turn off an audience more quickly than waiting interminably for you to get to the point.

✓ Practice delivering your introduction until you feel confident that you've got it right.

A good introduction serves to:

- Gain the audience's attention and willingness to listen.
- Preview the topic and purpose of the speech.
- Preview the main points of the speech.

- Motivate the audience to accept your goals.
- Make the topic relevant.
- Establish your credibility.

Gain Audience Attention

Some time-honored techniques for winning the audience's attention include using quotations, telling a story, posing questions, saying something startling, using humor, referring to the occasion, and expressing interest in the audience.

USE A QUOTATION   Theodore Roosevelt used to say, "Speak softly and carry a big stick." A good quotation, one that elegantly and succinctly expresses an idea, is a very effective way to draw the audience's attention. Quotations can be culled from literature, poetry, film, or directly from people.

TELL A STORY   Noted speechwriter and language expert William Safire once remarked that stories are "surefire attention getters."[2] Stories personalize issues, encouraging identification and making things relevant. Most important, they entertain. An **anecdote** is a brief story of interesting, humorous, or real-life incidents. As rhetorical scholar Edward Corbett notes, anecdotes are "one of the oldest and most effective gambits for seizing the attention."[3]

POSE QUESTIONS   Can you recall a speech that began with a question? As you can see, posing questions draws the audience's attention to what you are about to say. Questions can be real or rhetorical. **Rhetorical questions** (like the one that opens this paragraph) do not invite actual responses. Instead, they make the audience think.

SAY SOMETHING STARTLING   Did you know that virtually no one is having babies anymore in parts of Western Europe? Surprising audience members with startling or unusual facts and statistics is one of the surest ways to get their attention. Statistics are a powerful means of illustrating consequences and relationships and tend to quickly bring things into focus.

USE HUMOR   Handled well, humor is an excellent way to build rapport, put people at ease, make key points, and introduce the theme of a speech. Caution is in order, however. As one notes, "Humor goes beyond language; it takes us into of cultural understanding."[4] Speech humor should the audience, topic, purpose, and occasion.

REFER TO THE OCCASION   Introductions that include references to the speech occasion and to any relevant facts about the audience tend to capture attention and, crucially, establish good will. People appreciate the direct reference to the event, and they are interested in the meaning the speaker assigns to it.

EXPRESS INTEREST IN THE AUDIENCE   Audiences are won over when speakers express interest in them. Focusing on your listeners demonstrates interest and respect, and it thereby builds speaker credibility.

Preview the Topic and Purpose

The introduction should alert the audience to the speech topic and purpose. In the attention-getting phase of the introduction, you may already have alluded to your topic, sometimes very clearly. If not, however, you now need to declare what your speech is about and what you hope to accomplish.

Topic and purpose are clearly explained in this introduction to a speech by Marvin Runyon, postmaster general of the United States:

> This afternoon, I want to examine the truth of that statement—"Nothing moves people like the mail, and no one moves the mail like the U.S. Postal Service." I want to look at where we are today as a communications industry, and where we intend to be in the days and years ahead.[5]

Preview the Main Points

Introductions should preview the main points of the speech. A **preview statement** identifies the main points of the speech, thus helping audience members to mentally organize the speech structure. It also helps you, the speaker, to keep their attention. Preview statements are straightforward. You simply tell the audience what the main points will be and in what order you will address them.

Robert L. Darbelnet effectively introduces his topic, purpose, and main points with this preview statement:

> My remarks today are intended to give you a sense of AAA's ongoing efforts to improve America's roads. Our hope is that you will join your voices to ours as we call on the federal government to do three things:
>
> Number one: Perhaps the most important, provide adequate funding for highway maintenance and improvements.

Number two: Play a strong, responsible yet flexible role in transportation programs.

And Number three: Invest in highway safety.

Let's see what our strengths are, what the issues are, and what we can do about them.[6]

Motivate the Audience to Accept Your Goals

A final function of the introduction is to motivate the audience to care about your topic and believe what you have to say about it. For this to occur, audience members must believe that (1) the topic is relevant and (2) you are qualified to address it.

MAKE THE TOPIC RELEVANT   One way to demonstrate why your listeners should care about your topic is to describe the practical implications it has for them. Another is to convince them that your speech purpose is consistent with their motives and values. Yet another strategy is to specify what the audience stands to gain by listening to you. A student speech about groundwater shows how this can be accomplished:

Anytime we are thirsty, water is available through a tap or drinking fountain. None of us ever stops to think about where water comes from or how it's processed. It may surprise you to learn that frequently in the United States simple tap water has been found to contain dozens of pollutants and impurities. Fertilizers from irrigation fields, petroleum products from leaking underground storage facilities, and even the motor oil your neighbor dumped in the alley may end up in your drinking water.

ESTABLISH CREDIBILITY AS A SPEAKER   During the introduction, audience members make a decision about whether they are interested not just in your topic but also in you. They

---

QUICK TIP

When Credibility Is Key

Although it is always important to establish your credibility in the introduction, it is particularly so in situations where the audience does not know you well and where you must clearly establish your professionalism.[7] In these situations, be sure to stress the reasons why audience members should trust you and believe what you have to say.

want to know why they should believe you, and they will look to you for reasons to do so. To build your credibility, make a simple statement of your qualifications for speaking on the topic at the particular occasion and to the specific audience. Briefly emphasize some experience, knowledge, or perspective you have that is different from or more extensive than that of your audience.

CHECKLIST: How Effective Is Your Introduction?

Does your introduction . . .

____ 1. Capture the audience's attention?

____ 2. Alert listeners to the speech purpose and topic?

____ 3. Motivate listeners to accept your speech goals?

____ 4. Make the topic relevant with listeners and establish your credibility?

Preparing the Conclusion

A well-constructed conclusion ensures that you go out with a bang and not a whimper. Conclusions give you the opportunity to drive home your purpose and make the kind of impression that will accomplish the goals of your speech.

CHECKLIST: Guidelines for Preparing the Conclusion

✓ As with the introduction, prepare the conclusion after you've completed the speech body.

✓ Keep the conclusion brief — as a rule, no more than about one-sixth of the body of the speech, and conclude soon after you say you are about to end.

✓ Carefully consider your use of language. More than in other parts of the speech, the conclusion can contain words that inspire and motivate (see Chapter 16 on using language).

✓ Practice delivering your conclusion until you feel confident that you've got it right.

A good conclusion serves to:

- Signal to the audience that the speech is coming to an end and to provide closure.
- Summarize the key points.
- Reiterate the topic and speech purpose.
- Challenge the audience to respond.
- End the speech memorably.

Signal the Close of the Speech and Provide Closure

People who listen to speeches have taken a journey of sorts, and they want and need the speaker to acknowledge the journey's end. The more emotional the journey, as in speeches designed to touch hearts and minds, the greater the need for logical and emotional closure.

One way to alert the audience that a speech is about to end is to use a transition statement or phrase (see Chapter 12 for more on transitions). Phrases such as *Finally, Looking back, In conclusion,* and *Let me close by saying* all signal closure.

You can also signal closure more subtly, by your manner of delivery. For example, you can vary your tone, pitch, rhythm, and rate of speech to indicate that the speech is winding down (see Chapter 18).

Once you've signaled the end of your speech, do so in short order (though not abruptly).

QUICK TIP

Length of Introductions and Conclusions
Although there are no hard-and-fast rules about length, as a general rule about one-sixth of the speech can be spent on the introduction, one-sixth on the conclusion, and the remaining four-sixths on the body of the speech.[8]

Summarize the Key Points

One bit of age-old advice for giving a speech is "Tell them what you are going to tell them, tell them, and tell them what you told them." The idea is that emphasizing the main points three times will help the audience to remember them. In the introduction, you tell listeners what you are going to tell them. In the body of the speech, you tell them. In the conclusion, you tell them what you've told them. The summary or review should be more than a rote recounting, however.

Consider how Holger Kluge, in a speech titled "Reflections on Diversity," summarized his main points:

> I have covered a lot of ground here today. But as I draw to a close, I'd like to stress three things.
>
> First, diversity is more than equity. . . .
>
> Second, weaving diversity into the very fabric of your organization takes time. . . .
>
> Third, diversity will deliver bottom line results to your businesses and those results will be substantial, if you make the commitment. . . .[9]

A restatement of points like this brings the speech full circle.

Reiterate the Topic and Speech Purpose

The conclusion should reiterate the topic and speech purpose — to imprint it in the audience's memory. In the conclusion to a speech about preventing school violence, William Kirwan reminds his listeners of his central idea:

> What I've tried to convey this afternoon are the kinds of efforts it will take for us to save the next Nick Johnson and all the other tragedies like his. . . . We can build a network of metal detectors and surveillance cameras and hope that we catch a future Nick before he fires. Or, we can build a community that could save him long before he turns down the road toward destruction. Do we want to catch him, or do we want to save him?[10]

Challenge the Audience to Respond

A strong conclusion challenges audience members to put to use what the speaker has taught them. In *informative speeches,* the speaker challenges audience members to use what they've learned in a way that benefits them. In *persuasive speeches,* the challenge to audience members usually comes in the form of a **call to action**, a challenge to see the problem in a new way, change their beliefs about the problem, or change both their actions and their beliefs about the problem.

Hillary Rodham Clinton makes a specific call to action in her conclusion to an address presented to the United Nations Fourth World Conference on Women:

> We have seen peace prevail in most places for a half century. We have avoided another world war. But we have not solved

older, deeply rooted problems that continue to diminish the potential of half the world's population. Now it is time to act on behalf of women everywhere. If we take bold steps to better the lives of women, we will be taking bold steps to better the lives of children and families too. . . . Let this conference be our — and the world's — call to action.[11]

Make the Speech Memorable

A good conclusion increases the odds that the speaker's message will linger after the speech is over. A speech that makes a lasting impression is one that listeners are most likely to remember and act on. To do this, make use of the same devices for capturing attention described for use in introductions — quotations, stories, questions, startling statements, humor, and references to the audience and the occasion.

QUICK TIP

Create a Memorable Conclusion
Using a quotation that captures the essence of the speech, either in the form of a poem or memorable statement, can be a very effective way to close a speech. A short concluding story can bring the entire speech into focus very effectively. Yet another technique is to pick up on a story or an idea that you mentioned in the introduction, bringing the speech full circle.

CHECKLIST: How Effective Is Your Conclusion?

Does your conclusion . . .

___ 1. Alert the audience that the speech is ending?

___ 2. Come to an end soon after you say you will finish?

___ 3. Last no more than about one-sixth of the speech body?

___ 4. Reiterate the main points?

___ 5. Remind listeners of the topic and speech purpose?

___ 6. Challenge the audience to respond?

___ 7. Make a lasting impression?

16 Using Language

In public speaking, choosing the right words is crucial to connecting with your audience and helping listeners understand, believe in, and retain your message.[1] **Style** is the specific word choices and **rhetorical devices** (techniques of language) speakers use to express their ideas. A speaker's style can make a speech colorful and convincing or bland and boring.

Write Your Speeches for the Ear

Unlike readers, listeners have only one chance to understand a spoken message. Speeches should therefore be written for the ear:

- Use familiar words, easy-to-follow sentences, and straightforward syntax (subject-verb-object agreement).
- Steer clear of terms that are difficult to pronounce (and therefore difficult to decipher).
- Use frequent transitions, internal previews, and summaries (see Chapter 12).
- Judiciously use the personal pronouns "I" and "you" to personalize the occasion and foster a sense of inclusion.
- Use vivid imagery that will help listeners "see" what you are saying.
- Create a cadenced arrangement of language through rhetorical devices such as repetition, alliteration, and parallelism.

Choose Language That Encourages Shared Meaning

To encourage shared meaning with your audience, choose language that is culturally sensitive and unbiased, simple, concise, concrete, and vivid.

Use Language That Is Culturally Sensitive and Unbiased

Demonstrate **cultural sensitivity** to listeners by being considerate of cultural beliefs, norms, or traditions that are different from your own. Review your speeches for any **biased language**—language that relies on unfounded assumptions; negative descriptions; or stereotypes of a given group's age, class, gender, disability, and geographic, ethnic, racial, or religious characteristics.

Strive for Simplicity

When selecting between two synonyms, choose the simpler term. Translate **jargon**—or the specialized language of a given profession—into commonly understood terms. As speech-writer Peggy Noonan notes in her book *Simply Speaking:*

> Good hard simple words with good hard clear meanings are good things to use when you speak. They are like pickets in a fence, slim and unimpressive on their own but sturdy and effective when strung together.[2]

Be Concise

As a rule, try to use fewer rather than more words to express your thoughts. Consider the following examples. Which would you rather hear?

> It is difficult to believe that the United States government is attempting to tax us at every level of our personal and professional lives, whether it be capital gains taxes, value-added taxes, or, of course, your favorite and mine: income taxes.

> It's hard to believe but true. The U.S. government is taxing us to death. It's got its hands in every conceivable pocket. Capital gains taxes. Value-added taxes. And, of course, your favorite and mine: income taxes.

QUICK TIP

Experiment with Phrases and Sentence Fragments
To add punch to your speech, experiment with using phrases *and* sentence fragments *in place of full sentences:*
Intrapreneurialism. One-minute management. Strategic alliances. Leveraged recapitalizations. Right-brain thinking. These are some of the exotic plants that grow in management's magic garden. . . .[3]

Choose Concrete Words

As you draft your speeches, try to avoid **abstract language** that is open to interpretation—unless that is your intent. Instead, choose concrete nouns and verbs to convey meaning that is specific, tangible, and definite:

ABSTRACT		LESS ABSTRACT		CONCRETE
Summer	→	hot weather	→	sweltering heat
Congestion	→	traffic jam	→	gridlock

Use Vivid Imagery

Enliven your speech by selecting colorful and concrete words. Do this by modifying nouns and verbs with descriptive adjectives and adverbs. For example, rather than characterizing the sky merely as "blue," specify it as "faint blue" or "blue with pillows of dark gray." Use language that appeals to the listeners' sense of smell, taste, sight, hearing, and touch.

Figures of speech are rhetorical devices that make striking comparisons that help the listener to visualize, identify with, and understand your ideas.

A **simile** explicitly compares one thing to another, using *like* or *as*: "He works like a dog" and "The old woman's hands were as soft as a baby's." A **metaphor** also compares two things but does so by describing one thing as actually being the other: "Education is an uphill climb" and "Life is a parade."

An **analogy** is an extended metaphor or simile that clarifies an unfamiliar concept by comparing it to a more familiar one.[4] For example, note how African American minister Phil Wilson used metaphoric language when he preached to his congregation in Los Angeles about the dangers of AIDS:

> Our house is on fire! The fire truck arrives, but we won't come out, because we're afraid the folks from next door will see that we're in that burning house. AIDS is a fire raging in our community and it's out of control![5]

Choose Language That Builds Credibility

To build trust and credibility, language must be both truthful in expression and correct in usage. Steer clear of **slander** (defamatory speech; see Chapter 2 on ethics, p. 7), and avoid the **malapropism**—the inadvertent use of a word or phrase in place of one that sounds like it[6] ("It's a strange receptacle" for "It's a strange spectacle").

Use Appropriate Language

As a rule, when drafting a speech or presentation, strive to uphold the conventional rules of grammar and usage associated with standard English. The more diverse the audience, and the more formal the occasion, the closer you will want to

---

Denotative versus Connotative Meaning
*When drafting your speech or presentation, choose words that
are both denotatively and connotatively appropriate for the
audience. The* **denotative meaning** *of a word is its literal, or
dictionary, definition. The* **connotative meaning** *of a word is
the special association that different people bring to bear on
it. For example, you may like to be called "slender" but not
"skinny," or "thrifty" but not "cheap."*

---

remain within these bounds. Sometimes, however, especially
when the audience is more homogeneous, it may be appropriate to mix casual language, regional dialects, or even slang
in your speech. Consider the following excerpt:

> On the gulf where I was raised, *el valle del Rio Grande* in
> South Texas—that triangular piece of land wedged between
> the river *y el golfo* which serves as the Texas–U.S./Mexican
> border—is a Mexican *pueblito* called Hargill.[7]

Use the Active Voice

Voice is the feature of verbs that indicates the subject's relationship to the action. A verb is in the *active voice* when the
subject performs the action and in the *passive voice* when the
subject is acted upon or is the receiver of the action.[8] Speaking in the active voice will make your statements clear and
assertive instead of indirect and weak:

PASSIVE:	A test was announced by Ms. Carlos for Tuesday.
	A president is elected by the voters every four years.
ACTIVE:	Ms. Carlos announced a test for Tuesday.
	The voters elect a president every four years.

Choose Language That Creates a Lasting Impression

Oral language that is artfully arranged and infused with
rhythm leaves a lasting impression on listeners. You can create a cadenced arrangement of language through rhetorical
devices such as repetition, alliteration, and parallelism.

Repetition

Repeating key words, phrases, or even sentences at various intervals throughout a speech creates a distinctive rhythm and thereby implants important ideas in listeners' minds. Repetition works extremely well when delivered with the appropriate voice inflections and pauses. Note, for example, Ronald Reagan's wording in a speech prior to the fall of the Berlin Wall:

> "*Mr. Gorbachev,* open this gate! *Mr. Gorbachev,* tear down this wall."

In one form of repetition, called **anaphora**, the speaker repeats a word or phrase at the beginning of successive phrases, clauses, or sentences. One famous example of this is Dr. Martin Luther King Jr.'s speech, delivered in 1963 in Washington, D.C., in which he repeated the phrase "I have a dream" numerous times, each with an upward inflection followed by a pause.

Speakers have made use of anaphora since earliest times. For example, Jesus preached:

> Blessed are the poor in spirit. . . .
>
> Blessed are the meek. . . .
>
> Blessed are the peacemakers. . . .[9]

In a speech about becoming an organ donor, student Ed Partlow used anaphora this way:

> Today *I am going to talk about* a subject that can be both personal and emotional.
>
> *I am going to talk about* becoming an organ donor. . . .

Alliteration

Alliteration is the repetition of the same sounds, usually initial consonants, in two or more neighboring words or syllables. Examples of alliteration in speeches include phrases such as Jesse Jackson's "Down with dope, up with hope" and former U.S. vice president Spiro Agnew's disdainful reference to the U.S. press as "nattering nabobs of negativism."

When used well, alliteration drives home themes and leaves listeners with a lasting impression. On the other hand, if poorly crafted or hackneyed, alliteration can distract from, rather than enhance, a message.

Parallelism

The arrangement of words, phrases, or sentences in a similar form is known as **parallelism**. Parallel structure can help the speaker emphasize important ideas in the speech. Like repetition, it also creates a sense of steady or building rhythm.[10] You can easily make use of parallelism by doing the following:

- Orally numbering your points ("first," "second," and "third").

- Introducing material chronologically.

- Grouping speech concepts or ideas into three ("Of the people, by the people, and for the people").

- Setting off two ideas in balanced (parallel) opposition (the device of **antithesis**, e.g., "One small step for man, one giant leap for mankind").

- Repeating a key word or phrase that emphasizes a central or recurring idea of the speech, often in the introduction, body, and conclusion.

 CHECKLIST: Use Language Effectively

✓ Use familiar words, easy-to-follow sentences, and straightforward syntax.

✓ Root out biased language.

✓ Avoid unnecessary jargon.

✓ Use fewer rather than more words to express your thoughts.

✓ Make striking comparisons with *similes, metaphors,* and *analogies*.

✓ Use the active voice.

✓ Repeat key words, phrases, or sentences at various intervals (anaphora).

✓ Experiment with alliteration — words that repeat the same sounds, usually initial consonants, in two or more neighboring words or syllables.

✓ Experiment with parallelism — arranging words, phrases, or sentences in similar form.

Part 5
Delivery

17 Choosing a Method of Delivery

The delivery of a speech is the moment of truth. For most of us, delivery makes us feel anxious because this is the moment when all eyes are upon us. As communication scholar James McCroskey has noted, however, effective delivery rests on the same natural foundation as everyday conversation.[1] Focusing on the quality of naturalness can help you reduce the fear of delivery and make your presentations more effective.

Strive for Naturalness and Enthusiasm

Speakers who deliver well-received speeches or presentations share several characteristics at the podium: They are natural, enthusiastic, confident, and direct.

- *Strive for naturalness.* Think of your speech as a particularly important conversation. Rather than behaving theatrically, act naturally.

- *Show enthusiasm.* Inspire your listeners by showing enthusiasm for your topic and for the occasion. Speak about what interests and excites you.

- *Project a sense of confidence.* Focus on the ideas you want to convey rather than on yourself. Inspire the audience's confidence in you by appearing confident to them.

- *Be direct.* Engage your listeners by establishing eye contact, using a friendly tone of voice, and smiling whenever it is appropriate. Consider positioning yourself so that you are physically close to the audience.

QUICK TIP

Show Enthusiasm and Confidence

When you're speaking about something that excites you, confidence follows almost naturally. Instead of thinking about how you look and sound, you're thinking about what you're trying to say and how well your listeners are grasping it. An enthusiastic and confident delivery helps you to feel good about your speech, and it focuses your audience's attention on the message.

Select a Method of Delivery

Whether delivering formal public speeches or classroom or professional presentations, you can choose from four basic methods of delivery: speaking from manuscript; speaking from memory; speaking impromptu; and speaking extemporaneously.

Speaking from Manuscript

When **speaking from manuscript**, you read a speech verbatim—that is, from prepared written text that contains the entire speech, word for word. As a rule, speaking from manuscript restricts eye contact and body movement, and it may also limit expressiveness in vocal variety and quality. Watching a speaker read a speech can be monotonous and boring for the audience. Quite obviously, the natural, relaxed, enthusiastic, confident, and direct qualities of delivery are all limited by this method.

There are certainly times, however, when it is advisable or necessary to read a speech—for example, when you must convey a very precise message, when you will be quoted and must avoid misinterpretation, and when you must address an emergency and need to convey exact descriptions and directions.

If you must read from a prepared text, do what you can to deliver the speech naturally:

- Vary the rhythm of your words.
- Become familiar enough with the speech so that you can establish some eye contact.
- Consider using some compelling presentation aids.

Speaking from Memory

The formal name for **speaking from memory** is **oratory**. In oratorical style, you would put the entire speech, word for word, into writing and then commit it to memory. In the United States, instances of speaking from memory rarely occur anymore, though this form of delivery remains common in many parts of the world.[2]

Memorization is not a natural way to present a message. True eye contact with the audience is unlikely, and memorization invites potential disaster during a speech because there is always the possibility of a mental lapse or block. Some kinds of brief speeches, however, such as toasts and introductions, can be well served by memorization. Sometimes it's helpful to memorize a part of the speech, especially when you must present the same information many times in the same words, or when you use direct quotations as a form of support. If you do find an occasion to use memorization, learn that portion of your speech so completely that in actual delivery you can convey enthusiasm and directness.

Speaking Impromptu

Speaking impromptu involves speaking on relatively short notice with little time to prepare. Many occasions may require that you make some remarks on the spur of the moment. An instructor may invite you to summarize key points from an assignment, for example, or a fellow employee who was scheduled to speak on the new marketing plan may be sick and your boss has asked you to take his place.

Optimally, you will anticipate situations in which you might be called upon to speak and will prepare remarks beforehand, if only mentally. Otherwise, to succeed in delivering impromptu remarks, maximize the time you do have to prepare on the spot:

- Find a pen and a piece of paper as quickly as possible.
- Take a minute to reflect on how you can best address the audience's interests and needs.
- Take a deep breath, and focus on your expertise on the topic or on what you really want to say.
- Jot down in key words or short phrases the ideas you want to cover.
- Stay on the topic. Don't wander off track.
- If your speech follows someone else's, acknowledge that person's statements.
- State your ideas and then summarize them.
- Use transitions such as "first," "second," and "third," both to organize your points and to help listeners follow them.

As much as possible, try to organize your points into a discernible pattern. If addressing a problem, for example, such as someone's poor performance or a project failure or glitch, consider the problem-solution pattern or the cause-effect pattern of organizational arrangement (see Chapter 13). If called on to defend one proposal as superior to another, consider using the comparative advantages pattern, in which you illustrate various advantages of the favored proposal over other options (see Chapter 24 on persuasive speeches).

Speaking Extemporaneously

Speaking extemporaneously falls somewhere between impromptu and written or memorized deliveries. In an extemporaneous speech, you prepare well and practice in advance, giving full attention to all facets of the speech—content, arrangement, and delivery alike. Instead of memorizing or writing the speech word for word, you speak from an outline of key words and phrases (see Chapter 14), having concentrated throughout your preparation and practice on the ideas that you want to communicate.

More speeches are delivered by extemporaneous delivery than by any other method. Because extemporaneous speaking is the technique most conducive to achieving a natural, conversational quality of delivery, many speakers consider it to be the preferred method of the four types of delivery. Knowing your idea well enough to present it without memorization or manuscript gives you greater flexibility in adapting to the specific speaking situation. You can modify wording, rearrange your points, change examples, or omit information in keeping with the audience and the setting. You can have more eye contact, more direct body orientation, greater freedom of movement, and generally better control of your thoughts and actions than any of the other delivery methods allow.

Speaking extemporaneously is the preferred method of delivery in most situations, but several possible drawbacks exist. Because you aren't speaking from written or memorized text, you may become repetitive and wordy. Fresh examples or points may come to mind that you want to share, so the speech may take longer than you anticipated. Occasionally even a glance at your speaking notes will fail to jog your memory on a point that you wanted to cover, and you momentarily find yourself searching for what to say next. The remedy

> **QUICK TIP**
>
> ***Extemporaneous Delivery Is Often Preferred***
> *In most situations, select the extemporaneous method of delivery. Thoroughly prepare and practice your speech in advance of delivery. Speak from a key-word or phrase outline that has been adapted from a full-sentence outline (see Chapter 14).*

for these potential pitfalls is, of course, practice. If you frequently practice delivering your speech using a speaking outline, you will probably have no difficulty staying on target.

METHODS OF DELIVERY AND THEIR PROBABLE USES	
WHEN . . .	**METHOD OF DELIVERY**
√ Precise wording is called for; for instance, you want to avoid being misquoted or misconstrued, or you need to communicate exact descriptions and directions . . .	Consider *speaking from manuscript* (reading part or all of your speech from fully prepared text)
√ You must deliver a short special-occasion speech, such as a toast and introduction, or you plan on using direct quotations . . .	Consider *speaking from memory* (memorizing part or all of your speech)
√ You are called upon to speak without prior planning or preparation . . .	Consider *speaking impromptu* (organizing your thoughts with little or no lead time)
√ You have the time to prepare and practice developing a speech or presentation that achieves a natural conversational style . . .	Consider *speaking extemporaneously* (developing your speech in working outline and then practicing and delivering it with a phrase or key-word outline)

18 Controlling the Voice

Regardless of the quality and importance of your message, if you have inadequate mastery of your voice you may lose the attention of your audience and fail to deliver a successful speech. Fortunately, as you practice your speech, you can learn to control each of the elements of vocal delivery. These include volume, pitch, speaking rate, pauses, vocal variety, and pronunciation and articulation.

Adjust Your Speaking Volume

Volume, the relative loudness of a speaker's voice while delivering a speech, is usually the most obvious and frequently cited vocal element in speechmaking. If you do not speak loud enough for the entire audience to hear you, your speech is essentially a failure. *The proper volume for delivering a speech is somewhat louder than that of normal conversation.* Just how much louder depends on three factors: (1) the size of the room and the number of people in the audience, (2) whether or not you use a microphone, and (3) the level of background noise. The easiest way to judge whether you are speaking too loudly or too softly is to be alert to audience feedback.

CHECKLIST: Tips on Using a Microphone

✓ Always do a sound check with the microphone before delivering your speech.

✓ When you first speak into the microphone, ask your listeners if they can hear you clearly.

✓ Speak directly into the microphone; if you turn your head or body, you won't be heard.

✓ To avoid broadcasting private statements, beware of "open" mikes.

✓ When wearing a **lavaliere microphone** attached to your lapel or collar, speak as if you were addressing a small group. The amplifier will do the rest.

✓ When using a **hand-held** or **fixed microphone**, beware of *popping*. Popping occurs when you use sharp consonants such as *p, t,* and *d* and the air hits the mike. To prevent popping, move the microphone slightly below your mouth and about six inches away.[1]

Vary Your Intonation

Pitch is the range of sounds from high to low (or vice versa). Vocal pitch is important in speechmaking because it powerfully affects the meaning associated with spoken words. For example, say "stop." Now, say "Stop!" Hear the difference? As you speak, pitch conveys your mood, reveals your level of enthusiasm, expresses your concern for the audience, and signals your overall commitment to the occasion. When there is no variety in pitch, speaking becomes monotonous. A monotonous voice is the death knell to any speech.

Adjust Your Speaking Rate

Speaking rate is the pace at which you convey speech. The normal rate of speech for adults is between 120 and 150 words per minute. The typical public speech occurs at a rate slightly below 120 words per minute, but there is no standard, "ideal," or most effective rate. Being alert to the audience's reactions is the best way to know whether your rate of speech is too fast or too slow. An audience will get fidgety, bored, listless, perhaps even sleepy if you speak too slowly. If you speak too rapidly, listeners will appear irritated and confused, as though they can't catch what you're saying.

QUICK TIP

Control Your Rate of Speaking

One recent study suggests that speaking too fast will cause listeners to perceive you as tentative about your control of the situation.[2] To control your rate, choose 150 words from your speech and time yourself as you read them aloud. Do this until you achieve a comfortable speaking rate.

Use Strategic Pauses

Pauses enhance meaning by providing a type of punctuation, emphasizing a point, drawing attention to a key thought, or just allowing listeners a moment to contemplate what is being said. In short, they make a speech far more effective than it might otherwise be. Both the speaker and the audience *need* pauses.

QUICK TIP

Avoid Meaningless Vocal Fillers

*Many novice speakers are uncomfortable with pauses. It's as if there were a social stigma attached to any silence in a speech. We often react the same way in conversation, covering pauses with unnecessary and undesirable **vocal fillers** such as "uh," "hmm," "you know," "I mean," and "it's like." Like pitch, however, pauses are important strategic elements of a speech. Use them strategically, taking care to eliminate distracting vocal fillers.*

Strive for Vocal Variety

Rather than operating separately, all the vocal elements described so far—volume, pitch, speaking rate, and pauses—work together to create an effective delivery. Indeed, the real key to effective vocal delivery is to vary all these elements. One key to achieving effective **vocal variety** is enthusiasm. Vocal variety comes quite naturally when you are excited about what you are saying to an audience, when you feel it is important and want to share it with them.

CHECKLIST: Practice Check for Vocal Effectiveness

____ 1. As you practice, does your voice project authority?

____ 2. Is your voice too loud? Too soft?

____ 3. Do you avoid speaking in a monotone? Do you vary the stress or emphasis you place on words to clearly express your meaning?

____ 4. Is your rate of speech comfortable for listeners?

____ 5. Do you avoid unnecessary vocal fillers, such as "uh," "hmm," "you know," and "I mean"?

____ 6. Do you use pauses for strategic effect?

____ 7. Does your voice reflect a variety of emotional expressions? Do you convey enthusiasm?

Carefully Pronounce and Articulate Words

Few things distract an audience more than improper pronunciation or unclear articulation of words. **Pronunciation** is the correct formation of word sounds. **Articulation** is the clarity or forcefulness with which the sounds are made, regardless of whether they are pronounced correctly. In other words, you can be articulating clearly but pronouncing incorrectly. It is therefore important to pay attention to and work on both areas.

Articulation problems are also a matter of habit. A very common pattern of poor articulation is **mumbling**—slurring words together at a low level of volume and pitch so that they are barely audible. Sometimes the problem is **lazy**

speech. Common examples are saying "fer" instead of "for," "wanna" instead of "want to," "gonna" instead of "going to," "theez' er" instead of "these are," and so on.

Like any habit, poor articulation can be overcome by unlearning the problem behavior:

- If you mumble, practice speaking more loudly and with emphatic pronunciation.

- If you tend toward lazy speech, put more effort into your articulation.

- Consciously try to say each word clearly and correctly.

- Practice clear and precise enunciation of proper word sounds. Say *articulation* several times until it rolls off your tongue naturally.

- Do the same for these words: *want to, going to, Atlanta, chocolate, sophomore, California.*

- As you practice, consider words that might pose articulation and pronunciation problems for you. Say them over and over until doing so feels as natural as saying your name.

COMMONLY MISPRONOUNCED WORDS[3]		
CORRECT SPELLING	**WRONG PRONUNCIATION**	**RIGHT PRONUNCIATION**
AC*TS*	*AKS*	AK*TS*
A*SKED*	*AKS*	A*SKT*
ET*C*ETERA	*EK SET ER UH*	E*T SET ER UH*
FA*CT*S	*FAKS*	FA*KT*S
FI*F*TH	*FI TH* or *FIF*	FI*F*TH
GEN*UI*NE	*JEN YU W INE*	JEN YU I*N*
HUND*RE*D	*HUN DERT*	HUN D*RED*
IN*T*ERNATIONAL	*INNERNASHUNAL*	IN *T*ER NA SHUH NAL
IN*TRO*DUCE	*INNERDOOS*	IN *TRO* DYOOS
NU*CL*EAR	*NOOKYOULUHR*	NOO KL*EE* UHR
PI*C*TURE	*PI CHUR*	PI*K CHUR*
PRODUCTS	*PRAH DUKS*	PRAH DUK*TS*
R*E*COG*NIZED*	*REKUNIZED*	RE *KUG* NIZED

19 Using the Body

Pay Attention to Body Language

Audience members are quick to detect discrepancies between what you say and how you say it. As they listen to you, they are simultaneously evaluating the messages sent by your facial expressions, eye behavior, gestures, and general body movements. Audiences do not so much listen to a speaker's words as "read" the **body language** of the speaker who delivers them.[1]

Animate Your Facial Expressions

From our facial expressions, audiences can gauge whether we are excited about, disenchanted by, or indifferent to our speech—and the audience to whom we are presenting it.

Few behaviors are more effective for building rapport with an audience than *smiling*. A smile is a sign of mutual welcome at the start of a speech, of mutual comfort and interest during the speech, and of mutual goodwill at the close of a speech. In addition, smiling when you feel nervous or otherwise uncomfortable can help you relax and gain heightened composure. Of course, facial expressions need to correspond to the tenor of the speech. Doing what is natural and normal for the occasion should be the rule.

CHECKLIST: Tips for Using Effective Facial Expressions

✓ Use animated expressions that feel natural and express your meaning.

✓ Avoid a deadpan expression; never use expressions that are out of character for you or inappropriate for the speech occasion.

✓ In practice sessions, loosen your facial features with exercises such as widening the eyes and moving the mouth.

✓ Establish rapport with the audience by smiling naturally where appropriate.

Maintain Eye Contact

If smiling is an effective way to build rapport, maintaining eye contact is mandatory in establishing a positive relationship with your listeners. Having eye contact with the audience is one of the most, if not *the* most, important physical actions in public speaking. Eye contact does the following:

- Maintains the quality of directness in speech delivery.
- Lets people know they are recognized.
- Indicates acknowledgment and respect.
- Signals to audience members that the speaker sees them as unique human beings.

With an audience of one hundred to more than a thousand, it's impossible to look at every listener. But in most speaking situations you are likely to experience, you should be able to look at every person in the audience by using a technique called **scanning**. When you scan an audience, you move your gaze from one listener to another and from one section to another, pausing as you do so to gaze briefly at each individual.

QUICK TIP

Focus on Three Visual Anchors

To maintain eye contact with audience members, one speaking pro suggests following the "rule of three": Pick three audience members to focus on—one in the middle, one on the right, and one on the left of the room; these audience members will be your anchors as you scan the room.[2] Initially, this may be difficult. But with just a little experience, you will find yourself doing it naturally.

Use Gestures That Feel Natural

Words alone seldom suffice to convey what we want to express. Head, arm, hand, and even leg gestures are often critical in helping to clarify the meanings we try to convey in words. Physical gestures fill in the gaps, as in illustrating the size or shape of an object (e.g., by showing the size of it by extending two hands, palms facing each other), expressing the depth of an emotion (e.g., by pounding a fist on a podium), or emphasizing a certain word (e.g., by using one's index finger to "write" the word in the air while saying it).

To achieve a natural, relaxed quality in delivery, use gestures to fill in meaning gaps, as you would in everyday conversation. Gestures should arise from genuine emotions and should conform to your personality:[3]

- Use natural, spontaneous gestures.
- Avoid exaggerated gestures, but use gestures that are broad enough to be seen by each audience member.
- Eliminate distracting gestures, such as fidgeting with pens or pencils, brushing back hair from your eyes, or jingling coins in your pockets.
- Analyze your gestures for effectiveness in practice sessions.
- Practice movements that feel natural to you.

Be Aware of General Body Movement

General body movement is also important in maintaining audience attention and processing of your message. Audience members soon tire of listening to a "**talking head**" that remains steadily positioned in one place behind a microphone or a podium. As space and time allow, try to get out from behind the podium and stand with the audience. As you do, move around at a comfortable, natural pace.

QUICK TIP

Stand Straight
A speaker's posture sends a definite message to the audience. Listeners perceive speakers who slouch as being sloppy, unfocused, and even weak. Strive to stand erect, but not ramrod straight. The goal should be to appear authoritative but not rigid.

Dress Appropriately

Superficial as it may sound, the first thing an audience is likely to notice as you approach the speaker's position is your clothing. The critical criteria in determining appropriate dress for a speech are audience expectations and the nature of the speech occasion. If you are speaking as a representative of your business, for example, you will want to complement your company's image.[4]

An extension of dress is the possession of various objects on or around your person while giving a speech — pencil and pen, a briefcase, a glass of water, or papers with notes on them. Always ask yourself if these objects are really necessary. A sure way to distract an audience from what you're saying is to drag a briefcase or a backpack to the speaker's stand and open it while speaking, or to fumble with a pen or other object.

CHECKLIST: Broad Dress Code Guidelines

✓ For a "power" look, wear a dark-colored suit.

✓ Medium-blue or navy suits paired with white shirts or blouses will enhance your credibility.

✓ The color yellow conveys friendliness.

✓ The color red focuses attention on you.

✓ Flashy jewelry distracts listeners.

Practice the Delivery

Practice is essential to effective delivery. The more you practice, the greater your comfort level will be when you actually deliver the speech. More than anything, it is uncertainty that breeds anxiety. By practicing your speech using a fully developed speaking outline (see Chapter 14), you will know what to expect when you actually stand in front of an audience.

Focus on the Message

The purpose of your speech is to get a message across, not to display extraordinary delivery skills. Keep this goal foremost in your mind. Psychologically, too, focusing on your message is likely to make your delivery more natural and confident.

Plan Ahead and Practice Often

If possible, begin practicing your speech at least several days before you are scheduled to deliver it:

• Practice with your speaking notes.

• Revise those parts of your speech that aren't satisfactory, altering your speaking notes as you go.

• Focus on your speech ideas rather than on yourself.

- Time each part of your speech—introduction, body, and conclusion.

- Practice with any presentation aids you plan to use (see Chapters 20–22).

- Practice your speech several times, and then record it with a tape recorder.

- If possible, videotape yourself twice—once after several practice sessions, and again after you've worked to incorporate any changes into your speech.

- Visualize the setting in which you will speak and practice the speech under realistic conditions, paying particular attention to projecting your voice to fill the room.

- Practice in front of at least one volunteer, and seek constructive criticism.

- Schedule your practice sessions early in the process so that you have adequate time to prepare.

QUICK TIP

Practice Five Times

Many expert speakers recommend practicing your speech about five times in its final form. Given that few speeches are longer than twenty minutes, and most are shorter, this represents a maximum of two hours of practice time—time that is certainly well spent.

Part 6
Presentation Aids

20 Types of Presentation Aids

Presentation aids help listeners to understand and remember key points, to see relationships among concepts, and to grasp complex ideas quickly.[1] Used wisely, they spark audience members' interest, convey information in a timesaving fashion, and enhance speaker credibility. Indeed, research findings indicate that we remember only about 20 percent of what we hear, but more than 50 percent of what we see *and* hear.[2] As the saying goes, "Seeing is believing."

Effective presentation aids draw audience members into a speech and provide stimulation that keeps them interested. Presentation aids allow listeners to engage the right side of their brains—the hemisphere that plays an important role in such nonverbal tasks as visualization, music, and drawing. By expressing difficult thoughts and ideas without lengthy explanations, presentation aids facilitate concise communication and save time.

QUICK TIP

Use Presentation Aids to Supplement Your Main Ideas

The strength of a presentation aid lies in the context in which it is used. No matter how powerful a photograph or chart or video may be, the audience will be less interested in merely gazing at it than in discovering how you will relate it to a specific point. If even superior-quality aids are poorly related to the speech, listeners will be turned off. Thus presentation aids should be used to supplement rather than to serve as the main source of your speech ideas.

Select an Appropriate Aid

Presentation aids include props and models, graphs, charts, video, audio, and multimedia. Carefully consider which aid, or combination of aids, will illustrate your speech points most effectively.

Consider a Prop or Model

A **prop** can be any inanimate or live object—a stone or a snake, for instance—that captures the audience's attention and illustrates or emphasizes key points. A **model** is a three-dimensional, scale-size representation of an object. Presentations in engineering, architecture, medicine, and many other disciplines often make use of models.

When using a prop or model,

- Make sure it is big enough for everyone to see (and read, if applicable).
- Keep the prop or model hidden until you are ready to use it, in most cases.
- Practice your speech using the prop or model.

Create a Graph

A **graph** represents the relationship between variables. Four types of graphs that speakers use include line graphs, bar graphs, pie graphs, and pictograms.

A *line graph* displays one measurement, usually plotted on the horizontal axis, and units of measurement or values, which are plotted on the vertical axis. Each value or point is connected with a line. Line graphs are especially useful in representing information that changes over time, such as trends (see Figure 20.1).

A *bar graph* (see Figure 20.2) uses bars of varying lengths to compare quantities or magnitudes. *Multidimensional bar graphs,* or bar graphs distinguished by different colors or markings, compare two or more different kinds of information or quantities in one chart.

When creating line and bar graphs,

- Label both axes appropriately.
- Start the numerical axis at zero.

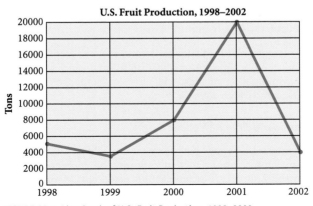

FIGURE 20.1 Line Graph of U.S. Fruit Production, 1998–2002

Vertical Bar Graphs

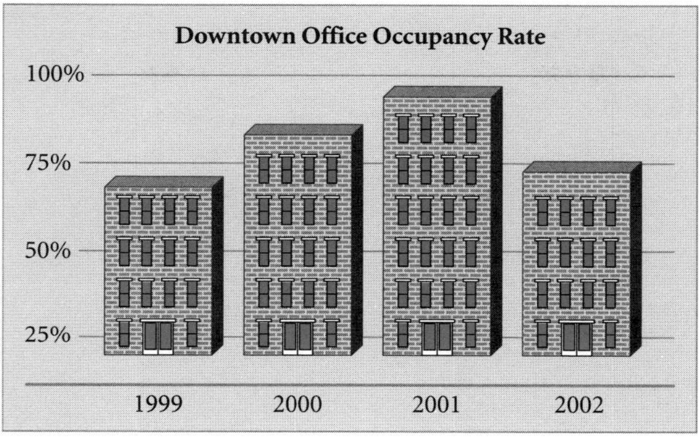

FIGURE 20.2 Bar Graph

- Compare only like variables.
- Put no more than two lines of data on one line graph.
- Assign a clear title to the graph.

A *pie graph* depicts the division of a whole into slices. Each slice constitutes a percentage of the whole. When creating pie graphs,

- Restrict the number of pie slices to a maximum of seven.
- Identify and accurately represent the values or percentages of each pie slice.
- Consider using color or background markings to distinguish the different slices of the pie.

A *pictogram* uses picture symbols (icons) to illustrate relationships and trends, such as using a generic-looking human figure repeated in a row to demonstrate increasing enrollment in college over time (see Figure 20.3).

When creating pictograms,

- Clearly label what the pictogram symbolizes.
- To avoid confusing the eye, make all pictograms the same size.
- Clearly label the axes of the pictogram.

New College Freshmen

👥 = 1 million	1970	1980	1990	2000
Private Universities	👥👥👥👥	👥👥👥👥	👥👥👥	👥👥👥
Public Universities	👥👥👥👥👥👥👥👥👥	👥👥👥👥👥👥👥👥👥👥👥	👥👥👥👥👥👥👥	👥👥👥👥👥👥👥👥👥👥👥👥👥👥👥👥👥👥👥👥

FIGURE 20.3 Pictogram Showing Increase in College Students

Produce a Chart

Like a graph, a **chart** visually represents data and its relationship to other data in meaningful form. Several different types of charts help listeners grasp key points:

> A *flowchart* diagrams the progression of a process, helping viewers visualize sequence or directional flow (see Figure 20.4).

> A **diagram** (also called a "schematic drawing") visually plots how something works or is made or operated (see Figure 20.5).

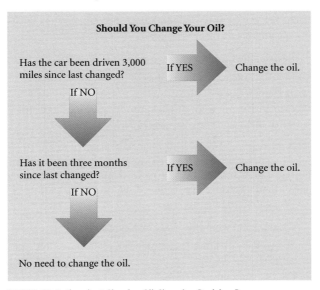

FIGURE 20.4 Flowchart Showing Oil-Changing Decision Process

A tabular chart, or **table**, systematically groups data in column form, allowing viewers to examine and make comparisons about information quickly. The table on p. 124, for example, summarizes the best uses of different types of graphs and charts.

Incorporate Audio and Video

Introducing an *audio clip*—a short recording of sounds, music, or speech—into a speech can add interest, illustrate ideas, and even bring humor to the mix. *Video*—including movie, television, and other recording instruments—can

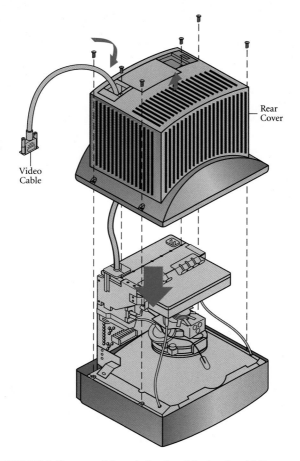

FIGURE 20.5 Diagram or Schematic Drawing of Monitor Stand Cables

BEST USE OF DIFFERENT TYPES OF GRAPHS AND CHARTS	
TYPE OF GRAPH OR CHART	**BEST USE**
Line graph	To represent trends or information that changes over time
Bar graph	To compare individual points of information, magnitudes
Pie graph	To show proportions such as sales by region, shares
Pictogram	To show comparisons in picture form
Flowchart	To diagram processes
Diagram	To show how something works or is constructed
Table	To show large amounts of information in an easily viewable form

also be a powerful presentation aid that combines sight, sound, and movement. With presentation software programs such as Microsoft's PowerPoint (see Chapter 22), you can also incorporate audio and video into an electronic presentation. **Multimedia** combines several media (stills, sound, video, text, and data) into a single production. When incorporating audio and video into your presentation:

- Cue the audio or videotape to the appropriate segment before the presentation.
- Alert audience members to what they will be viewing before you show the tape.
- Reiterate the main points of the audio or video clip once it is over.
- Check to see whether the audio or video material you are using is copyrighted, and check that you are using it in a manner that is consistent with copyright laws.

Choose a Method of Display

Options for presenting the aids to the audience include, on the more traditional side, overhead transparencies, slide transparencies, flip charts, chalkboards, and handouts. Many presenters display computer-generated graphics with LCD panels and projectors.

Project Overhead Transparencies

An **overhead transparency** (also called "overhead acetate") is an image printed on a transparent sheet of acetate that can be viewed by projection. If the speaker writes on the transparency during the presentation, it can be used much like a chalkboard. Parts of the transparency can be covered with paper and revealed progressively during the presentation. Alternatively, transparencies can be laid one on top of the other so that successive details can be added.

When using overhead transparencies,

- Ensure that the projector is in good order: Make sure it does not block the audience's view; have a spare projector bulb available; and tape the power cord to the floor.

- Stand to the side of the projector and face the audience, not the projected image.

- Use a pointer to indicate specific sections of a transparency—point to the transparency, not to the screen.

- If creating transparencies by writing or drawing during the presentation, use a water-soluble transparency pen and make sure to write clearly.

- Cover the transparencies when you are done using them. Use heavy paper or cardboard so they will not be moved by the projector's fan.[3]

- Practice using your transparencies before your presentation.

Use LCD Panels or Video Projectors

With presentation software programs such as Microsoft's PowerPoint, speakers create *computer-generated graphics*, displaying them with **LCD** (liquid crystal diode) **panels** and **projectors** or transferring the graphics to overhead transparencies. Used most frequently in large-scale settings, *video projectors* display an image through three lenses (red, green, blue) and project high-resolution images of up to twenty-five feet.

Prepare a Flip Chart

A **flip chart** is simply a large (27–34 inches) pad of paper on which a speaker can draw visual aids. They are often prepared in advance; then, as you progress through the speech, you simply flip through the pad to the next exhibit. You can also write and draw on the paper as you speak.

Use Posters

A **poster** is (generally) a large (36 × 56 inches) stiff paper board on which the speaker places, alone or in combination, text, data, and pictures. Speakers use posters to introduce topics or concepts to survey a topic. Many disciplines make use of posters in a form of presentation called the *poster session* (see Chapter 26). You can create posters by hand or generate them using Microsoft PowerPoint (see Chapter 22).

Pass Out Handouts

A **handout** is a page-size item that conveys information that either is impractical to give to the audience in another manner or is intended to be kept by audience members after the presentation. Handouts can also be used when it is best to have audience members follow along with you while you go over information. To avoid distracting listeners, unless you specifically want them to read the information as you speak, *wait until you are done before you distribute the handout.* If you do want the audience to view a handout during the speech, pass it out only when you are ready to talk about it.

CHECKLIST: Incorporating Presentation Aids into Your Speech

✓ Talk to your audience rather than to the screen — insofar as possible, don't turn your back to the audience.

✓ Maintain eye contact with the audience.

✓ Avoid putting the aid directly behind you. Place it to one side so that the entire audience can see it.

✓ Display the aid only when you are ready to discuss it, and put it away when you are finished.

✓ Practice your speech with the aids until you are confident that you can handle them without causing undue distractions.

✓ If you decide to use a pointer, don't brandish it about. Once you've indicated your point, put it down.

✓ In case problems arise, make sure that you are prepared to give your presentation without presentation aids.

21 Designing Presentation Aids

Whether you fashion presentation aids with pen and paper or generate them on a computer, apply the principles of simplicity and continuity to each aid you create.

Strive for Simplicity

Presentation aids that try to communicate too many messages will quickly overwhelm the audience. On average, viewers see slides or hand-wrought aids for about thirty seconds, so don't jam too much information onto any single visual:

- Present one major idea per aid.
- Follow the **eight by eight rule**; that is, don't use more than eight words in a line and more than eight lines on one slide.
- Where possible, state your points in short phrases.
- Where possible, construct your text in active verb form and parallel grammatical structure.
- Create concise titles that tell viewers what to look for and that reinforce your message.

Use Design Elements Consistently

Apply the same design decisions you make for one presentation aid to all of the aids you display in a speech. Doing so will ensure that viewers don't become distracted by a jumble of unrelated visual elements. Carry your choice of any key design elements—colors, fonts, upper- and lowercase letters, styling (boldface, underlining, italics), background color, page layout, repeating elements such as titles and logos—through to each aid.

Select Appropriate Typeface Styles and Fonts

A **typeface** is a specific style of lettering, such as Arial, Times Roman, and Courier. Typefaces come in a variety of **fonts**, or sets of sizes (called the point size), and upper and lower cases.

Designers divide the thousands of available typefaces into two categories: serif and sans serif. (Additional categories, such as script typefaces, aren't recommended for presentation aids because they are difficult to read from a distance.) **Serif typefaces** include small flourishes, or strokes, at the tops and bottoms of each letter. **Sans serif typefaces** are more blocklike and linear; they are designed without these tiny strokes.

Whether you are using a hand-drawn poster board or a computer-generated graphic, check your lettering for legibility, taking into consideration the audience's distance from the aid. Use a typeface that is simple and easy to read.

• Check that your lettering stands apart from your background; that is, don't put black type on a dark blue background.

• Use upper- and lowercase type; this combination is easier to read than all capital letters.

• Don't overuse **boldface**, <u>underlining</u>, or *italics*. Use them sparingly to emphasize the most important points.

• Experiment with 36-point type for major headings; 24-point type for subheads; and 18-point type for text. Use nothing smaller than 18-point type, and for larger rooms consider 24-point or larger.

• Use a sans serif typeface for major headings. Experiment with a serif typeface for the body of the text.

• Avoid ornate fonts — they are difficult to read.

• Use no more than two different typefaces in a single visual aid.

QUICK TIP

Using Serif and Sans Serif Type

For reading a block of text, serif typefaces are easiest on the eye (see Figure 21.1). Small amounts of text, however, such as headings, are best viewed in sans serif type. Thus, consider a sans serif typeface for the heading and a serif typeface for the body of the text. If you include only a few lines of text, consider using sans serif text throughout.

Use Color Carefully

The skillful use of color can draw attention to key points, helping listeners see comparisons, contrasts, and emphases. On the other hand, poor color combinations will set the wrong mood, render an image unattractive, or make it just plain unreadable.

• Use colors consistently across all aids.

• Keep the background color of your presentation con-

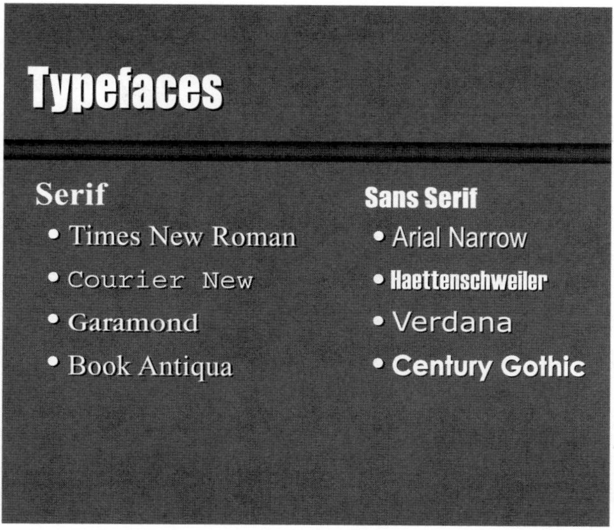

FIGURE 21.1 Serif and Sans Serif Typefaces

stant, and avoid dark backgrounds. Use light blues or
greens, or neutral colors such as tans or whites.

- For type and graphics, use colors that contrast rather
  than clash with or blend into the background.
- Use bold, bright colors to emphasize important points.
  Warm colors move to the foreground of a field. Yellow,
  orange, and red rank highest in visibility, so use these colors to highlight text or objects within a frame. But be

---

QUICK TIP

Beware of Color Associations

*Different audiences will make subjective interpretations
of color, depending on their professional and cultural
orientations, so take care not to summon a meaning, or
even a mood, that you don't intend. In the United States,
combinations of orange and black evoke Halloween, and red
and green, Christmas. In the professional arena, financial
managers react positively to green; it reminds health care
workers of infection. Internationally, Africans associate red
with death, while the Chinese link it with joy and prosperity,
and so forth.*

careful: These colors can be difficult to see from a distance.

- Limit the number of colors you use in a graphic. Use no more than four colors; using two or three is even better.
- Use softer, lighter colors to de-emphasize less important areas of a presentation.

CHECKLIST: Apply the Principles of Simplicity and Continuity

✓ Concentrate on presenting one major idea per visual aid.

✓ Apply design decisions consistently to each aid.

✓ Use type that is large enough for audience members to read comfortably.

✓ Use color to highlight key ideas and enhance readability.

✓ Check that colors contrast rather than clash.

22 A Brief Guide to Microsoft PowerPoint

A variety of presentation software packages offer public speakers powerful tools for creating and displaying professionally polished visual aids. With just the click of a mouse, you can transform your ideas into eye-catching graphics. You can project the aids directly from the computer via an LCD panel or projector or convert them into handouts or overhead transparencies. Presentation software programs also allow you to import video and sound into your presentation as part of a multimedia presentation.

With Microsoft's PowerPoint, one of the most popular presentation programs on the market today, you can generate slides containing text, artwork, photos, charts, graphs, tables, clip art, video, and sound. PowerPoint also allows you to produce handouts, outlines, and notes based on the slide presentation. In this section, we offer a brief overview of PowerPoint's features based on PowerPoint 2000. For more information, good references include *PowerPoint 2000* by Microsoft Press and *PowerPoint®2002 for Dummies®* by Doug Lowe.

QUICK TIP

It's a Speech, Not a Slide Show
Some speakers may become so enamored of generating electronic aids that they forget that their primary mission is to communicate through the spoken word and their physical being. Presentation aids can help you make your points and can even reduce speech anxiety, but only as long as your message and the audience remain your primary focus. As author Ron Hoff notes, "It's OK to be partially electronic—everybody can use a bit of glitz—but when all votes are counted and all scores are in, the presenter who is most alive will carry the day."[1]

PowerPoint's Presentation Options

After you launch the program, PowerPoint automatically displays a dialog box that allows you to choose from three options for creating a new presentation: *AutoContent Wizard, Design Template,* and *Blank Presentation* (see Figure 22.1). (To revise a presentation you have already created, select "Open an existing presentation.")

AutoContent Wizard

Of the three options, *AutoContent Wizard* offers the greatest degree of help (see Figure 22.2). With this option, you first choose from one of about two dozen organizational options, including *Marketing Plan, Introducing a Speaker,* and *Presenting a Technical Report.* Each option provides a predetermined organization and design. After you select a presentation medium (On-screen, Web, Overheads) and enter some basic information, the AutoContent Wizard sets up an index of customizable slides (generally from six to twelve) with preloaded slide titles, points, subpoints, color, and designs.

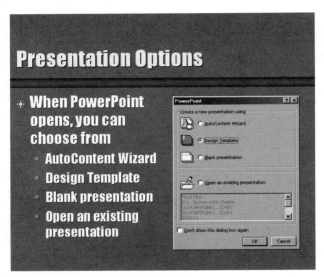

FIGURE 22.1 Options for Creating Presentations

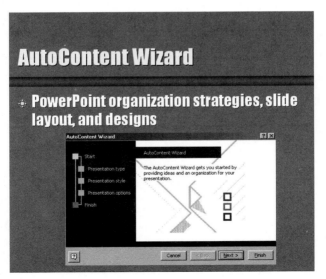

FIGURE 22.2 AutoContent Wizard

Template Option

For more flexibility in designing a presentation, the *Template* option includes approximately forty-eight predesigned templates to choose from. With the Template option, you decide how to organize your points and subpoints; the template you select then applies a consistent layout and color scheme to each slide in the presentation.

PowerPoint includes two kinds of templates: *presentation templates* and *design templates* (see Figure 22.3). The former provide layout and basic organizational outlines for particular presentations, such as business plans and progress reports. The latter offer only a design; the user determines the layout and content for each slide (see Figure 22.4).

Blank Presentation Option

In *Blank Presentation* mode, users customize every aspect of the presentation: layout, color, font type and size, organization of content, and graphics. Of the three options, Blank Presentation allows the greatest degree of creativity and flexibility. The downside is that each slide design essentially starts from scratch.

To create a new "blank" presentation, select Blank Presentation from the initial pop-up menu, select Blank Presentation from the New section of the File menu, or select the New File icon on the standard toolbar.

Open an Existing Presentation Option

Use this option to open, view, and edit an existing PowerPoint presentation.

PowerPoint Views

In the latest versions of PowerPoint, you can view the aids you create in *normal view, slide sorter view,* and *slide show view.* Each can be found in the View menu on the toolbar.

- *Normal view* allows you to view one entire slide on the screen and edit it; appearing right next to it is an outline of the entire presentation.
- *Slide sorter view* provides a snapshot of all slides. In this view, you can click and drag slide icons to reorganize or delete slides.

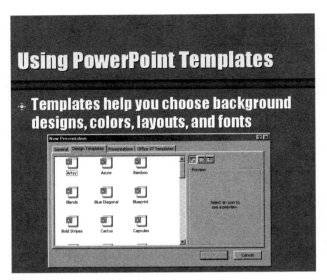

FIGURE 22.3 Using PowerPoint Templates

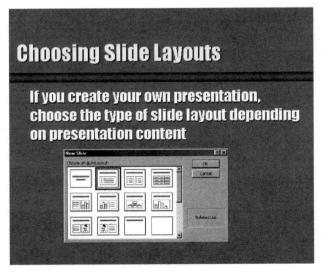

FIGURE 22.4 Choosing Slide Layouts

- *Slide show view* is used during projection to an audience. The slide takes up the entire screen and starts with the first slide.

PowerPoint Masters

For every graphic you create, PowerPoint creates a set of "masters": a *Slide Master*, a *Title Master,* a *Handout Master,* and a *Notes Master.* Slide Masters contain the elements (text or pictures) that you want to appear on every presentation slide, such as a logo, image, or line of text. To display a master, go to the View menu, scroll down to Master, and choose an option from a submenu: Slide Master, Title Master, Handout Master, or Notes Master.

Transition and Animation Effects

When moving from one slide to another in your presentation, or from one point to another within a single slide, you may wish to add special effects in the form of transitions and text animations. *Transition effects* add motion and sound effects as you move from one slide to another. To set transition effects in a presentation,

1. On the Slide Show menu, click Slide Transition.
2. In the Effect box, click the transition you want.
3. To apply the transition to the selected slide, click Apply. To apply the transition to all the slides, click Apply All.

Animation effects—sometimes referred to as *builds*—allow you to reveal text or graphics within a slide during a presentation. You can reveal one letter, word, or paragraph at a time, for example, as you discuss each item. Or you can make text or objects look dimmer or change color when you add another element.

PowerPoint 2000 comes with both preset and custom animations. *Preset animations* determine the options for you—such as whether an object flies in from the top, bottom, left, or right of the slide. *Custom animations* allow you to select your own options. To apply an animation,

1. Select the object you want to animate. For example, select a text placeholder or a piece of art that you would like to highlight.
2. On the Slide Show menu, click Preset Animation or Custom Animation.

3. Click the animation effect you want.

4. To edit the preset settings for this object after assigning a preset animation, go to Custom Animation on the Slide Show menu and make the changes you want.

QUICK TIP

Using Animation Effects
Used sparingly, transitions and animations can add zip to a presentation, but beware of using them so much that they distract from your message. Keep all text animations consistent from one slide to the next; for example, if you use the "fly in from left" effect for one slide, use it on all slides that you build. The same guidelines apply to slide transitions. Keep them consistent throughout the entire slide show or within different sections.

Entering and Editing Text

Whenever you choose a slide layout (other than blank layout), you replace the sample text in a placeholder with your own text. To select a *text placeholder,* click within the placeholder. The faint outline is replaced by a wide hashed border, the sample text disappears, and a flashing insertion point appears, indicating that you can now insert text. When you finish entering the text, deselect the placeholder by clicking a blank area of the slide. To add text when you do not have a placeholder, follow these steps:

1. Click the Text Box button in the Drawing toolbar.

2. Position the pointer where you want the top left corner of the text box to be.

3. Click and drag the mouse diagonally down and to the right to form a box of the appropriate width.

4. Release the mouse button and enter text.

Inserting Objects into Slides

PowerPoint allows you to create or import drawings, clip art, tables, worksheets, movies, and sounds in slides.

Clip Art

The PowerPoint ClipArt Gallery contains more than 1,000 drawings that cover a wide range of topics. Online, Microsoft's Clip Gallery Live, <http://cgl.microsoft.com/clipgallerylive>, contains more than 120,000 graphic images and sounds. PowerPoint also has the ability to insert video files.

You can insert clip art into a slide in several ways. If you are using AutoLayout, you simply double-click on the clip-art placeholder. You also can choose the Insert ClipArt command, select an option from the category list (Clip-Art, Pictures, Sounds, Videos), select a picture, and then choose OK.

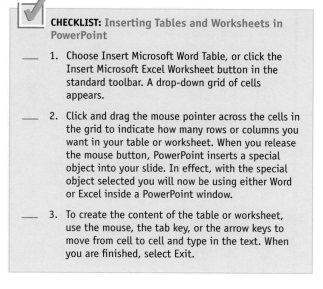

CHECKLIST: Inserting Tables and Worksheets in PowerPoint

___ 1. Choose Insert Microsoft Word Table, or click the Insert Microsoft Excel Worksheet button in the standard toolbar. A drop-down grid of cells appears.

___ 2. Click and drag the mouse pointer across the cells in the grid to indicate how many rows or columns you want in your table or worksheet. When you release the mouse button, PowerPoint inserts a special object into your slide. In effect, with the special object selected you will now be using either Word or Excel inside a PowerPoint window.

___ 3. To create the content of the table or worksheet, use the mouse, the tab key, or the arrow keys to move from cell to cell and type in the text. When you are finished, select Exit.

Movies and Sounds

PowerPoint comes with a variety of built-in movie and sound clips, or you can import clips from other sources. PowerPoint can also play a track from a compact disk inserted into your computer.

Running the Presentation

There are several ways to run a PowerPoint slide show. You can run an on-screen slide show by completing the following steps:

1. Open the presentation.
2. Choose any view.
3. Choose the View Slide Show command, click the Slide Show button in the lower left corner of the PowerPoint window, or hit F5. The Slide Show dialog box appears.
4. In the Slides section of the dialog box, choose All.
5. In the Advance section, choose Manual Advance or Use Slide Timings; then click Show. Your slide presentation begins running.

CHECKLIST: Tips for Successfully Incorporating Electronic Presentations

✓ Make sure that your presentation will work on the equipment in the presentation room.

✓ Don't let the technology get in the way of relating to your audience.

✓ As with nonelectronic presentations, talk to your audience rather than to the screen. Maintain eye contact as much as possible.

✓ Have a backup plan in case of technical errors; prepare a hard copy of your presentation.

✓ If you use a pointer of any kind (laser or otherwise), turn it off and put it down as soon as you have made your point.

✓ Never shine a laser pointer into anyone's eyes. It will damage them!

✓ As you practice your speech, incorporate the aids into your session until you feel confident that they won't get in the way of delivering your core message.

Part 7
Types of Speeches

23 Informative Speaking

To *inform* is to communicate knowledge. An **informative speech** provides an audience with new information, new insights, or new ways of thinking about a topic. Your speech might be an in-depth analysis of a complex subject; an explanation of a new policy or concept; a vivid description of a person, place, or event; or a physical demonstration of how something works. As long as your **general speech purpose** is to increase the listeners' understanding and awareness (see Chapter 8), your options are nearly limitless.

Identify Your Listeners' Information Needs

To make an informative speech truly effective, you must gauge what your listeners already know about a topic, as well as what they want and need to know about it (see Chapter 7 on audience analysis). You can then use this information to help listeners identify with the topic, see its relevance to their lives, and follow it to its logical conclusion.

Determine Your Speech Type

Informative speeches may be about people, events, processes, objects, concepts, or issues. These are by no means hard-and-fast categories — for example, many topics can be about both processes and people, concepts and events, and so forth — but they can be useful in organizing your thoughts and presenting your topic.

TYPE OF SPEECH	REPRESENTATIVE SUBJECTS
Speeches about objects — about anything animate or inanimate, other than humans	• digital cameras • the brain • survey of weight-loss diets • caring for a corn snake
Speeches about people — about any person or group of people that meets the informational goal	• war refugees • Saddam Hussein • Jim Calhoun, champion basketball coach
Speeches about events — about any current or historical event that meets the informational goal	• the history of St. Patrick's Day • 1937 Paris World's Fair

TYPE OF SPEECH	REPRESENTATIVE SUBJECTS
Speeches about processes—about anything that is best explained in terms of how it is made, how it works, or how it is performed	• pruning trees • isolating DNA in cells • how laughter improves health • how lightning forms
Speeches about concepts—about any abstract or complex concept that requires explanation	• Einstein's theory of relativity • justice • understanding the status of endangered species
Speeches about issues—about any issue or problem, as long as the speaker focuses on enlarging the audience's understanding and awareness rather than on advocating one position versus another	• racial profiling • your legal rights • political issues in the Middle East

Choose a Strategy for Presenting Content

Speeches that inform depend on one or, more often, a combination of the following approaches to presenting information: definition, description, explanation, and demonstration. Some informative speeches rely almost exclusively on a single approach (e.g., their main purpose is to demonstrate how something works or to describe what something is). Many speeches, however, employ a combination of strategies.

DEFINITION   Clearly defining terms is critical to any kind of speech; it is especially so when the explicit goal is to impart understanding and awareness. When you define information, you identify the essential qualities and meaning of something. When your speech focuses on addressing the meaning of a complex concept or one that is new to the audience—such as "What is a chaos theory?" or "What is a black box?"—pay particular attention to using definition to clarify your points. Regardless of the type of informative speech you deliver, however, you will likely make use of definition somewhere within it.

Defining information may sound straightforward, but there are in fact a number of ways to define something, including the following:

• Defining the topic by explaining what it does (**operational definition**); for example, *A computer is something that processes information.*

• Defining the topic by describing what it is not (**definition by negation**); for example, *Courage is not the absence of fear.*

• Defining the topic by providing several concrete examples of it (**definition by example**); for example, *Medical professionals include doctors, nurses, EMTs, and ambulance drivers.*

• Defining the topic by comparing it to something with which it is synonymous (**definition by synonym**); for example, *A friend is a comrade or a buddy.*

• Defining the topic by illustrating the root meaning of the term in question (**definition by etymology** [word origin]); for example, *Our word <u>rival</u> derives from the Latin word <u>rivalis</u>, "one living near or using the same stream."*[1]

DESCRIPTION   Whether recounting bullfighting in Pamplona, Spain, to a general audience or presenting a technical proposal to a group of experts, listeners want enough detail to allow them to form a mental picture of the person, place, event, or process under consideration. Use description, in the form of vivid details, to help them do this.

EXPLANATION   When you explain something, you provide reasons or causes, demonstrate relationships, and offer interpretation and analysis. Conveying information this way is particularly important when addressing difficult or confusing scientific theories or explaining the meaning of a historical movement, a period of literature or art, or an individual work.

DEMONSTRATION   Another approach to presenting information is to explain how something works or to actually demonstrate it. Use demonstration to convey information when working with an actual object, a representation or model, or a visual aid.

Arrange Main Points in a Pattern

An appropriate organizational pattern or patterns will help listeners follow main points.[2] Informative speeches can be organized using any of the patterns described in Chapter 13, including the topical, chronological, spatial, problem-solution, cause-effect, circle, and narrative patterns. A speech defining the French Impressionist movement in painting, for example, could be organized in a chronological pattern, in which main points are arranged in sequence from the movement's early period to its later falling out of favor. A speech explaining the glycemic index could be organized in a topical pattern (by logical grouping), in which each main point introduces a separate function of the index.

In a student speech on "How to Buy a Guitar," Richard Garza organizes his main points chronologically:

THESIS STATEMENT:	Buying and caring for a guitar involve knowing what to look for when purchasing it and understanding how to maintain it once you own it.
MAIN POINTS:	I. Decide what kind of guitar you need.
	II. Inspect the guitar for potential flaws.
	III. Care for the guitar.

In a speech on the nonmonetary uses of gold, Krista Kim organizes her main points topically:

THESIS STATEMENT:	Little known to the general population are gold's many nonmonetary applications in medicine and science.
MAIN POINTS:	I. Gold's general unique and useful qualities
	II. Gold's applications in medicine
	III. Gold's applications in the NASA space program

Help Listeners Follow Along

Audience members are not simply empty vessels into which you can pour facts and figures and expect them to recognize and remember all that information. Before they can retain information, they must be able to recognize and understand it.[3] Incorporating the steps described here into your speech will help listeners follow along.

CHECKLIST: Possible Matches of Organizational Patterns with Speech Types

✓ Objects — spatial, topical

✓ People — chronological, topical, narrative

✓ Events — chronological, cause-effect, narrative

✓ Processes — chronological, narrative

✓ Concepts — topical, circle, cause-effect

✓ Issues — chronological, cause-effect, topical, circle

Preview Main Points

Give listeners a sense of the whole before plunging into particulars, and offer them specific guideposts they can follow. Do this in the introduction by previewing your main points and summarizing what you want them to gain from the speech; for example,

> I'll begin by . . . Next I will . . . By the end of this presentation, I hope that you will not only be more familiar with cars but will have gained enough knowledge to know when you are being deceived at the repair shop.

See also the section on preview statements, Chapter 15, p. 91.

QUICK TIP

Demonstrate the Topic's Relevance

Early on in your speech (in your preview statement, for example), tell the audience why they should listen to you. Do this by pointing out how what they will learn from your presentation will benefit them. Giving listeners a reason to care will motivate them to pay attention to your message.

Define Your Terms

Consider how familiar your listeners are with your topic, and evaluate the terms you are using against this level of knowledge. Err on the side of caution by planning to explain any terms that may be unclear.

Include Neither Too Much Nor Too Little

Find the right balance between saying too much and offering too little information. Rather than including material simply because it is of interest to you, evaluate the information in terms of your listeners' interests and needs.

Present New and Interesting Information

Audiences seek knowledge, which means they like learning something new. To satisfy this drive, try to uncover information that is fresh and compelling. Seek out unusual sources (but make certain they are credible), novel (but sound) interpretations, startling facts, compelling examples, and moving stories.

Reinforce Your Message through Repetition and Parallelism

Repeating key words or phrases (parallelism) at various intervals in your speech creates a distinctive rhythm and thereby implants important ideas in listeners' minds (see Chapter 16 on language).

Relate the Unknown to the Familiar

To help listeners understand new concepts, draw comparisons (analogies; see Chapter 16) to concepts with which audience members are familiar. Once you have established a common ground of understanding, your listeners will have an easier time venturing into new territory, especially if the information you present contradicts misconceptions they might have.

Use Visualization

Language that is vivid and concise helps turn abstract concepts into concrete examples and builds interest in your topic. Rhetorical devices such as similes, metaphors, analogies, and the various techniques of repetition described in Chapter 16 help listeners grasp and retain information.[4]

QUICK TIP

Incorporate Presentation Aids

People process and retain information best when they receive information in more than one format. Messages that are reinforced visually and otherwise, in the form of presentation aids — such as Microsoft PowerPoint, objects, props, pictures, graphics, video, and audio — are often more memorable and believable than those that are simply verbalized.

CHECKLIST: Guidelines for Communicating Your Informative Message

✓ Tell audience members in your introduction what you hope they will learn from your message.

✓ Stress the topic's relevance to your listeners, and describe how they will benefit from the information.

✓ Use definition, description, explanation, and demonstration to convey your ideas.

✓ Select examples that will be clear to all audience members.

✓ Introduce concepts that may be new to the audience by relating them to something with which listeners are already familiar; use analogies, similes, and metaphors.

✓ Reinforce important ideas through repetition of key words or phrases.

✓ Base your choice of organizational pattern on your communication goals, the nature of your topic, and the needs of your audience.

✓ Consider how presentation aids can reinforce and expand upon your speech points.

SAMPLE INFORMATIVE SPEECH

In the following informative speech, Pete Weissman delivers a highly useful and engaging speech about the craft of writing speeches. A speechwriter himself, Weissman practices what he preaches, applying the advice he dispenses in the speech *to* his speech. Weissman's speech is nearly "textbook-perfect" in its clear development of ideas, relevant examples,

and frequent use of transitions, including a preview statement, internal previews and summaries, and signposts (see
Chapter 12). Just as he counsels, he builds the speech around
his audience, targeting and addressing their interests and
needs.

In terms of categorizing it, Weissman's speech is mainly
about a process (that of being an effective speechwriter) and
incidentally about a person (Senator Patty Murray). Weissman makes ample use of explanation to make his methods
clear to listeners, detailing the steps he takes to analyze an
audience, speaking in plain English and in a style suitable for
the speaker, and capturing the audience's attention.

As you read through this excerpted version of the speech,
note how Weissman adheres to the advice offered in this
chapter, including previewing main points, defining terms,
and presenting new and interesting information.

Speechwriting Secrets from the Senate

PETE WEISSMAN
Speechwriter and Deputy Communications Director,
United States Senator Patty Murray (D-Wash)

Delivered to the Washington Speechwriters Roundtable,
Washington, D.C., November 18, 2002

Thank you Ed [Vilade, vice president]. I want to thank   1
everyone at AARP for hosting us today. I know many of
you in this room write speeches for cabinet secretaries,
leaders of associations, and presidents of
universities. One of the things I love about   The speaker
this group is that it gives me a chance to   acknowledges the
peek into the lives of other speechwriters   expertise of his
and find out if their jobs are in fact better   audience and gains
than mine. [*Laughter*]   attention with a
  laugh.

Today, I want to lift up the curtain and tell you about   2
my job as a speechwriter in the United
States Senate. I'm going to show you the   The speaker provides
techniques I use to write Senate speeches—   a clear preview
everything from how to captivate the audi-   statement of what he
ence to how to produce a clear, memorable   will address.
text. While I use these techniques in the Senate, the truth
is these tips can help anyone who has to write or give a
speech.

I'm going to focus on three things. First, I want to   3
give you a flavor of the person I write for, Senator Patty

Murray, because she shapes everything I do. Then, I want to turn to what it's like to write speeches in the Senate. . . . Finally, I want to close with two things I wish I knew on my first day as a speechwriter—and one thing I did.

Let me begin with a word about my boss, U.S. Senator   4
Patty Murray of Washington State. She is not the average senator, and I mean that literally. The average senator is: a man, a millionaire, a lawyer, someone with a healthy ego, and tall. Patty Murray is none of those things. . . .

. . . Everyone who meets her can see that she is down   5
to earth and does not have a big ego like many politi-
cians. She'd rather get things done in a Senate committee than go on all the Sunday   Weissman uses
morning talk shows and just talk about get-   descriptive language
ting things done. One Washington State   about Senator
columnist described her as a workhorse,   Murray to gain
not a show horse. . . .   attention.

I share those examples with you because her back-   6
ground really affects the type of speeches she gives and the way she communicates.

I know that many speechwriters are frustrated because   7
they don't have the access they need to their principal. Fortunately, Senator Murray is very accessible and has very clear ideas about what she wants to say and how she wants to say it. She often sends me emails with her ideas for upcoming speeches. In every speech, much of the content and most of the ideas come straight from her. . . .

. . . I use seven steps to transform a
rough draft into a polished speech.   The speaker
First, I take the policy content from the   organizes his points
[Senator's] staff and translate it into En-   chronologically,
glish. Some of you work with lawyers. Oth-   step-by-step.
ers work with engineers and scientists. We all face the same challenge of removing the jargon and making the text clear.

Second, I build the speech around the audience. Aside   10
from the Senator, I'm the only person in our office who
thinks about what the audience will experi-
ence when the senator speaks. Everyone   The speaker suggests
else in our office is thinking from a legisla-   considering the
tive or press perspective. I'm the one who   timing and order of a
says, "Hmm, we've got 400 people sitting   speech in assessing
outside at the dedication of a library.   the audience's likely
They've just listened to seven state and lo-   disposition to a
   message.
cal officials. Senator Murray is last speaker on the agenda. The audience is probably bored and tired. They are not

going to want to hear a 20 minute treatise on the finer points of the Library Act."

I always try to put myself in the audience's shoes. In 11 fact, I keep this sign above my desk, which says, "Pete Weissman, Audience Advocate." It reminds me that my job is to be the advocate for that poor soul stuck in the last row of an auditorium at an event that has gone on too long.

The third thing I do to transform a speech is give it a 12 solid structure. Speeches are different than written communication. In a book, a reader can glance at a table of contents to understand the structure. In a speech, the speaker must explain how the speech is organized at the very start. I add signposting and explain the main sections of the speech. I also make sure there is a captivating introduction and a rousing conclusion. In some cases, I may develop a theme to hold the speech together. Generally, a speech needs a theme if it's more than 10 minutes long or if it has a bunch of unrelated parts that need to be unified rhetorically.

Fourth, I try to make the speech as persuasive as pos- 13 sible. I make sure there are statistics, quotes and data to support every point.

Fifth, I make the speech "media friendly." After all, very few people will actually see the speech in person. Most people will hear about it through the media. I want to make sure there's a short, clear quote that summarizes what Senator Murray is trying to accomplish.

> The speaker reminds students of advice he has followed in his speech — to provide clear and compelling support for each point.

Sixth, I make sure the speech fits her style. Patty Mur- 15 ray is not a stuffy, formal, ceremonial speaker. She's down to earth, determined and friendly. She won't say, "It is a deep personal honor for me to be here today with the educators of America." Instead, she'll say with energy and passion, "I'm thrilled to be here with people who are fighting for students every day, and together we've got to do four things."

Finally, I put the speech in the right format for her, 16 which thankfully does not involve a million little index cards. I'll provide either a double-spaced text with large bold letters or a short outline. Throughout those seven steps, I'm also getting edits directly from the Senator and incorporating those into her speech. Those are the seven steps I follow

> Weissman uses effective full-sentence transitions, internal previews, and transitional phrases such as "first," "second," and "third."

when things go right, but in the Senate I run into a lot of challenges. . . .

. . . I want to turn to the last part of my speech and leave you with two things I wish I knew on my first day — and one thing that I did know back then. [17]

First, I wish I knew the importance of the person introducing the Senator before she begins a speech. National associations will spend thousands of dollars putting on a convention, but when it's time to introduce the Senator, they just read the old biography from her website. That biography is so general that it doesn't show her expertise on the topic she's about to address. These days before a big speech, I'll send a few talking points to the introducer about her work on the topic at hand. It's always up to them whether they use it or not, but it often means a better introduction that is tailored to the interests of that audience. . . . [18]

[Second], I wish I knew the importance of addressing audience objections at the start of a speech. Every vote a Senator casts upsets some group of constituents, and they usually don't forget it. That can get in the way of an effective speech, unless you

> In a persuasive speech, this corresponds to the refutative pattern of organization (see Chapter 24).

address those concerns early in the speech. For example, Senator Murray may speak to a group of business leaders who are unhappy with her vote on a labor bill last year. They're really not going to listen to her with an open mind if they're still sore about that vote. She needs to address that objection upfront at the top of her speech. She may say, "I know that many of you disagree with my vote on last year's labor bill. After my speech, I'll be happy to answer all of your questions about that vote. In the end, we may just agree to disagree. But this session, there's a bill that's scheduled to come to the floor next week that will have a big impact on all of your businesses. For the next minute, I'd like to ask your indulgence so I can explain how this bill will impact your company." By acknowledging their concern up front, audience members are more likely to listen with an open mind.

This brings me to my final point. There is one thing I did know on my first day. It's something that has served me well and can help a speechwriter or speaker at any stage in their career. On my first day, I knew that I needed to learn from every speech. That's why I attend every [20]

> The final transition signals the close of the speech.

speech I can. I stand in the back of the room and watch to see if people in that last row are paying attention or if they're talking to each other. After the speech, I talk to the conference planner—and even audience members—to find out what they thought. I know I can't write perfect speeches every time, but I am committed to learning from each speech. Whether you're just starting out today as a speechwriter or you've written for presidents as some of our members have, I encourage you to learn from every speech. Thank you.

> Weissman concludes on a positive note that is likely to be inspirational to an audience of speechwriters.

24 Persuasive Speaking

To persuade is to advocate, or to ask others to accept your views. The goal of a **persuasive speech** is to influence the attitudes, beliefs, values, and acts of others. Some persuasive speeches attempt to modify audience attitudes and values such that they move in the direction of the speaker's stance. Others aim for an explicit response, as when a speaker urges listeners to donate money for a cause or to vote for a candidate. Sometimes a speech will attempt to modify both attitudes and actions.

Success in persuasive speaking requires attention to human psychology—to what motivates listeners. Audience analysis is therefore extremely important in persuasive appeals.

You can increase the odds of achieving your persuasive speech goal if you:

- Make your message personally relevant to the audience.[1]

- Clearly demonstrate how any change you propose will benefit the audience.[2]

- Expect minor rather than major changes in your listeners' attitudes and behaviors.

- Target issues that audience members feel strongly about. If they don't much care about an issue, it is unlikely that they will pay much attention to the speech.[3]

- Demonstrate how an attitude or a behavior might keep listeners from feeling satisfied and competent, thereby encouraging receptivity to change.

- Expect to be more successful when addressing an audience whose position differs only moderately from yours.
- Establish your credibility with the audience.

QUICK TIP

Expect Modest Results
Regardless of how thoroughly you have conducted audience analysis, or how skillfully you present your point of view, don't expect your audience to respond immediately or completely to a persuasive appeal. Persuasion does not occur with a single dose. Changes tend to be small, even imperceptible, especially at first.

Balance Reason and Emotion

Persuasion is a complex psychological process of reasoning and emotion, and effective persuasive speeches target not one but both processes in audience members. Emotion gets the audience's attention and stimulates a desire to act; reason provides the justification for the action.

Appeals to reason and logic — or to what Aristotle termed **logos** — are critical when an audience needs to make an important decision or reach a conclusion regarding a complicated issue. Such appeals make considerable use of **arguments** — stated positions, with support for or against an idea or issue.

To be truly persuasive, however, you must also convince listeners to care about your argument by appealing to their emotions — to what Aristotle termed **pathos.** Feelings such as pride, love, anger, shame, and fear underlie many of our actions and motivate us to think and feel as we do.

Two means of invoking emotions in a speech are *vivid description* and *emotionally charged words.* In a speech to the Democratic National Convention on July 16, 1984, Mario Cuomo used vivid description to praise the values of America's working class and the freedom given them by a democratic government to pursue their dreams. Using his father as an example, Cuomo evokes emotions of boldness and pride:

> I watched a small man with thick calluses on both hands work fifteen and sixteen hours a day. I saw him once literally bleed from the bottoms of his feet, a man who came here uneducated, alone, unable to speak the language, who taught

me all I needed to know about faith and hard work by the simple eloquence of his example. . . .[4]

QUICK TIP

Base Your Emotional Appeals on Sound Reasoning
Although emotion is a powerful means of moving an audience, relying solely on naked emotion will probably fail. What actually persuades an audience is the interplay of emotion with logic. When using emotions to appeal to an audience, always do so on the basis of sound reasoning.

Stress Credibility

Audiences want more than information, arguments, and even appeals to their emotions; they want what's relevant to them from someone who cares. Aristotle termed this effect of the speaker **ethos**, or moral character. Modern-day scholars call it **speaker credibility**. Audience members' feelings about your credibility strongly influence how receptive they will be toward your message. Attitude change is related to the extent to which the speaker is perceived to be telling the truth and to be credible in general.[5] To build credibility in a persuasive speech, do the following:

- Demonstrate trustworthiness by presenting your topic honestly and by showing concern for your listeners.
- Reveal your personal moral standards vis-à-vis your topic early in the speech.
- For speeches that involve a lot of facts and analysis, stress your expertise on the topic.
- For speeches on matters of a more personal nature, emphasize commonality with the audience.
- Display high regard for the speech occasion, even if it is outside your primary areas of interest.

QUICK TIP

Balancing Logos, Pathos, and Ethos
To evoke an effective balance of reason (logos), emotion (pathos), and speaker credibility (ethos), identify and target (1) your audience members' needs, (2) their likely approach to receiving the message, and (3) their underlying motivations for feeling and acting.

Target Listeners' Needs

Audience members are motivated to act on the basis of their needs; thus one way to persuade listeners to adopt changes in attitudes, beliefs, or behavior is to point to some need they want fulfilled and then give them a way to fulfill it. According to psychologist Abraham Maslow's classic **hierarchy of needs** (Figure 24.1), each of us has a set of basic needs ranging from the essential, life-sustaining ones to the less critical, self-improvement ones. Our needs at the lower, essential levels (physiological and safety needs) must be fulfilled before the higher levels (social, self-esteem, and self-actualization needs) become important and motivating. Using Maslow's hierarchy to persuade your listeners to wear seat belts, for example, you would appeal to their need for safety.

Following are five basic needs identified by Maslow and examples of corresponding appeals to these needs in listeners:

NEED	SPEECH ACTION
Physiological needs (basic sustenance, including food, water, and air)	• Plan for and accommodate the audience's physiological needs — are they likely to be hot, cold, hungry, or thirsty?

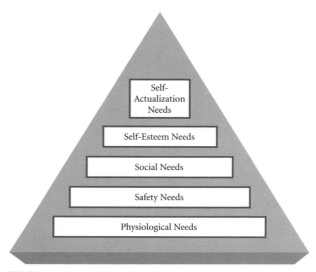

FIGURE 24.1 Maslow's Hierarchy of Needs

NEED	SPEECH ACTION
Safety needs (to feel protected and secure)	• Appeal to safety benefits— how wearing seat belts or voting for a bill to stop pollution will remove a threat or protect the audience members from harm.
Social needs (to find acceptance; to have lasting, meaningful relationships)	• Appeal to social benefits— if you want teenagers to quit smoking, stress that if they quit they will appear more physically fit and attractive to their peers.
Self-esteem needs (to feel good about ourselves; self-worth)	• Appeal to emotional benefits—when proposing a change in attitudes or behavior, stress that the proposed change will make listeners feel better about themselves.
Self-actualization needs (to achieve goals; to reach our highest potential)	• Appeal to your listeners' need to fulfill their potential— stress how adopting your position will help them "be all that they can be."

QUICK TIP

Show Them the Money

In order for change to endure, listeners must be convinced that they will be rewarded in some way. For example, to persuade people to lose weight and keep it off, you must make them believe that they will be healthier and happier if they do so. Skillful persuaders motivate their listeners to help themselves.

Encourage Mental Engagement

Audience members will mentally process your persuasive message by one of two routes, depending on their degree of involvement in the message.[6] When they are motivated and able to think critically about a message, they engage in **central processing**. That is, these listeners seriously consider what your message means to them and are the ones who are most likely to act on it. When listeners lack the motivation (or the ability) to pay close attention to the issues, they engage in **peripheral processing** of information—they pay little attention and respond to the message as being irrelevant, too complex to follow, or just plain unimportant. Even though such listeners may sometimes "buy into" your message, they will do so not on the strength of the arguments but on the basis of such superficial factors as reputation, entertainment value, or personal style. Listeners who use peripheral processing are unlikely to experience meaningful changes in attitudes or behavior.

To encourage listeners to engage in central rather than peripheral processing (and thus increase the odds that your persuasive appeal will produce lasting, rather than fleeting, changes in their attitudes and behavior), make certain to do the following:

- Present your message at an appropriate level of understanding.
- Make your message relevant to your listeners.
- Establish your credibility.

Construct Sound Arguments

Persuasive speeches use arguments to present one alternative as superior to others. In an argument, you ask listeners to accept a conclusion about some state of affairs by providing evidence and reasons that show that the evidence logically supports the claim. The **claim** states the speaker's conclusion, based on evidence. The **evidence** substantiates the claim.

Depending on the nature of the issue being addressed, a persuasive speech can consist of three different kinds of claims: of fact, of value, and of policy. Each type of claim requires evidence to support it (see the section on using convincing evidence).

- **Claims of fact** focus on whether something is or is not true or whether something will or will not happen. They usually address issues for which two or more competing answers exist, or those for which an answer does not yet exist. An example of the first is "Does affirmative action discriminate against nonminority job applicants?" An example of the second is "Will a woman president be elected in the United States within the next ten years?"

- **Claims of value** address issues of judgment by attempting to show that something is right or wrong, good or bad, worthy or unworthy. Examples include "Is assisted suicide ethical?" and "Should late-term abortions be permitted when a woman's health is at stake?" The evidence in support of a value claim tends to be more subjective than for a fact claim.

- **Claims of policy** recommend that a specific course of action be taken or approved of. Such claims often use the word *should* and often involve claims of fact and value as well. Examples include "Full-time students who commute to campus should be granted reduced parking fees" and "Property taxes should be increased to fund classroom expansions in city elementary schools." Notice that in each claim the word *should* appears. A claim of policy speaks to an "ought" condition, proposing that certain better outcomes would be realized if the proposed condition were met. To build a strong case for a claim of policy, organize your speech around a three-part justification consisting of (1) a need or a problem, (2) a solution, and (3) evidence of the solution's feasibility. (See the later discussion of the problem-cause-solution pattern.)

CHECKLIST: Structure the Claims in Your Persuasive Speech

✓ When addressing whether something is or is not true, or whether something will or will not happen, frame your argument as a *claim of fact*.

✓ When addressing issues that rely upon individual judgment of right and wrong for their resolution, frame your argument as a *claim of value*.

✓ When proposing a specific outcome or solution to an issue, frame your argument as a *claim of policy*.

Use Convincing Evidence

Every key claim must be supported with convincing *evidence*, or supporting material that provides grounds for belief.

Chapter 9 describes several forms of evidence: examples, narratives, testimony, facts, and statistics. These forms of evidence—called "external evidence"—are most powerful when imparting new information that the audience has not previously used in forming an opinion.[7] Thus, seek out information your audience is not likely to know but will find persuasive.

You can also use *audience's knowledge and opinions* and your own *speaker expertise* as evidence for your claims. *Audience's knowledge and opinions* refers to what listeners already think and believe. Nothing is more persuasive to listeners than a reaffirmation of their own attitudes, beliefs, and values, especially for claims of value and policy. To use this form of evidence, identify what the audience knows and believes about the topic and then present information that confirms these beliefs.

Finally, when the audience will find your opinions credible and convincing, consider using your own *speaker expertise* as evidence. Beware, however, that few persuasive speeches can be convincingly built on speaker experience and knowledge alone.

QUICK TIP

Address the Other Side of the Argument
All attempts at persuasion are subject to counterpersuasion. Listeners may be persuaded to accept your claims, but once they are exposed to counterclaims they may change their minds. If listeners are aware of counterclaims and you ignore them, you risk a loss of credibility.[8] Yet you need not painstakingly acknowledge and refute all opposing claims. Instead, raise and refute the most important counterclaims and evidence that the audience would know about. Ethically, you can ignore counterclaims that don't significantly weaken your argument.[9]

Avoid Fallacies in Reasoning

A **logical fallacy** is either a false or an erroneous statement or an invalid or deceptive line of reasoning.[10] In either case you need to be aware of fallacies in order to avoid making them in your own speeches and to be able to identify them in the speeches of others. Many fallacies of reasoning exist; the following are merely a few.

LOGICAL FALLACY	EXAMPLES
Begging the question An argument that is stated in such a way that it cannot help but be true, even though no evidence has been presented	• "The television special on PBS proved that chlorine causes cancer in humans." • "War kills."
Bandwagoning An argument that uses (unsubstantiated) general opinion as its (false) basis	• "Nikes are superior to other brands of shoes because everyone wears Nikes."
Either-or fallacy An argument stated in terms of two alternatives only, even though there may be many additional alternatives	• "If you don't send little Susie to private school this year, she will not gain admission to college."
Ad hominem argument An argument that targets a person instead of the issue at hand in an attempt to incite an audience's dislike for that person	• "I'm a better candidate than X because, unlike X, I work for a living."
Red herring An argument that relies on irrelevant premises for its conclusion	• "The recent tax hike by Governor Lambert has hurt working families across the state. Therefore you should vote against Mr. Morales for mayor."

Strengthen Your Case with Organization

Once you've developed your speech claims, the next step is to structure your speech points using one (or more) of the organizational patterns described in Chapter 13 and in this chapter.

A key factor to consider when deciding how to arrange your persuasive speech is what your **target audience** knows about the topic and how they stand in relation to it. Persuasion scholar Herbert Simon describes four types of potential audiences and suggests a different organizational pattern for each:[11]

PERSUASIVE STRATEGIES AND AUDIENCE TYPE	
AUDIENCE	**STRATEGIES**
Hostile audience or those that strongly disagree	• Stress areas of agreement. • Address opposing views. • Don't expect major change in attitudes. • Consider the refutation pattern (see p. 165). • Wait until the end before asking audience to act, if at all.
Critical and conflicted audience	• Present strong arguments and evidence. • Address opposing views, perhaps by using the refutation pattern.
Sympathetic audience	• Use motivational stories (the narrative pattern; emotional appeals) to reinforce positive attitudes. • Stress your commonality with listeners. • Clearly tell audience what you want them to think or do.
Uninformed, less educated, or apathetic audience	• Focus on capturing their attention. • Stress personal credibility and "likeability." • Arrange points logically, perhaps using a topical pattern.

Problem-Solution Pattern

One commonly used design for persuasive speeches, especially those based on claims of policy and claims of fact, is the **problem-solution pattern** (see Chapter 13). Here you organize speech points to demonstrate the nature and significance of a problem and then to provide justification for a proposed solution:

I. Problem (define what it is)

II. Solution (offer a way to overcome the problem)

Many problem-solution speeches require more than two points to adequately explain the problem and to substantiate the recommended solution. Thus a **problem-cause-solution pattern** may be in order:

I. The nature of the problem (explain why it's a problem, for whom, etc.)

II. Reasons for the problem (identify its causes, incidence)

III. Proposed solution (explain why it's expected to work, noting any unsatisfactory solutions)

Claims of policy can be organized effectively using these patterns. Another way to organize a claim of policy is to use four points of justification consisting of (1) a need or a problem, (2) reasons for the problem, (3) a solution to the need or problem, and (4) evidence of the solution's feasibility. This can be seen in the following claim of policy about changing the NBA draft:

THESIS: The NBA draft should be changed so that athletes like you aren't tempted to throw away their opportunity for an education.

I.   The NBA draft should be revamped so that college-age athletes are not tempted to drop out of school *(need/problem)*.

II.   Its present policies lure young athletes to pursue unrealistic goals of superstardom while weakening the quality of the game with immature players *(reasons for the problem)*.

III.   The NBA draft needs to adopt a minimum age of 20 *(solution to the problem)*.

IV.   National leagues in countries X and Y have done this successfully *(evidence of the solution's feasibility)*.

Monroe's Motivated Sequence

The **motivated sequence**, developed in the mid-1930s by Alan Monroe,[12] is a five-step process that begins with arousing listeners' attention and ends with calling for action. This time-tested variant of the problem-solution pattern is particularly effective when you want the audience to do something—buy a product, donate to a cause, and so forth. Yet it is equally useful when you want listeners to reconsider their present way of thinking about something or to continue to believe as they do but with greater commitment.

STEP 1: ATTENTION   The *attention step* addresses listeners' core concerns, making the speech highly relevant to them. Here is an excerpt from a student speech by Ed Partlow on becoming an organ donor:

> Today I'm going to talk about a subject that can be both personal and emotional. I am going to talk about becoming an organ donor. Donating an organ is a simple step you can take that will literally give life to others — to your husband or wife, mother or father, son or daughter — or to a beautiful child whom you've never met.
>
> There is one thing I want to acknowledge from the start. Many of you may be uncomfortable with the idea of becoming an organ donor. I want to establish right off that it's OK if you don't want to become a donor.
>
> Many of us are willing to donate our organs, but because we haven't taken the action to properly become a donor, our organs go unused. As a result, an average of 15 people die every day because of lack of available organs.

STEP 2: NEED   The *need step* isolates and describes the issue to be addressed. If you can show the members of an audience that they have an important *need* that must be satisfied or a problem that must be solved, they will have a reason to listen to your propositions. Continuing with the organ donor speech, here the speaker establishes the need for donors:

> According to the U.S. Department of Health and Human Services, there are approximately 80,000 people on the waiting list for an organ transplant. Over 50,000 are waiting for a kidney transplant alone, and the stakes are high: ninety percent of patients who receive a kidney from a living donor live at least 10 years after the transplant. One of the people on the waiting list is Aidan Malony, who graduated two years ago from this college. Without a transplant, he will die. It is agonizing for his family and friends to see him in this condition. And it is deeply frustrating to them that more people don't sign and carry organ donor cards. I have always carried my organ donor card with me, but didn't realize the extreme importance of doing so before talking to Aidan.
>
> Every 16 minutes another name joins that of Aidan Malony and is added to the National Transplant Waiting List.

STEP 3: SATISFACTION   Next, the *satisfaction step* identifies the solution. This step begins the crux of the speech, offering the audience a proposal to reinforce or change their attitudes, beliefs, and values regarding the need at hand. Here is an example from the speech on organ donation:

It takes only two steps to become an organ donor. First, fill out an organ donor card and carry it with you. You may also choose to have a note added to your driver's license next time you renew it.

Second and most important, tell your family that you want to become an organ donor and ask them to honor your wishes when the time arrives. Otherwise, they may discourage the use of your organs should something happen to you. Check with your local hospital to find out about signing a family pledge—a contract where family members share their wishes about organ and tissue donation. This is an absolutely essential step in making sure the necessary individuals will honor your wish to become an organ donor.

STEP 4: VISUALIZATION   The *visualization step* provides the audience with a vision of anticipated outcomes associated with the solution. The purpose of this step is to carry audience members beyond accepting the feasibility of your proposal to seeing how it will actually benefit them:

There are so many organs and such a variety of tissue that may be transplanted. One organ donor can help up to 50 people. Who can forget the story of 7-year-old American Nicholas Green, the innocent victim of a highway robbery in Italy that cost him his life? Stricken with unfathomable grief, Nicholas's parents, Reg and Maggie Green, nevertheless immediately decided to donate Nicholas's organs. As a direct result of the donation, seven Italians thrive today, grateful recipients of Nicholas's heart, corneas, liver, pancreas cells, and kidneys. Today, organ donations in Italy are twice as high as in 1993, the year preceding Nicholas's death. The Italians called this phenomenon, "The Nicholas Effect."

STEP 5: ACTION   Finally, in the *action step* the speaker asks audience members to act according to their acceptance of the message. This may involve reconsidering their present way of thinking about something, continuing to believe as they do but with greater commitment, or implementing a new set of behaviors. Here, the speaker makes an explicit call to action:

It takes courage to become an organ donor.
You have the courage to become an organ donor!
All you need to do is say yes to organ and tissue donation on your donor card and/or driver's license and discuss your decision with your family.
Be part of "The Nicholas Effect."

CHECKLIST: Steps in the Motivated Sequence

✓ *Step 1: Attention*   Address listeners' core concerns, making the speech highly relevant to them.

✓ *Step 2: Need*   Show listeners that they have an important need that must be satisfied or a problem that must be solved.

✓ *Step 3: Satisfaction*   Introduce your proposed solution.

✓ *Step 4: Visualization*   Provide listeners with a vision of anticipated outcomes associated with the solution.

✓ *Step 5: Action*   Make a direct request of listeners that involves changing or strengthening their present way of thinking or acting.

Comparative Advantage Pattern

When your audience is already aware of an issue or problem that needs a solution, consider the **comparative advantage pattern**. In this arrangement, speech points are organized to show how your viewpoint or proposal is superior to one or more alternatives. To maintain credibility, make sure to identify alternatives that your audience is familiar with and ones supported by opposing interests.

With the comparative advantage pattern, the main points in a speech addressing the best way to control the deer population might look like these:

THESIS: Rather than hunting, fencing, or contraception alone, the best way to reduce the deer population is by a dual strategy of hunting and contraception.

I.   A combination strategy is superior to hunting alone because many areas are too densely populated by humans to permit hunting; in such cases, contraceptive darts and vaccines can address the problem (*advantage over alternative #1, hunting*).

II.   A combination strategy is superior to relying solely on fencing because fencing is far too expensive for widespread use (*advantage over alternative #2, fencing*).

III. A combination strategy is superior to relying solely on contraception because only a limited number of deer are candidates for contraceptive darts and vaccines (*advantage over alternative #3, contraception*).

The Refutation Pattern

When you feel confident that the opposing argument is vulnerable, consider the **refutation organizational pattern**, in which each main point addresses and then refutes (disproves) an opposing claim to your position. Note that it is important to refute strong rather than weak objections to the claim, since refuting weak objections won't sway the audience.[13] If done well, refutation may influence audience members who either disagree with you or are conflicted about where they stand.

Main points arranged in a refutation pattern follow a format similar to this:

Main Point I: State the opposing position.

Main Point II: Describe the implications or ramifications of the opposing claim.

Main Point III: Offer arguments and evidence for your position.

Main Point IV: Contrast your position with the opposing claim to drive home the superiority of your position.

Consider the speaker who argues for increased energy conservation versus a policy of drilling for oil in protected land in Alaska.

THESIS: Rather than drilling for oil in Alaska's Arctic National Wildlife Refuge (ANWR), as the Bush Administration proposes, we should focus on energy conservation measures as a way of lessening our dependence on foreign oil.

I.   Bush claims that drilling in the Arctic Refuge is the only way to increase our energy independence; that it will have little negative impact on the environment; and that without this step our reliance on foreign energy will increase (*describes opposing claims*).

II. By claiming that drilling in the Refuge is the only solution, Bush sidesteps the need for stricter energy conservation policies and the need to protect one of the last great pristine lands (*describes implications and ramifications of opposing claims*).

III. The massive construction needed to access the Tundra will disturb the habitat of thousands of species and shift the focus from energy conservation to increased energy consumption, when the focus should be the reverse (*offers arguments and evidence for the speaker's position, as developed in subpoints*).

IV. Bush's plan would encourage consumption and endanger the environment; my plan would encourage energy conservation and protect one of the world's few remaining wildernesses (*contrasts the speaker's position with opposing claims, to drive home the superiority of this position*).

SAMPLE PERSUASIVE SPEECH

The following persuasive speech is by community college student Amy Taber. Amy's specific speech purpose is to raise awareness among her audience members and to convince them that, along with society as a whole, they need to practice disability awareness.

Amy's speech is both impassioned and well reasoned. In it, she targets listeners' feelings by pointing out that any of us could become disabled at any time. She also appeals to audience members' reasoning by offering credible evidence demonstrating the good that can come from increased awareness. Although not mentioned in the speech, the fact that Amy is part of the disabled community increased her credibility, or *ethos*.

Amy offers a variety of evidence in support of her thesis, including external evidence such as facts and statistics, as well as audience knowledge and opinions (the speech was delivered in Simsbury, Connecticut, and Amy refers to a new "boundless" playground the community recently erected). Amy organizes her speech along the lines of Monroe's motivated sequence.

The Need for Disability Awareness

AMY TABER

Manchester Community and Technical College

Imagine being in a bad car crash. One day you're on the men's or women's basketball team. The next day you're paralyzed and wheelchair bound. Will you be ready to drop all your dreams just like that?

> The speaker gains audience attention by personalizing the topic with the second-person point of view and by making it relevant to listeners—the first step in the motivated sequence.

Until very recently, we lived in a world where having a disability—either as a result of an accident of birth or of fate—meant the death of your dreams. At best, you were invisible. You were kept apart from the mainstream of society. You were seen as less than a whole person. "Normal" people assumed you couldn't make decisions for yourself. You were treated as if you would never amount to anything. Legally, you had no rights to fight such discrimination.

Today persons with disabilities [PWD] are no longer so invisible or powerless. The Civil Rights Movement of 1964, the Americans with Disabilities Act of 1990, and the heroic efforts of disability rights activists have helped to change all this. Many people with disabilities now attend regular public schools. They are an active part of the workforce. They can live independently. And when they meet discrimination, they have legal recourse to do something about it.

Each of these so-called "now open doors" represents a milestone for people with disabilities. But the battle is far from over. The disabled have successfully overcome many legal hurdles, but disability awareness in the general population remains low. As a result, we have yet to enact much of what the Americans with Disabilities Act promises us. Today the need is less for legal remedies than for disability awareness. By raising our level of what being disabled entails, we can ensure that it doesn't mean the automatic death of our dreams.

> The speaker identifies the need as individual lack of awareness of disabilities, and then she states her thesis: Disability awareness is a greater need than legal remedies.

Let me begin by describing a little about the Americans with Disabilities Act [ADA]. The first President George Bush signed the law on July 26, 1990; it protects the civil rights of individuals with disabilities and guarantees them equal opportunity in the workplace, public accommodation (such as access to public parks and buildings), transportation, public services, and telecommunications. The model for this landmark legislation was the 1964 Civil Rights Act, which prohibits discrimination based on race, color, sex, religion, and national origin.

A person is considered to have a *disability* if he or she ⁶ has, and I quote from the ADA, "a physical or mental impairment that substantially limits one or more major life activities, has a record of such an impairment, or is regarded as having such an impairment." As you can see, disabilities can be both *visible* and *invisible*. Disabled people may be sight- or hearing impaired or wheelchair bound. They may suffer from mental illness or a history of alcoholism from which they are recovering. They may have a physical and/or emotional impairment as the result of a violent crime. They may have been born with a genetic condition, such as Down Syndrome or Autism, that endows them with special needs.

The speaker effectively describes the scope and prevalence of disabilities using a formal definition and statistics as evidence.

According to the latest U.S. government figures, some 54 million Americans have some sort of disability. With a total population of some 281 million people, this translates into one out of every five people in the U.S. Any of us can become disabled at any time. No one is exempt from this risk. Not those of us who plan on having children. Not those who, like Christopher Reeve, decide one day to go horseback riding. Not those who, like the thousands of spinal cord injury victims, become injured in the course of their daily lives. We are all vulnerable, and we are all valuable. This is why it is so very important to understand and practice disability awareness.

The speaker demonstrates listener need, step 2 of the motivated sequence: They face a problem (they may become disabled) that must be addressed (they will need access to opportunity).

Sheer numbers suggest that we need to practice disability awareness. Spiritually and morally, the call is stronger still to "desegregate" the disabled through widespread disability awareness. Only by doing this can we realize the full potential offered by the Americans with Disabilities Act. The government cannot and should not be expected to enact all of the provisions of the Act. This volunteer nation of ours must take that spirit into the realm of disability awareness.

Amy again personalizes her message by stressing that it is up to individuals to enact change. The strong words "spiritually and morally" appeal to *pathos*.

What exactly is disability awareness? At the broadest level, it means understanding

Amy proposes that the solution to the need is participation by all (step 3 ["satisfaction"] of the motivated sequence).

and accepting people with disabilities in our midst—in our communities. Disability awareness means changing our attitudes about people with disabilities. It means recognizing that people with disabilities is the largest minority group in the United States and in the world. Practicing disability awareness means being aware of how we use language to talk about disability. Another is courtesy—how we behave towards those with disabilities. It means getting to know people with disabilities. Asking them questions. Thinking before you speak or act.

On a practical level, disability awareness means taking action whenever and wherever we can to bring our society "up to code." As a result of disability awareness in concert with the American Disabilities Act, ramps appear when none existed. Curb

> Here Amy moves to the visualization step, offering concrete examples of what practicing disability awareness can accomplish.

cuts let people maneuver their wheelchairs. City playgrounds sprout newly accessible surfaces and paths. Visual alarms notify patrons who are deaf or hard of hearing of an emergency. Untimed standardized tests permit more qualified people to enter schools of law and medicine. Casey Martin, a golfer with a rare disability that limits his ability to walk, can compete in the PGA using a golf cart. And it's wonderful that so many previously locked doors are now open as a result of disability awareness.

The Americans with Disabilities Act came about be-   11 cause of disability awareness on the part of dedicated individuals. Today, 13 years later, it is our responsibility to ensure that we fulfill the promise it represents. I urge you to take a lesson from the residents of San Antonio, Texas, who made their beautiful 2.5-mile Riverwalk truly wheelchair-friendly. Follow the lead of residents of Simsbury, Connecticut, who erected a "boundless" playground. Like the

> Moving to the action step, Amy concludes with examples of the kinds of specific actions her audience can take to increase their own disability awareness.

residents of Fernandina Beach, Florida, work with your local officials to install pool lifts in your public pools. Most important, try to be aware of and sensitive to issues related to disability on a daily basis.

Sources

1. Disabilityinfo.gov Web site. <http://www.disabilityinfo.gov/>
2. Americans with Disabilities Act Homepage. <http://www.ada.gov/>

25 Speaking on Special Occasions

A **special occasion speech** is one that is prepared for a specific occasion and for a purpose dictated by that occasion. Special occasion speeches can be either informative or persuasive or, often, a mix of both. However, neither of these functions is the main goal; the underlying function of a special occasion speech is to entertain, celebrate, commemorate, inspire, or set a social agenda:

- In speeches that *entertain,* listeners expect a lighthearted, amusing speech; they may also expect the speaker to offer a certain degree of insight into the topic at hand.

- In speeches that *celebrate* (a person, place, or event), listeners look to the speaker to praise the subject of the celebration; they also anticipate a degree of ceremony in accordance with the norms of the occasion.

- In speeches that *commemorate* an event or person (at dedications of memorials or at gatherings held in someone's honor), listeners expect the speaker to offer remembrance and tribute.

- In speeches that *inspire* (including inaugural addresses, keynote speeches, and commencement speeches), listeners expect to be motivated by examples of achievement and heroism.

- In speeches that *set social agendas* (such as occur at gatherings of cause-oriented organizations, fund-raisers, campaign banquets, conferences, and conventions), listeners expect the articulation and reinforcement of the goals and values of the group.

Special occasion speeches include (but are not limited to) speeches of introduction, speeches of acceptance, speeches of presentation, roasts and toasts, eulogies and other speeches of tribute, after-dinner speeches, and speeches of inspiration.

Speeches of Introduction

The object of a **speech of introduction** is to prepare or "warm up" the audience for the speaker—to heighten audience interest and build the speaker's credibility. A good speech of introduction balances four elements: the speaker's background, the subject of the speaker's message, the occasion, and the audience.

- *Describe the speaker's background and qualifications.* Describe the speaker's achievements, offices held, and other facts to demonstrate why the speaker is relevant to the occasion. Mention the speaker's achievements, but not so many that the audience glazes over.

- *Briefly preview the speaker's topic.* Give the audience a sense of why the subject is of interest, bearing in mind that it is not the introducer's job to evaluate the speech or otherwise comment on it at length. The rule is: Get in and out quickly with a few well-chosen remarks.

- *Ask the audience to welcome the speaker.* This can be done simply by saying something like "Please welcome Anthony Svetlana."

- *Be brief.* Speak just long enough to accomplish the goals of preparation and motivation. One well-known speaker recommends a two-minute maximum.[1]

CHECKLIST: Preparing a Speech of Introduction

✓ Identify the speaker correctly. Assign him or her the proper title, such as "vice president for public relations" or "professor emeritus."

✓ Practice a difficult-to-pronounce name several times before introducing the speaker.

✓ Contact the speaker ahead of time to verify any facts about him or her that you plan to cite.

✓ Consider devices that will capture the audience's attention, such as quotes, short anecdotes, and startling statements (see Chapter 15).

Speeches of Acceptance

A **speech of acceptance** is made in response to receiving an award. Its purpose is to express gratitude for the honor bestowed on the speaker. The speech should reflect that gratitude.

- *Prepare in advance.* If you know or even suspect that you are to receive an award, decide before the event what you will say.

- *Express what the award means to you.* Convey to the audience the value you place on the award. Express yourself genuinely and with humility.

*   *Express gratitude.* Thank by name each of the relevant persons or organizations involved in giving you the award. Acknowledge any team players or others who helped you attain the achievement for which you are being honored.

Speeches of Presentation

The goal of the **speech of presentation** is twofold: to communicate the meaning of the award and to explain why the recipient is receiving it.

*   *Convey the meaning of the award.* Describe what the award is for and what it represents. Mention the sponsors and describe the link between the sponsors' goals and values and the award.
*   *Explain why the recipient is receiving the award.* Explain the recipient's achievements and special attributes that qualify him or her as deserving of the award.
*   *Plan the physical presentation.* To avoid any awkwardness, consider logistics before the ceremony. For example, if you hand the award to the recipient, do so with your left hand so that you can shake hands with your right.

Roasts and Toasts

A **roast** is a humorous tribute to a person, one in which a series of speakers jokingly poke fun at him or her. A **toast** is a brief tribute to a person or an event being celebrated. Both roasts and toasts call for short speeches whose goal is to celebrate an individual and his or her achievements.

*   *Prepare.* Impromptu though they might appear, the best roasts and toasts reflect time spent drafting and rehearsing. As you practice, time the speech.
*   *Highlight remarkable traits of the person being honored.* Restrict your remarks to one or two of the person's most unique or recognizable attributes. Convey the qualities that have made him or her worthy of celebrating.
*   *Be positive.* Even if the speech is poking fun at someone, as in a roast, keep the tone positive. Remember, your overall purpose is to pay tribute to the honoree.
*   *Be brief.* Usually several speakers are involved in roasts and toasts. Be considerate of the other speakers by refraining from taking up too much time.

Eulogies and Other Tributes

The word **eulogy** derives from the Greek word meaning "to praise." Those delivering eulogies, usually close friends or family members of the deceased, are charged with celebrating and commemorating the life of someone while consoling those who have been left behind.

- *Balance delivery and emotions.* The audience looks to the speaker for guidance in dealing with the loss and for a sense of closure, so stay in control. If you do feel that you are about to break down, pause, take a breath, and focus on your next thought.

- *Refer to the family of the deceased.* Families suffer the greatest loss, and a funeral is primarily for their benefit. Show respect for the family, and mention each family member by name.

- *Be positive but realistic.* Emphasize the deceased's positive qualities while avoiding excessive praise.

QUICK TIP

Commemorate Life — Not Death

A eulogy should pay tribute to the deceased person as an individual and remind the audience that he or she is still alive, in a sense, in our memories. Rather than focus on the circumstances of death, focus on the life of the person. Talk about the person's contributions and achievements, and demonstrate the person's character. Consider telling an anecdote that illustrates the type of person you are eulogizing. Even humorous anecdotes may be appropriate if they effectively humanize the deceased.

After-Dinner Speeches

Its name notwithstanding, the contemporary **after-dinner speech** is just as likely to occur before, during, or after a lunch seminar or other type of business, professional, or civic meeting as it is to follow a formal dinner. In general, an after-dinner speech is expected to be lighthearted and entertaining. At the same time, listeners expect to gain insight into the topic at hand.

- *Recognize the occasion.* Connect the speech with the occasion. Delivering a speech that is unrelated to the event

may leave the impression that the speech is **canned**—one
that the speaker uses again and again in different settings.

- *Keep remarks sufficiently low-key to accompany the diges-
tion of a meal.* Even when charged with addressing a serious topic, keep the tone somewhat low-key.

Speeches of Inspiration

A **speech of inspiration** seeks to uplift the members of the
audience. Effective speeches of inspiration touch on deep
feelings in the audience. Through emotional force, they urge
us toward purer motives and harder effort and remind us of
a common good.

- *Appeal to audience members' emotions.* Two means of
invoking emotion are *vivid description* and *emotionally
charged words.* These and other techniques of language,
such as repetition, alliteration, and parallelism, can help
transport the audience from the mundane to a loftier
level (see Chapter 16).

- *Use real-life stories.* Few things move us as much as real-
life examples and stories, such as that of an ordinary person whose struggles result in triumph over adversity and
the realization of a dream.

- *Be dynamic.* If it fits your personality, use a dynamic
speaking style to inspire through delivery. Combining an
energetic style with a powerful message can be one of the
most successful strategies for inspirational speaking.

- *Make your goal clear.* Inspirational speeches run the risk
of being vague, leaving the audience unsure about what
the message was. Whatever you are trying to motivate
your listeners to do, let them know.

- *Consider a distinctive organizing device.* Many successful
inspirational speakers use devices such as **acronyms** or
steps to help the audience to remember the message. For
example, a football coach speaking at a practice session
might organize an inspirational speech around the word
WIN. His main points might be "Work," "Intensity," and
"No excuses," forming the acronym *WIN.*

- *Close with a dramatic ending.* Use a dramatic ending to
inspire your audience to feel or act. Recall from Chapter 15 the various methods of concluding a speech,
including quotations, stories, rhetorical questions, and a
call to action.

> ### QUICK TIP
>
> **Tailor Your Message to the Audience and Occasion**
> *Always plan your special occasion speech with audience expectations firmly in mind. People listening to a eulogy, for example, will be very sensitive to what they perceive to be inappropriate humor or lack of respect. Those attending a dedication ceremony for a war memorial will expect the speaker to offer words of inspiration. When a speaker violates audience expectations in situations like these, audience reaction will usually be pronounced.*

SAMPLE SPECIAL OCCASION SPEECH

The loss of the space shuttle *Columbia,* which exploded on Saturday, February 1, 2003, was a national tragedy. And because the crew of the doomed *Columbia* included the first astronaut from Israel and the first woman astronaut born in India, it was an international loss as well.

President Bush delivered a eulogy three days later at the Johnson Space Center in Houston, Texas. The president's speech follows the main guidelines for a eulogy. This was a moving event for him: He had to appear authoritative in his role as the nation's leader, but without fully masking his own bereavement. He names each astronaut in turn and notes something unique and memorable about his or her life's ambitions, professional achievements, or contributions to the mission. He is positive about each one without appearing insincere, and in several cases tells brief but informative anecdotes about how the individuals' lives had led them to become astronauts. President Bush also mentions some of the family members, friends, and colleagues of the deceased, acknowledging their significant grief and courage, thus humanizing his message and intimating that he knows the event is really for them, the survivors. He mentions the tragedy itself, at the beginning of the speech, but does not dwell on it. Rather, throughout the speech he commemorates the kinds of persons the astronauts were and how important their service was to their countries. President Bush concludes on the uplifting note that the country will long remember these astronauts.

Eulogy of the Columbia *Space Shuttle Astronauts*

PRESIDENT GEORGE W. BUSH

Delivered at the Johnson Space Center, Houston, Texas, February 4, 2003

Their mission was almost complete and we lost them so close to home. The men and women of the *Columbia* had journeyed more than 6 million miles and were minutes away from arrival and reunion. The loss was sudden and terrible, and for their families the grief is heavy. 1

Our nation shares in your sorrow and in your pride.

We remember not only one moment of tragedy, but seven lives of great purpose and achievement.

> President Bush begins by acknowledging that the greatest loss was suffered by the astronauts' loved ones. He seeks to comfort them in their loss by referring not only to "sorrow" but also to "pride."

To leave behind Earth and air and gravity is an ancient dream of humanity. For these seven it was a dream fulfilled. Each of these astronauts had the daring and discipline required of their calling.

Each of them knew that great endeavors are inseparable from great risk. And each of them accepted those risks willingly, even joyfully, in the cause of discovery.

> Rather than focusing on the circumstances of their deaths, President Bush uses stories to celebrate the astronauts' characters.

Rick Husband was a boy of four when he first thought of being an astronaut. As a man and having become an astronaut, he found it was even more important to love his family and serve his Lord.

> The speaker names each of the deceased astronauts in turn and notes something unique and memorable about his or her life and achievements.

One of Rick's favorite hymns was "How Great Thou Art," which offers these words of praise: "I see the stars. I hear the mighty thunder. Thy power throughout the universe displayed."

David Brown was first drawn to the stars as a little boy with a telescope in his backyard. He admired astronauts, but as he said: "I thought they were movie stars. I thought I was kind of a normal kid." 8

David grew up to be a physician, an aviator who could land on the deck of a carrier in the middle of the night and a shuttle astronaut. His brother asked him several weeks ago, what would happen if something went wrong on their mission? David replied, "This program will go on." 9

Michael Anderson always wanted to fly planes and 10
rose to the rank of lieutenant colonel in the Air Force.
Along the way, he became a role model, especially for his
two daughters and for the many children he spoke to in
schools.

He said to them, "Whatever you want to be in life, 11
you're training for it now."

He also told his minister, "If this thing doesn't come 12
out right, don't worry about me, I'm just going on higher."

Laurel Salton Clark was a physician and a flight sur-
geon who loved adventure, loved her work, loved her husband and her son. A friend who heard
Laurel speaking to mission control said,
"There was a smile in her voice."

Laurel conducted some of the experiments as *Columbia* orbited the Earth and
described seeing new life emerge from a
tiny cocoon. "Life," she said, "continues in a
lot of places, and life is a magical thing."

Mentions of family,
friends, and
colleagues of
the deceased
acknowledge
their grief and
personalize the
message.

None of our astronauts traveled a longer path to space 15
than Kalpana Chawla. She left India as a student, but she
would see the nation of her birth, all of it, from hundreds
of miles above.

When the sad news reached her hometown, an admin- 16
istrator at her high school recalled, "She always said she
wanted to reach the stars." She went there and beyond.

Kalpana's native country mourns her today and so 17
does her adopted land.

Ilan Ramon also flew above his home, the land of 18
Israel. He said, "The quiet that envelops space makes the
beauty even more powerful, and I only hope that the
quiet can one day spread to my country."

Ilan was a patriot, the devoted son of a Holocaust sur- 19
vivor, served his country in two wars.

"Ilan," said his wife Rona, "left us at his peak moment, 20
in his favorite place, with people he loved."

The *Columbia*'s pilot was Commander Willy McCool, 21
whom friends knew as the most steady and dependable of
men. In Lubbock today, they're thinking back to the Eagle
Scout who became a distinguished naval officer and a
fearless test pilot.

One friend remembers Willy this way, "He was blessed, 22
and we were blessed to know him."

Our whole nation was blessed to have such men and 23
women serving in our space program. Their loss is deeply

felt, especially in this place where so many of you called them friends, the people in NASA are being tested once again.

In your grief, you are responding as your friends 24 would have wished, with focus, professionalism, and unbroken faith in the mission of this agency.

Captain Brown was correct, America's space program 25 will go on.

This course of exploration and discovery is not an option we choose. It is a desire written in the human heart where that part of creation seeks to understand all creation. We find the best among us, send them forth into unmapped darkness and pray they will return. They go in peace for all mankind, and all mankind is in their debt.

President Bush commemorates how important the space program was to the astronauts.

Yet, some explorers do not return, and the law settles 27 unfairly on a few.

The families here today shared in the courage of those 28 they loved, but now they must face life and grief without them. The sorrow is lonely, but you are not alone.

In time, you will find comfort and the grace to see you 29 through. And in God's own time, we can pray that the day of your reunion will come.

And to the children who miss your mom or dad so 30 much today, you need to know, they love you, and that love will always be with you.

They were proud of you, and you can be proud of 31 them for the rest of your life.

The final days of their own lives were spent looking 32 down upon this Earth, and now, on every continent, in every land they can see, the names of these astronauts is known and remembered. They will always have an honored place in the memory of this country, and today, I offer the respect and gratitude of the people of the United States.

The speech concludes on a relatively uplifting note that the country will long remember these astronauts.

May God bless you all.   33

Part 8
The Classroom and Beyond

26 Typical Classroom Presentation Formats

Often, you will be called upon to prepare oral presentations in your major classes, in other general-education courses, and in the business and professional world. Oral presentations are forms of **presentational speaking**—reports delivered by individual speakers addressing groups of classmates, colleagues, clients, or customers, as well as multiple members of work groups addressing similarly composed audiences. This form of address has much in common with formal public speaking, yet important differences exist[1]:

- *Degree of formality.* Presentational speaking is *less formal* than public speaking; on a continuum, it would lie midway between public speaking at one end and conversational speaking at the other.

- *Audience composition.* Audiences attending public speeches range from those that are relatively small to those composed of thousands. The audience for a presentation can be as small as three people. Additionally, public-speaking audiences are more likely to be self-selected or voluntary, and they expect to be attending a onetime event. Attendees of oral presentations are more likely to be part of a "captive" audience, as in a classroom. As a group they are also more similar than audiences for public speeches, in that there is an ongoing relationship among the participants.

- *Speaker expertise.* Listeners generally assume that a public speaker has more expertise or firsthand knowledge than they do on a topic. Presentational speakers, in contrast, are more properly thought of as "first among equals."

No matter which major you select or what profession you choose, presentational speaking most likely will be required. Chapters 27–32 provide a review of course-specific presentation formats. In this chapter, we review typical oral-presentation formats assigned across the curriculum. These include team presentations, debates, reviews of academic articles, and poster sessions.

Typical Audiences

Depending upon the course, professors may require that you tailor your oral presentations to a hypothetical on-the-job audience, with your classmates representing that audience.

TYPES OF AUDIENCES IN THE WORKING WORLD	
TYPE OF AUDIENCE	**CHARACTERISTICS**
Expert or insider audience	People who have intimate knowledge of the topic, issue, product, or idea being discussed
Colleagues within the field	People who share the speaker's knowledge of the general field under question (e.g., psychology or computer science) but who may not be familiar with the specific topic under discussion (e.g., short-term memory or voice recognition systems, respectively)
Lay audience	People who have no specialized knowledge of the field related to the speaker's topic or of the topic itself
Mixed audience	An audience composed of a combination of people — some with expert knowledge of the field and topic and others with no specialized knowledge. This is perhaps the most difficult audience to satisfy

These audiences include the **expert or insider audience, colleagues within the field**, the **lay audience**, and the **mixed audience**. Note: Individual instructors or people in the working world may not use the same terminology employed here. (See also Chapter 28 on technical courses.)

Team Presentations

Team presentations are oral presentations prepared and delivered by a group of three or more individuals. Often used in the classroom as well as in the business and professional environment, successful team presentations require cooperation and planning (see Chapter 33, "Communicating in Groups").

Designate a Team Leader

First, designate a leader to map out a strategy for presenting the information and to ensure coordination among all members. Once the strategy is in place, the team should assign roles and tasks.

Assign Roles and Tasks

In some group presentations, one person may present the introduction, one or several others may deliver the body of the speech, and another may conclude the presentation. Together with the group leader, members must decide who will do what.

- Choose the person with the strongest presentation style and credibility level for the opening.
- Put the weaker presenters in the middle of the presentation.
- Select a strong speaker to conclude the presentation.
- Assign someone to handle the presentation aids.
- Assign someone to manage the question-and-answer session.[2]

Establish a Consistent Format

The verbal and the audiovisual portions of the presentation should follow a consistent format. Members should use shared terminology, and all visual aids such as slides should be similarly formatted. One person should be designated to check that these elements are consistent in terms of style, content, and formatting.

Establish Transitions between Speakers

Work out transitions between speakers ahead of time — for example, whether one team member will introduce every speaker or whether each speaker will introduce the next speaker upon the close of his or her presentation.

Rehearse the Presentation

Together with the whole group, members should practice their portions of the presentation in the order they will be given in the final form, and they should do so until the presentation proceeds smoothly. Apply the techniques for rehearsal described in Chapter 19 on delivery.

QUICK TIP

Practice for a Balanced Group Delivery
Audiences become distracted by marked disparities in style, such as hearing a captivating speaker followed by an extremely dull one. As in individual presentations, practice is key to overcoming such disparities and achieving a good balance of delivery styles.

CHECKLIST: Team Presentation Tips

✓ Find out who will be attending and what audience members expect to hear.

✓ Write out each member's responsibilities regarding content and presentation aids.

✓ Practice introductions and transitions to create a seamless presentation.

✓ Determine how introductions will be made — all at once at the beginning or having each speaker introduce the next one.

✓ Establish an agreed-upon set of hand signals that will indicate when a speaker is speaking too loud or soft, or too slow or fast.

✓ Rehearse the presentation several times from start to finish.

Debates

Debates offer a unique perspective to the challenge of public speaking, calling upon skills in persuasion (especially the reasoned use of evidence), in delivery, and in the ability to think quickly and critically. Much like a political debate, in an academic debate two individuals or groups consider or argue an issue from opposing viewpoints. Generally there will be a winner and a loser, lending this form of speaking a competitive edge.

Take a Side

Opposing sides in a debate are taken by speakers in one of two formats. In the **individual debate format**, one person takes a side against another person. In the **team debate format**, multiple people (usually two) take sides against another team, with each person on the team assuming a speaking role.

The *pro* side (also called "affirmative") in the debate supports the topic with a *resolution* — a statement asking for change or consideration of a controversial issue. "Resolved, that the United States government should severely punish flag burners" is a resolution that the affirmative side must support and defend. The pro side tries to convince the audience (or judges) that the topic under consideration should be addressed, supported, or agreed with. The *con* side (also called "negative") in the debate attempts to defeat the resolution by dissuading the audience from accepting the pro side's arguments.

Advance Strong Arguments

Whether you take the affirmative or negative side, your primary responsibility is to advance strong arguments in support of your position. Arguments usually consist of the following three parts (see also Chapter 24):[3]

- **Claim**— A claim makes an assertion or declaration about an issue. "Females are discriminated against in the workplace." Depending on your debate topic, your claim may be one of fact, value, or policy (see Chapter 24).

- **Reasoning**— Reasoning is a logical explanation of the claim. "Females make less money and get promoted less frequently than males."

- **Evidence**— Evidence is the support offered for the claim. "According to a recent report by the U.S. Department of Labor, women make 28 percent less than men in comparable jobs and are promoted 34 percent less frequently."

Debates are characterized by *refutation,* in which each side attacks the arguments of the other. Refutation can be made against an opponent's claim, reasoning, evidence, or some combination of these elements. In the previous argu-

---

QUICK TIP

Flowing the Debate

In formal debates (in which judges take notes and keep track of arguments), debaters must attack and defend each argument. "Dropping" or ignoring an argument can seriously compromise the credibility of the debater and her or his side. To ensure that you respond to each of your opponent's arguments, try using a simple technique adopted by formal debaters called "flowing the debate" (see Figure 26.1). Write down each of your opponent's arguments, and then draw a line or arrow to indicate that you (or another team member) have refuted it.

Affirmative	Negative	Affirmative	Negative	Affirmative	Negative
Nonviolent prisoners should be paroled more often.	Nonviolent prisoners can become violent when they are paroled.	Studies show nonviolent prisoners commit fewer crimes upon their release.	Those studies are outdated and involve only a few states.	My studies are recent and include big states like New York and California.	The studies from New York and California were flawed due to poor statistics.

FIGURE 26.1 Flowchart of the Arguments for the Resolution "Resolved That Nonviolent Prisoners Should Be Paroled More Often"

ment, an opponent might refute the evidence by arguing "The report used by my opponent is three years old, and a new study indicates that we are making substantial progress in equalizing the pay among males and females; thus we are reducing discrimination in the workplace."

Refutation also involves rebuilding arguments that have been refuted or attacked by the opponent. This is done by adding new evidence or attacking the opponent's reasoning or evidence.

CHECKLIST: Tips for Winning a Debate

✓ Present the most credible and convincing evidence you can find.

✓ Before you begin, describe your position and tell the audience what they must decide.

✓ If you feel that your side is not popular among the audience, ask them to suspend their own personal opinion and judge the debate on the merits of the argument.

✓ Don't be timid. Ask the audience to specifically decide in your favor, and be explicit about your desire for their approval.

✓ Point out the strong points from your arguments. Remind the audience that the opponent's arguments were weak or irrelevant.

✓ Be prepared to think on your feet (see Chapter 17 on impromptu speaking).

✓ Don't hide your passion for your position. Debate audiences appreciate enthusiasm and zeal.

Review of Academic Articles

A commonly assigned speaking task across disciplines is the
review of academic articles. A biology instructor might ask
you to review a study on cell regulation published in *Cell
Biology,* for example, while a psychology teacher may require
that you talk about a study on fetal alcohol syndrome published in the journal *Neuro-Toxicology.* Typically, when you
are assigned to review an academic article, your instructor
will expect you to do the following:

- Identify the author's thesis, and explain the methods by
  which the author arrived at his or her conclusions.
- Explain the author's findings.
- Identify the author's theoretical perspective, if applicable.
- Evaluate the study's validity, if applicable.
- Describe the author's sources, and evaluate their
  credibility.
- Show how the findings of the study might be applied to
  other circumstances, and make suggestions on how the
  study might lead to further research.[4]

Poster Sessions

A **poster session** presents information about a study or an
issue concisely and visually on a large (usually a 3' 8" by 5' 8")
poster. Presenters display their findings on posters, which are
hung on freestanding boards; on hand are copies of the written report, with full details of the study. When you prepare
for a poster session, pay particular attention to the following:

- Select a concise and informative title.
- Include an **abstract** (a brief summary of the study).
- Present two to three key points from each section of your
  paper.
- In the upper-right-hand corner of the poster, place a
  concise introduction that indicates the purpose of the
  presentation.
- In the lower-right-hand corner of the poster, place your
  conclusions and summary.
- Select a muted color for the poster, such as gray, beige,
  light blue, or white.
- Make sure your type is large enough to be read comfortably from at least three feet away.

- Design figures and diagrams to be viewed from a distance, and label each one.
- Include a concise summary of each figure in a legend below each one.
- Be prepared to provide brief descriptions of your poster and to answer questions; keep your explanations short.[5]

27 Science and Mathematics Courses

Oral presentations in the sciences and mathematics often describe the results of original or replicated research. Instructors want to know the processes by which your experimental results were obtained. For example, your biology instructor may assign an oral report on the extent to which you were able to replicate an experiment on cell mitosis. A mathematics instructor may ask you to apply a mathematical concept to an experiment or issue facing the field. In a geology course, you might describe the findings of your fieldwork.

QUICK TIP

What Do Science-Related Courses Include?
Science-related disciplines *include the physical sciences (e.g., chemistry and physics), the natural sciences (e.g., biology and medicine), and the earth sciences (e.g., geology, meteorology, and oceanography). Fields related to mathematics include accounting, statistics, physics, and applied math.*

Original Research Presentation

In the **original research presentation** (also called **oral scientific presentation**), you describe original research you have done, either alone or as part of a team. The research presentation usually follows the model used in scientific investigation and includes the following elements:

1. Introduction describing the research question or issue and the scope and objective of the study

2. Description of methods used to investigate the research question, including where it took place and the conditions under which it was carried out

3. Results of the study describing the key results and highlighting the answers to the questions/hypotheses investigated

4. Conclusion (also called "Discussion"), in which the speaker interprets the data or results and discusses their significance

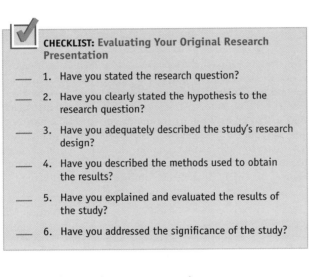

CHECKLIST: Evaluating Your Original Research Presentation

____ 1. Have you stated the research question?

____ 2. Have you clearly stated the hypothesis to the research question?

____ 3. Have you adequately described the study's research design?

____ 4. Have you described the methods used to obtain the results?

____ 5. Have you explained and evaluated the results of the study?

____ 6. Have you addressed the significance of the study?

Methods/Procedure Presentation

Some instructors may require you to describe how an experimental or mathematical process works and under what conditions it can be used. This is generally a ten- to fifteen-minute individual presentation. In a theoretical math class, for example, your assignment might be to describe an approach to solving a problem, such as the use of the Baum Welch algorithm, including examples of how this approach has been used, either inappropriately or appropriately. This type of **methods/procedure presentation** generally does the following:

1. Identifies the conditions under which the process should be used

2. Offers a detailed description of the process
3. Discusses the benefits and shortcomings of the process

The Research Overview

The **research overview presentation** provides background for a research question that will form the basis of an impending experiment or investigation. Instructors often ask students to organize research overviews with the following sections:

1. Overview of research that is relevant to the question at hand
2. Discussion of key studies that are central to the question
3. Analysis of the strengths and weaknesses of research in light of the current hypothesis or question

The format for the research overview may be an individual presentation or a **panel discussion**, with several individuals exploring specific lines of research that contribute to a general hypothesis or question. (See Chapter 33 for a review of panel discussions.)

Field Study Presentation

You may sometimes be called on to describe a field study project. A geology student may report on a dig, for example. The **extended research or field study presentation** can be delivered individually, in teams, or in poster-session format (see Chapter 26).

Whatever the format, included in the extended research study are the following details:

1. Overview of the field research
2. Methods used in the research
3. Analysis of the results of the research
4. Timeline indicating how the research results will be used in the future

Features of Effective Presentations

Science and mathematics instructors will expect your presentations to be grounded in the scientific method and to provide detailed information about methods used in gathering and analyzing data. Credible presentations must clearly illustrate the nature of the research question and the means by which results were achieved. Instructors will expect you to do the following:

- Use observation, proofs, and experiments as support.
- Be selective in your focus on details, highlighting critical information but not overwhelming listeners with details they can learn about by referring to the written paper and the cited sources.

Depending on the nature of the report, instructors may also expect you to recount experiences in the field or to offer observations of experimental findings (e.g., describe what happened to the chemicals in a chemistry experiment or to the physical objects in a physics experiment).

QUICK TIP

Use Presentation Aids to Illustrate Processes
Clearly executed presentation aids often are critical to effective scientific and mathematical presentations, and instructors generally require them. Aids can range from slides generated with presentation software programs and computer simulations to equations drawn on a chalkboard. Remember that the more simply you can render complex information (without distorting findings), the more likely it is that audience members will grasp your points.

 CHECKLIST: Tips for Preparing Successful Scientific Presentations

✓ Create an informative title.

✓ Place your presentation in the context of a major scientific principle.

✓ Focus on a single issue, and adjust it to the interests of your audience.

✓ Identify the underlying question you will address, divide it into subquestions, and answer each question.

✓ Follow a logical line of thought.

✓ Explain scientific concepts unambiguously, with a minimum of jargon.

✓ End with a clearly formulated conclusion related to your chosen scientific principle.[1]

28 Technical Courses

Oral presentations in technical courses often relate to a project, whether it is a set of plans for a building, a prototype robot, or an innovative computer circuit design. Rather than addressing prior research, as is often the case in oral scientific and social scientific reports, the focus of technical presentations usually rests on the product or design itself.

Several of the types of presentations you are likely to deliver in a technical course are reviewed in Chapter 34, including the *progress report* (see pp. 210–211). Other kinds include (but are not limited to) the design review and the request for funding.

QUICK TIP

What Are the Technical Disciplines?
Technical disciplines *include the range of engineering fields (mechanical, electrical, chemical, civil, aerospace, industrial, nuclear), computer science–oriented fields (computer science, computer engineering, software engineering), and design-oriented fields (industrial design, architecture, graphic design).*

The Design Review

The **design review** provides information on the results of a design project. Many capstone-engineering courses require that students prepare design reviews, which are generally informative in nature, although their purpose may include convincing the audience that the design decisions are sound. Design reviews often incorporate a prototype demonstration. A **prototype** is a model of the design. Typically, design reviews are delivered as team presentations (about twenty-five to thirty minutes in length) or in poster-session format.

Design reviews typically include the following:

1. Overview of the design
2. Description of the unique specifications of the design
3. Discussion of any experimental testing that has been completed on the design
4. Discussion of future plans and unresolved problems
5. Discussion of marketing and economic issues

191

The Request for Funding

In the **request for funding**, a team member or the entire team provides evidence that a project, a proposal, or a design idea is worth funding. As such, this kind of presentation is persuasive in nature. Requests for funding are usually organized as follows:

1. Overview of customer specifications and needs
2. Analysis of the market and its needs
3. Overview of the design idea or project and how it meets those needs
4. Projected costs for the project
5. Specific reasons why the project should be funded

The request for funding may be delivered as an individual or team presentation. On the job, the audience for the request for funding is made up of people who are concerned with the marketing, economic, and customer aspects of the idea or project (e.g., "colleagues within the field"; see p. 181).

QUICK TIP

Lead with Results
Technical disciplines such as engineering are about results — the end product. When organizing a technical presentation, consider telling the audience the most important result first. Then fill in the details.[1]

Features of Effective Technical Presentations

Technical presentations rely heavily on visual aids, sell an idea, provide hard data, and are results oriented:[2]

- *Gear information to the appropriate level.* Because of its complexity, it is especially important to deliver technical information at a level appropriate to the audience. Typically, people who attend technical presentations possess a range of technical knowledge, from little or none to an expert understanding of the topic at hand (see representative types of audiences, Chapter 26). A **mixed audience** is one composed of a combination of people — some with expert knowledge of the field and topic and others with no specialized knowledge. (See the following checklist for direction on presenting to a mixed audience.)

- *Use ample visual aids.* Use diagrams, prototypes, and drawings, including design specifications, computer simulations, physical models, and spreadsheets. Construct aids early in the process, and use them continually in practice and revision.

- *Sell your ideas.* On the job and in class, the technical presenter must persuade clients, managers, or classmates that a design, idea, or product is a good one. As one instructor notes, "You can never assume that your product or design will just sell — you have to do that."[3]

- *Provide hard data.* Good technical presentations are detailed and specific in their use of experimental results and numbers as evidence. Instead of making general, sweeping statements, provide hard data and clearly stated experimental results.

CHECKLIST: Presenting a Technical Report to a Mixed Audience

✓ Find out as much information as you can about the audience.

✓ Prepare both detailed and general content.

✓ Alert the audience to the order of your coverage — each audience segment will know what to expect and when.

✓ Consider devoting one-half to two-thirds of your time to an overview of your subject and saving highly technical material for the remaining time.[4]

✓ Be clear about the level at which you are speaking: "I am going to present the primary results of this project with minimal detailed information, but I'll be happy to review the statistics or experimental results in more detail following the presentation."

✓ If you notice that listeners are experiencing discomfort, consider stopping and asking for feedback about what they want. You might then change course and opt for a different approach.[5]

29 Social Science Courses

Students in the social sciences (including psychology, sociology, political science, and communication) learn to evaluate and conduct **qualitative research** (in which the emphasis is on observing, describing, and interpreting behavior) as well as **quantitative research** (in which the emphasis is on statistical measurement).[1] Research methods and areas of investigation can be far-ranging, from experiments on the behavior of neuroreceptors to surveys of homelessness.

Social scientists often focus on explaining or predicting human behavior or social forces, answering questions such as "What?," "How?," and "Why?"[2] Instructors may ask you to evaluate a theory or body of research, debate an issue, review the relevant literature, or make policy recommendations. Additionally, as in science and mathematics courses, you might prepare a research, field study, or methods/procedure presentation (see Chapter 27).

QUICK TIP

Define and Explain the Research
Use the strategies for presenting information discussed in Chapter 23 to offer clear descriptions and explanations of research. Clearly define *terms (by identifying their essential qualities and meaning);* explain *research and theories (by interpreting and analyzing findings, offering reasons or causes, and demonstrating relationships); and use* description *to make your points clear (by providing relevant details and examples).*

Debates

Students in the social sciences often must prepare for *debates* on controversial issues (see Chapter 26 for more on debates). Sometimes an assignment involves advocating a position that you do not support. For example, a sociology instructor may require students who oppose school vouchers to defend the policy. Whatever side of an issue you address, you will need to prepare a well-composed argument with strong supporting evidence (see Chapter 9).

Review of the Literature

Some instructors may require that you review the body of research related to a given topic or issue and offer conclusions about the topic based on this research. A psychology student, for example, might review the literature on psychological dysfunction in the military family. In addition to describing the available research, the student would offer conclusions uncovered by the research and suggest directions for future research. A **review of the literature presentation** typically includes the following:

1. Description of the available research
2. Evaluation and conclusions about the research
3. Suggested directions for future study

Explanatory Research Report

As stated earlier, social scientists often attempt to explain social or psychological phenomena by answering "What?," "How?," and "Why?" The **explanatory research presentation** reports on studies that attempt to analyze and explain a phenomenon, such as teen alcohol abuse or infant neglect. Such presentations typically address the following:

1. Description of the phenomenon under discussion (e.g., What is taking place?)
2. Description of how the phenomenon occurs
3. Explanation or theory of why it occurs

Evaluation Research Report

In addition to explaining phenomena, social scientists often measure the effectiveness of programs developed to address these issues. In preparation for on-the-job delivery, instructors may ask you to evaluate a program or policy. Typically, the **evaluation research presentation** includes the following:

1. What is the program's mission?
2. What does the program actually accomplish?
3. How well or poorly has the program met its stated objectives?

The Policy Recommendation

Psychologists, sociologists, communications specialists, and others are often asked to offer advice and recommendations on a current issue or problem. These professionals gather ideas and present them to the person or body commissioning the report. This *lay audience* (see p. 181) usually has a vested interest in the problem but is unfamiliar with the intricacies of the field. As preparation for such situations, instructors sometimes direct a team of students to deliver a mock **policy recommendation report**, which typically includes the following:

1. Definition of the problem
2. Recommendations to solve the problem or address the issue
3. Plan for implementation of these recommendations
4. Discussion of future needs or parameters to fulfill these recommendations

Features of Effective Social Scientific Presentations

Good social scientific presentations clearly explain the research question, refer to current research, and use timely data.

- *Illustrate the research question.* Pay special attention to clearly illustrating the nature of the research question and the means by which results were achieved.
- *Refer to current research.* Credible social scientific presentations refer to recent findings in the field. Instructors are more likely to accept experimental evidence if it is replicable over time and is supported by current research.
- *Use timely data.* Instructors expect student presentations to include timely data and examples. A report on poverty rates for a sociology course must provide up-to-date data, because poverty rates change yearly. A review of treatments for the mentally ill, for example, should accurately reflect current treatments.

30 Arts and Humanities Courses

Speaking assignments in arts and humanities courses (including English, philosophy, foreign languages, art history, theater, music, religion, and history) often require that you interpret the meaning of a particular idea, event, person, story, or artifact. Your art history professor, for example, may ask you to identify the various artistic and historical influences on a sculpture or a painting. An instructor of literature may ask you to explain the theme of a novel or a poem. A theater instructor may ask you to offer your interpretation of a new play.

Rather than focusing on quantitative research, presentations in the arts and humanities often rely on the speaker's analysis and interpretation of the topic at hand. These interpretations are nonetheless grounded in the conventions of the field and build on research within it.

Oral presentation assignments in arts and humanities courses can range from informative speeches of explanation to individual and team debates.

Informative Speeches of Explanation

Often in the arts and humanities, students prepare informative speeches (see Chapter 23) in which they explain the relevance of a historical or contemporary person or event; school of philosophical thought; or piece of literature, music, or art. For example, an art history professor may require students to discuss the artist Bernini's contribution to St. Peter's Cathedral in Rome. Visual aids are often a key part of such presentations; here, audiences would expect to see relevant reproductions and photographs.

Presentations That Compare and Contrast

Instructors in the arts and humanities often ask students to compare and contrast events, stories, people, or artifacts in order to highlight similarities or differences. For example, you might compare two works of literature from different time periods or two historical figures or works of art. These presentations may be informative or persuasive in nature. Presentations that compare and contrast include the following items:

1. *Thesis statement* outlining the connection between the events, stories, people, or artifacts

2. *Discussion of main points,* including several examples that highlight similarities and differences

3. *Concluding evaluative statement* about the comparison (e.g., if the presentation is persuasive, why one piece of literature was more effective than another; if informative, a restatement of similarities and differences)

Debates

Often students will engage in debates on opposing ideas, historical figures, or philosophical positions. In a history class, for example, students might argue whether sixteenth-century women in Western Europe experienced a Renaissance. The speaker must present a brief assertion (two to three minutes) about the topic; the opposing speaker then responds with a position. Whatever side of an issue you address, prepare a well-composed argument with strong supporting evidence (see Chapter 26).

QUICK TIP

Be Prepared to Lead a Discussion
Many students taking arts and humanities courses must research a question and then lead a classroom discussion on it. For example, a student of English may lead a discussion on Anton Chekov's play The Cherry Orchard. *The speaker would be expected to provide a synopsis of the plot, theme, and characters and offer an analysis of the play's meaning. For directions on leading a discussion, see Chapter 31.*

Features of Effective Arts and Humanities Presentations

Effective presentations in the arts and humanities help the audience to think of the topic in a new way by providing an original interpretation of the topic under consideration. A presentation on the historical significance of the success of Hitler's National Socialist Party, for example, will be more effective if you offer a new way of viewing the topic rather than reiterating what other people have said or what is already generally accepted knowledge. A debate on two philosophical ideas will be most effective when you assert issues and arguments that are different from those that the audience has thought of before. Because many speaking events in the arts and humanities call for interpretation, the more original the interpretation (while remaining logical and supported with evidence), the more compelling will the audience perceive the presentation to be.

31 Education Courses

In education courses (including subfields such as curriculum and instruction, physical education, secondary and elementary education, and education administration), the most common and practical speaking event is *teaching in a classroom.* Assignments in education courses often focus on some form of instructional task, such as giving a lecture or demonstrating an activity. In a mathematics education course, you may give a mini-lecture on a particular geometric theorem. In a learning-styles course, you may tailor an activity to a variety of different learners.

Delivering a Lecture

A **lecture** is an informational speech for an audience of new student learners. Standard lectures range from fifty minutes to an hour and a half in length; a mini-lecture presentation, designed to give students an opportunity to synthesize information in a shorter form, generally lasts about fifteen to twenty minutes. Structure your lecture as follows:

1. Overview
2. Statement of the thesis
3. Statement of the connection to previous topics covered
4. Discussion of the main points
5. Preview of the next assigned topic

Facilitating a Group Activity

In the **group activity presentation**, the speaker facilitates a postlecture group activity by providing the following:

1. A brief review of the lecture thesis
2. A description of the goal of the activity
3. Directions on carrying out the activity
4. A preview of the discussion session following the activity

Facilitating a Classroom Discussion

In the **classroom discussion presentation**, the speaker facilitates a discussion following a lecture by offering brief preliminary remarks and then guiding the discussion as it proceeds. To lead such a discussion:

1. Outline critical points to be covered.
2. Prepare several general guiding questions to launch the discussion.
3. Prepare relevant questions and examples for use during the discussion.

Features of Effective Education Presentations

Good presentations in education are marked by clear organization, integration of the material into the broader course content, and student-friendly supporting material.

- *Organize material logically.* Presentations in education must be tightly organized so that the audience can easily access information. Thus, pay careful attention to selecting an organizational pattern (see Chapters 13 and 24). In educational settings, the simpler the organizational structure, the better. Use organizing devices such as **preview statements** and **transitions** to help listeners follow ideas in a lecture, for example. Provide clear and logical directions for group activities.

- *Integrate discussion to overall course content.* Effective lectures, activities, and discussions are clearly connected to other parts of the course, topic, or content. Describe how the lecture for the day relates to yesterday's lecture to help students connect topics. Within a discussion, make clear connections between students' comments and other topics that have been raised or topics that will be raised in the future.

- *Tailor examples and evidence to the audience.* Effective educational presentations use familiar examples and evidence that the audience can grasp easily. The successful instructor would not support an idea with a statistical proof, for example, unless the audience members were trained in statistics. Regardless of the audience, use examples that will enhance learning; those examples are often the ones that are closest to the students' experiences.

32 Business Courses

Critical to success in today's business and professional environment is the ability to communicate well. Responding to this need, business instructors often require students to deliver oral presentations. Chapter 34, on business and professional presentations, highlights five commonly delivered business and professional presentations: sales presentations, proposals, staff reports, progress reports, and crisis-response presentations. In the classroom, you will likely simulate most of these presentation types, especially sales reports and proposals. Another common presentation in the business school setting is the case study, described in detail below.

QUICK TIP

Integrate Presentation Aids

The use of presentation aids — handouts, posters, computer-generated slides, and so forth — has become extremely common in the workplace and thus in the business classroom. Aids help convey points quickly and, if designed well and used judiciously, build credibility. To prepare for your career, learn how to use computerized software programs and practice integrating aids in your presentations (see Chapters 20–22 for more on presentation aids).

Case Study Presentations

To help students understand business theory and concepts, instructors often require them to report orally on case studies, either alone or in teams. A **case study** is a detailed illustration of a real or hypothetical business situation. Students are typically expected to report on the following items, frequently accompanying them with an array of presentation aids:

1. Background of the case
2. Problems and issues involved
3. Extenuating circumstances not explicitly mentioned in the case
4. Potential solutions to the case problems
5. Final recommendations for how the case should be resolved

Build Career Skills
Approach your business presentation assignments as a way to build career skills. Many prospective employers will ask about such classroom experience, and you will deliver similar presentations throughout your business career. Entry-level employees with superior oral presentation skills tend to get promoted sooner than their co-workers.

Requirements of Effective Presentations

Regardless of the type of presentation required in your business class, bear in mind the following points when preparing and delivering your presentation.

- *Understand the requirements.* Make sure you understand the purpose of the presentation, its relationship to the assignment, and the expectations for its delivery, including time limits.

- *Give equal attention to oral and written assignments.* Don't assume that the oral presentation part of the assignment is less important than any written materials. Business instructors are especially sensitive to the needs for speaking skills among their graduates.

- *Prepare for follow-up questions.* Questions are just as likely to come from your student-peers as they are from the instructor. Make sure that you are familiar with all aspects of your subject even if you do not cover everything in your presentation.

- *Do timed rehearsals.* Many business students think their presentations are much shorter than they actually turn out to be, while business instructors are often strict about time limits. Don't get caught going over time and being penalized or — even worse — being cut off by your instructor.

- *Rehearse as a team.* In a team format, it is unlikely that all team members will be equally prepared for the presentation. To avoid a lopsided delivery, rehearse as a group (see Chapter 26 for more on team presentations).

33 Communicating in Groups

Most of us will spend a substantial portion of our educational and professional lives participating in **small groups** or teams[1] (usually between three and twenty people); and many of the experiences we have as speakers, in both the classroom and the workforce, occur in the group setting. Groups often report on the results they've achieved, and some groups form solely for the purpose of coordinating oral presentations (see Chapter 26 on team presentations). Thus understanding how to work cooperatively within the group setting is a critical skill.

Focus on Goals

How well or how poorly you meet the objectives of a group, whether they are coordinating a team presentation or solving an engineering dilemma, is largely a function of how closely you keep sight of the group's goals and avoid behaviors that detract from these goals. Setting an **agenda** can help participants stay on track by identifying items to be accomplished during a meeting; often it will specify time limits for each item.[2]

Adopt Productive Roles

In a group, you will generally assume dual roles, such as a task role and an interpersonal role. **Task roles** are the hands-on roles that directly relate to the group's accomplishment of its objectives. Examples include "recording secretary" (takes notes) and "moderator" (facilitates discussion).[3] Members also adopt various **interpersonal roles**, or styles of interacting in the group, such as "the harmonizer" (smooths out tension) and "the gatekeeper" (keeps the discussion moving and gets everyone's input).[4]

Task and interpersonal roles help the group achieve its mission. Conversely, **counterproductive roles** such as "hogging the floor" (not allowing others to speak), "blocking" (being overly negative about group ideas; raising issues that have been settled), and "recognition seeking" (acts to call attention to oneself rather than to group tasks) do not help with the group's goals and obviously should be avoided.

Center Disagreements around Issues

Whenever people come together to consider an important issue, conflict is inevitable. But conflict doesn't have to be destructive. In fact, the best decisions are usually those that emerge from productive conflict.[5] In *productive conflict,* group members clarify questions, challenge ideas, present counter-examples, consider worst-case scenarios, and reformulate proposals.

Productive conflict centers disagreements around issues rather than personalities. In *personal-based conflict,* members argue with one another instead of about the issues, wasting time and impairing motivation. On the other hand, *issues-based conflict* allows members to test and debate ideas and potential solutions. It requires each member to ask tough questions, press for clarification, and present alternative views.[6]

Resist Groupthink

For a group to be truly effective, members eventually need to form a *collective mind,* that is, engage in communication that is critical, careful, consistent, and conscientious.[7] At the same time, they must avoid **groupthink**, or the tendency to accept information and ideas without subjecting them to critical analysis.[8] Groups prone to groupthink typically exhibit these behaviors:

- Participants reach a consensus and avoid conflict so as to not hurt others' feelings, but without genuinely agreeing.
- Members who do not agree with the majority feel pressured to conform.
- Disagreement, tough questions, and counterproposals are discouraged.
- More effort is spent justifying the decision than testing it.

QUICK TIP

Optimizing Decision Making in Groups

Research suggests that groups can reach the best decisions by adopting two methods of argument: **devil's advocacy** *(arguing for the sake of raising issues or concerns about the idea under discussion) and* **dialectical inquiry** *(devil's advocacy that goes a step further by proposing a countersolution to the idea).[9] Both approaches help expose underlying assumptions that may be preventing participants from making the best decision.*

Be a Participative Leader

When called upon to lead a group, bear in mind the four broad styles of leadership and select the participative model:

- *autocratic* (leaders make decisions and announce them to the group)
- *consultive* (leaders make decisions after discussing them with the group)
- *delegative* (leaders ask the group to make the decision)
- *participative* (leaders make decisions with the group)[10]

Research suggests that the most effective leader is participative, that is, one that facilitates a group's activities and interaction in ways that will lead to a desired outcome.

Set Goals

As a leader, aim to be a catalyst in setting and reaching goals in collaboration with other group members. It is your responsibility to ensure that each group member can clearly identify the group's purpose(s) and goal(s).

Encourage Active Participation

Groups tend to adopt solutions that receive the largest number of favorable comments, whether these comments emanate from one individual or many. If only one or two members participate, it is their input that sets the agenda, whether or not their solution is optimal.[11] To encourage group participation, do the following:

- *Directly ask members to contribute.* Sometimes one person, or a few people, dominates the discussion. Encourage others to contribute by redirecting the discussion in their direction ("Patrice, we haven't heard from you yet" or "Juan, what do you think about this?").
- *Set a positive tone.* Some people are reluctant to express their views because they fear ridicule or attack. Minimize such fears by setting a positive tone, stressing fairness, and encouraging politeness and active listening.
- *Make use of devil's advocacy and dialectical inquiry.* Raise pertinent issues or concerns, and entertain solutions other than the one under consideration.

Facilitate Decision Making

To reach a decision or solution that all participants understand and are committed to, guide participants through the six-step process of reflective thinking shown in Figure 33.1, which is based on the work of educator John Dewey.[12]

Step 1   Identify the Problem
• What is being decided upon?
Group leader summarizes problem, ensures that all group members understand problem, and gains agreement from all members.

Step 2   Conduct Research and Analysis
• What information is needed to solve the problem?
Conduct research to gather relevant information.
Ensure that all members have relevant information.

Step 3   Establish Guidelines and Criteria
• Establish criteria by which proposed solutions will be judged.
Reach criteria through consensus and record criteria.

Step 4   Generate Solutions
• Conduct brainstorming session.
Don't debate ideas; simply gather and record all ideas.

Step 5   Select the Best Solution
• Weigh the relative merits of each idea against criteria. Select one alternative that can best fulfill criteria.
If more than one solution survives, select solution that best meets criteria.
Consider merging two solutions if both meet criteria.
If no solution survives, return to problem identification step.

Step 6   Evaluate Solution
• Does the solution have any weaknesses or disadvantages?
• Does the solution resemble the criteria that were developed?
• What other criteria would have been helpful in arriving at a better solution?

FIGURE 33.1   *Making Decisions in Groups: John Dewey's Six-Step Process of Reflective Thinking*

CHECKLIST: Guidelines for Setting Group Goals

✓ Identify the problem.

✓ Map out a strategy.

✓ Set a performance goal.

✓ Identify resources necessary to achieve the goal.

✓ Recognize contingencies that may arise.

✓ Obtain feedback.

34 Business and Professional Presentations

Rather than being formal public speeches, business and professional presentations are forms of **presentational speaking**—reports delivered by individuals addressing colleagues, managers, clients, customers, as well as multiple members of work groups addressing similarly composed audiences (see Chapter 26). As such, these presentations are generally less formal than public speeches. Audiences tend to be "captive," and as a group they are also more similar than audiences for public speeches, in that there is an ongoing relationship among the participants. In addition, topics for such reports are more specific, task-oriented, and management- or client-directed.

QUICK TIP

Prepare to Interact with the Audience

In business and professional presentations, verbal interaction between speaker and audience is the rule rather than the exception. Audience members ask questions and make comments during and after the talk, and it isn't unusual for a presentation to be stopped midway when a discussion ensues or time runs out. Anticipating this, introduce important information early on in your presentation, and prepare answers for likely questions.

Five of the most common types of business and professional presentations are sales presentations, proposals, staff
reports, progress reports, and crisis-response presentations.[1]

Sales Presentations

A **sales presentation** attempts to lead a potential buyer to
purchase a service or a product described by the presenter.
The general purpose of sales presentations is to persuade.

Audience

The audience for a sales presentation depends on who has
the authority to make the purchase under consideration.
Some sales presentations are invited by the potential buyer.
Others are "cold sales" in which the presenter/seller approaches a first-time potential buyer with a product or a service. In some cases the audience might be an intermediary—
a community agency's office manager, for example, who then
makes a recommendation to the agency director.

Sales presentations are most successful when you clearly
show how the product or service meets the needs of the potential buyer and you demonstrate how it surpasses other
options available.

Organization

Due to its inherently persuasive nature, plan on organizing a sales presentation as you would a persuasive speech
(see Chapter 24). Suitable patterns include the motivated
sequence, comparative advantage, and problem-solution or
problem-cause-solution models. The comparative-advantage
pattern works well when the buyer must choose between
competing products and seeks reassurance that the product
being presented is indeed superior. The problem-solution or
problem-cause-solution pattern is especially effective when
selling to a buyer who needs a product to solve a problem.

With its focus on audience needs, the **motivated sequence**
(sometimes called the *basic sales technique;* see Chapter 24)
offers an excellent means of appealing to buyer psychology.
To use it to organize a sales presentation, do the following:

1. Draw the potential buyer's attention to the product.
2. Isolate and clarify the buyer's need for the product.

3. Describe how the product will satisfy the buyer's need.
4. Invite the buyer to purchase the product.

QUICK TIP

Adapt the Motivated Sequence to the Selling Situation
When making a sales presentation following the motivated sequence, the extent to which you focus on each step depends on the nature of the selling situation. In cold-call sales situations, consider spending more time discovering the potential buyer's needs. For invited sales presentations, spend more time detailing the characteristics of the product and showing how it will satisfy the buyer's needs.

Proposals

Organizations must constantly make decisions based on whether to modify or adopt a product, procedure, or policy. Such information is routinely delivered as a **proposal**. Proposals may be strictly informative, as when a facilities manager provides information to his or her superiors. Often, proposals are persuasive in nature, with the presenter arguing in favor of one course of action over another.

Audience

The audience for a proposal can vary from a single individual to a large group; the individual or individuals have primary or sole decision-making responsibility. Because many proposals seek to persuade listeners, careful adaptation to the audience is critical to an effective presentation.

Organization

A proposal can be quite lengthy and formally organized or relatively brief and loosely structured. Organize lengthy proposals as follows:

1. Introduce the issue.
2. State the problem.
3. Describe the method by which the problem was investigated.
4. Describe the facts learned.

5. Offer explanations and an interpretation of the findings.
6. Offer recommendations.

Organize brief proposals as follows:

1. State your recommendations.
2. Offer a brief overview of the problem.
3. Review the facts on which the recommendations are based.

Staff Reports

A **staff report** informs managers and other employees of new developments that affect them and their work or it reports on the completion of a project or task.

Audience

The audience for a staff report is usually a group, but it can be an individual. The recipients of a staff report then use the information to implement new policy, to coordinate other plans, or to make other reports to other groups.

Organization

Formal staff reports are typically organized as follows:

1. State the problem or question under consideration (sometimes called a "charge" to a committee or a subcommittee).
2. Provide a description of procedures and facts used to address the issue.
3. Discuss the facts that are most pertinent to the issue.
4. Provide a concluding statement.
5. Offer recommendations.

Progress Reports

A **progress report** is similar to a staff report, with the exception that the audience can include people *outside* the organization as well as within it. A progress report updates clients or principals on developments in an ongoing project. On long-term projects, such reports may be given at designated intervals or at the time of specific task completions. On short-term projects, reports can occur daily.

Audience

The audiences for progress reports might be a group of clients or customers, developers and investors, next-line supervisors, company officers, media representatives, or same-level co-workers. Progress reports are commonplace in staff meetings where subcommittees report on their designated tasks. Audience questions are common at the end of progress reports (see Appendix B on handling question-and-answer sessions).

Organization

Organize a progress report as follows:

1. Briefly review progress made up to the time of the previous report.
2. Describe new developments since the previous report.
3. Describe the personnel involved and their activities.
4. Detail the time spent on tasks.
5. Explain supplies used and costs incurred.
6. Explain any problems and their resolution.
7. Provide an estimate of tasks to be completed for the next reporting period.

Crisis-Response Presentations

Crisis-response presentations (also called "crisis communication") are meant to reassure an organization's various audiences (its "publics") and restore its credibility in the face of an array of threats, such as contaminated products, layoffs, chemical spills, or bankruptcy. These are often conveyed via media such as television and radio.

Audience

Crisis-response presentations may target one, several, or multiple audiences. A personnel manager may address a group of disgruntled engineers unhappy over a new policy. Seeking to allay fears of ruin and shore up stockholder confidence, the CEO of an embattled corporation may target anxious employees and shareholders alike.

Organization

A variety of strategies exist for organizing a crisis presentation, ranging from simple denial to admitting responsibility
for a crisis and asking forgiveness.[2] Familiarity with a range
of *image restoration strategies* will allow the speaker to select
those techniques that best apply to the situation at hand.[3] In
essence, the crisis-response presentation is based on persuasion and argument. Sound reasoning and evidence are
essential to its effectiveness. Depending on the issue and
audience(s) involved, use one or another of the organizational patterns described in Chapter 24, especially problem-
solution and refutation.

QUICK TIP

Stick to Ethical Ground Rules

*As in public speeches, the ethical standards of trustworthiness,
respect, responsibility, and fairness (see Chapter 2) must
infuse any business or professional presentation you deliver.*
Business and professional ethics *define how people within
a company or profession integrate the "ethical ground rules"
into their policies and practices. Such ethics also involve
complying with legal standards and adherence to internal
rules and regulations.[4]*

Appendices

A Citation Guidelines

Instructors will often require that you include a bibliography of sources with your speech (see Chapters 2 and 10). You can document sources by following documentation systems such as *Chicago,* APA, MLA, CBE, and IEEE.

Chicago Style Documentation

Two widely used systems of documentation are outlined in *The Chicago Manual of Style,* fifteenth edition (2003). The first, typically used by public speakers in a variety of disciplines, provides for bibliographic citations in endnotes or footnotes. This method is illustrated below. The second form employs an author-date system: Sources are cited in the text with full bibliographic information given in a concluding list of references. For information about the author-date system—and more general information about Chicago style documentation—consult the *Chicago Manual,* Chapters 16 and 17.

1. BOOK BY A SINGLE AUTHOR Give the author's full name followed by a comma. Then italicize the book's title. In parentheses, give the city of publication followed by a colon, publisher's name followed by a comma, and publication date. Place a comma after the closing parenthesis; then give page numbers from which your paraphrase or quotation is taken.

1. Eric Alterman, *What Liberal Media? The Truth about Bias and the News* (New York: Basic Books, 2003), 180–85.

2. BOOK BY TWO OR MORE AUTHORS

2. Bill Kovach and Tom Rosenstiel, *The Elements of Journalism: What Newspeople Should Know and the Public Should Expect* (New York: Three Rivers Press, 2001), 57–58.

3. EDITED WORK

3. Joseph B. Atkins, ed., *The Mission: Journalism, Ethics, and the World* (Ames: Iowa State University Press, 2002), 150–57.

4. SELECTION IN AN ANTHOLOGY, OR CHAPTER IN A BOOK, WITH AN EDITOR

4. Jonathan Dube, "Writing News Online," in *Shop Talk and War Stories: American Journalists Examine Their Profession,* ed. Jan Winburn (Boston: Bedford/St. Martin's, 2003), 202.

5. ARTICLE IN A MAGAZINE

5. John Leo, "With Bias toward All," *U.S. News & World Report,* 18 March 2002, 8–9.

6. ARTICLE IN A JOURNAL   Give the author's full name, the title of the article in quotation marks, the title of the journal in italics, the volume and issue numbers, the year of publication in parentheses followed by a colon, and the pages used.

6. Tom Goldstein, "Wanted: More Outspoken Views: Coverage of the Press Is Up, but Criticism Is Down," *Columbia Journalism Review* 40 (2001): 144–45.

7. ARTICLE IN A NEWSPAPER

7. Felicity Barringer, "Sports Reporting: Rules on Rumors," *New York Times,* 18 February 2002, sec. C, p. 3.

8. WORLD WIDE WEB SITE   Give the name of the author (if available), the title of the page in quotation marks followed by a comma, the title of the Web site, the page's publication date (if available) followed by a comma, the site's address in angle brackets, and the date you accessed the site in parentheses.

8. "Challenging Hate Radio: A Guide for Activists," *Fairness and Accuracy in Reporting (FAIR),* n.d., <http://www.fair.org/activism/hate-radio.html> (5 February 2003).

9. E-MAIL MESSAGE

9. Grace Talusan, "Bias in the Media," 20 March 2002, personal e-mail (20 March 2002).

10. POSTING TO A DISCUSSION GROUP

10. Ola Seifert, "Reporting on Race, Religion, & Values," 23 August 2002, <SPJ-L@LISTS.PSU.EDU> via <http://f05n16.cac.psu.edu> (14 September 2002).

11. ELECTRONIC DATABASE

12. Mark J. Miller, "Tough Calls: Deciding When a Suicide Is Newsworthy and What Details to Include Are among Journalism's

More Sensitive Decisions." *American Journalism Review* 24, no. 10 (2002): 43. *Expanded Academic ASAP,* InfoTrac (1 March 2003).

12. GOVERNMENT DOCUMENT

12. U.S. Congress, *The Electronic Freedom of Information Improvement Act: Hearing before the Subcommittee on Technology and the Law of the Committee on the Judiciary,* 1992 (Washington, D.C.: GPO, 1993), 201.

13. PERSONAL COMMUNICATION

13. Soo Jin Oh, letter to author, 13 August 2000.

14. INTERVIEW

14. Walter Cronkite, interview by Daniel Schorr, *Frontline,* Public Broadcasting System, 2 April 1996.

15. FILM, VIDEO, OR DVD

15. *All the President's Men,* dir. Alan J. Pakula, 2 hr. 18 min., Warner Brothers, 1976, videocassette.

16. SOUND RECORDING

16. Noam Chomsky, *Case Studies in Hypocrisy,* read by Noam Chomsky (Oakland, CA: AK Press, 2000).

APA Documentation

Most disciplines in the social sciences — psychology, anthropology, sociology, political science, education, and economics — use the author-date system of documentation established by the American Psychological Association (APA). This citation style highlights dates of publication because the currency of published material is of primary importance in these fields.

In the author-date system, use an author or organization's name in a signal phrase or parenthetical reference within the main text to cite a source.

For example, you could cite Example 1 on p. 217 with the author's name in a signal phrase as follows:

Rabin (1999) states that an increase in environmental stresses increases the chances for contracting common types of influenza by twelve percent.

Or with a parenthetical reference as follows:

One study found that environmental stress increased the chances for contracting common types of influenza by twelve percent (Rabin, 1999).

Each in-text citation refers to an alphabetical *references* list that you must create.

In APA format, as well as in other citation styles, you must always acknowledge certain types of information from external sources. You should acknowledge direct quotations, facts that are not generally known, another person's opinions and ideas, statistics or visual aids you did not gather or create yourself, and help you received from others.

In APA format, it's usually sufficient to simply note in your speech personal Web sites, e-mail correspondence, and personal interviews.

For more information on APA format, see the *Publication Manual of the American Psychological Association,* fifth edition.

The numbered entries that follow introduce and explain some conventions of this citation style using examples from the topic of stress management.

1. BOOK BY A SINGLE AUTHOR   Begin with the author's last name and initials followed by the date of publication in parentheses. Next, italicize the book's title, and end with the place of publication and the publisher.

Rabin, B. S. (1999). *Stress, immune function, and health: The connection.* New York: Wiley-Liss.

2. BOOK BY TWO OR MORE AUTHORS OR EDITORS

Williams, S., & Cooper, L. (2002). *Managing workplace stress: A best practice blueprint.* New York: Wiley & Sons.

3. ARTICLE IN A REFERENCE WORK

Kazdin, A. E. (2000). Stress. In *Encyclopedia of psychology* (Vol. 7, pp. 479–489). New York: Oxford University Press.

4. GOVERNMENT DOCUMENT

U.S. Department of Health and Human Services. (1997). *Violence in the workplace: Guidelines for understanding and response.* Washington, DC: U.S. Government Printing Office.

5. JOURNAL ARTICLE   Begin with the author's last name and initials followed by the date of publication in parentheses. Next, list the title of the article and italicize the title of the journal in which it is printed, then give the volume and issue numbers. Italicize the volume number, but not the issue number. End with the inclusive page numbers of the article.

Dollard, M. F., & Metzer, J. C. (1999). Psychological research, practice, and production: The occupational stress problem. *International Journal of Stress Management, 6*(4), 241–253.

6. MAGAZINE ARTICLE

Quinn, J. (2002, April). Take time to relax. *Prevention, 43.*

7. NEWSPAPER ARTICLE

Goode, E. (2002, December 17). The heavy cost of chronic stress. *The New York Times,* p. D1.

8. UNSIGNED NEWSPAPER ARTICLE

Stress less: It's time to wrap it up. (2002, December 18). *Houston Chronicle,* p. A1.

9. DOCUMENT FROM A WEB SITE

Centers for Disease Control and Prevention. (1999, January 7). *Stress . . . at work.* Retrieved January 6, 2003, from http://www.cdc.gov/niosh/stresswk.html

10. POSTING TO A DISCUSSION GROUP

Roseman, J. (1997, September 2). OEM: Stress, health impact, and social work. Message posted to http://list.mc.duke.edu/cgi-bin/wa?A2=ind9709&L=occ-env-med-l&F=&S=&P=2391

11. MATERIAL FROM A CD-ROM OR ONLINE DATABASE

Waring, T. (2002). Stress management: A balanced life is good for business. *Law Society Journal, 40,* 66–68. Retrieved from Family & Society Studies Worldwide database.

12. ABSTRACT FROM AN INFORMATION SERVICE OR ONLINE DATABASE

Viswesvaran, C., Sanchez, J., & Fisher, J. (1999). The role of social support in the process of work stress: A meta-analysis.

Journal of Vocational Behavior, 54, 314–334. Abstract
retrieved January 3, 2003, from ERIC database.

MLA Documentation

Created by the Modern Language Association, MLA documentation style is fully outlined in the *MLA Handbook for Writers of Research Papers* (sixth edition, 2003). Disciplines that use MLA style include English literature, the humanities, and various foreign languages.

In MLA format, as well as the other forms of citation guidelines, you must always acknowledge certain types of information from external sources. You should acknowledge direct quotations, facts that are not generally known, another person's opinions and ideas, statistics or visual aids you did not gather or create yourself, and help you received from others.

In MLA format, you document materials from other sources with in-text citations that incorporate signal phrases and parenthetical references.

For example, you could cite Example 1 below with the author's name in a signal phrase as follows:

Berg notes that "'Chicano' is the term made popular by the
Mexican American civil rights movement in the 1960s and
1970s" (6).

Or with a parenthetical reference as follows:

The term 'Chicano' was "made popular by the Mexican
American civil rights movement in the 1960s and 1970s" (Berg,
1999).

Each in-text citation refers to an alphabetical *works cited* list that you must create.

The sample citations given here all relate to a single topic: film appreciation and criticism.

1. BOOK BY A SINGLE AUTHOR   Citations for most books are arranged as follows: (1) the author's name, last name first; (2) the title and subtitle, underlined; and (3) the city of publication, an abbreviated form of the publisher's name, and the date. Each of these three pieces of information is followed by a period and one space.

Berg, Charles Ramírez. <u>Latino Images in Film: Stereotypes, Sub-
version, and Resistance</u>. Austin: U of Texas P, 2002.

2. BOOK BY TWO OR MORE AUTHORS OR EDITORS   Give the first author's name, last name first, then list the name(s) of the other author(s) in regular order with a comma between authors and the word *and* before the last one. The final name in a list of editors is followed by a comma and *ed.* or *eds.*

Hill, John, and Pamela Church Gibson, eds. The Oxford Guide to
    Film Studies. New York: Oxford UP, 1998. 51-52.

3. ARTICLE IN A REFERENCE WORK, SELECTION IN AN ANTHOLOGY, OR CHAPTER IN A BOOK

Katz, Ephraim. "Film Noir." The Film Encyclopedia.
    4th ed. 2001.

4. GOVERNMENT DOCUMENT

United States. Cong. House. Committee on the Judiciary. National
    Film Preservation Act of 1996. 104th Cong., 2nd sess. H.
    Rept. 104-558. Washington: GPO, 1996.

5. ARTICLE IN A JOURNAL

Kingsley-Smith, Jane E. "Shakespearean Authorship in Popular
    British Cinema." Literature-Film Quarterly 30 (2002):
    159-61.

6. ARTICLE IN A MAGAZINE

Ansen, David. "Lights! Action! Cannes!" Newsweek 19 May 1997:
    76-79.

7. ARTICLE IN A NEWSPAPER

Sebastian, Pamela. "Film Reviews Have a Delayed Effect on Box-
    Office Receipts, Researchers Say." Wall Street Journal
    13 Nov. 1997: A1+.

8. EDITORIAL   If the editorial is signed, list the author's name first; otherwise, begin with the title.

"The Edgy Legacy of Stanley Kubrick." Editorial. New York Times
    10 Mar. 1999: A18.

9. ONLINE SCHOLARLY PROJECT OR REFERENCE DATABASE

"Origins of American Animation." American Memory.
     31 March 1999. Library of Congress. 26 June 2000 <http://
     memory.loc.gov/ammem/oahtml/oahome.html>.

10. PERSONAL OR PROFESSIONAL WEB SITE

"American Beauty." Crazy for Cinema. 24 Oct. 2000 <http://
     crazy4cinema.com/Review/FilmsA/f_american_beauty.html>.

11. ARTICLE IN AN ONLINE PERIODICAL

Taylor, Charles. "The Pianist." Salon 27 Dec. 2002. 1 Jan. 2003
     <http://www.salon.com/ent/movies/review/2002/12/27/
     pianist/index_np.html>.

12. POSTING TO A DISCUSSION GROUP

Granger, Susan. "Review of The Cider House Rules."
     Online posting. 30 Mar. 2000. Rotten Tomatoes. 2 Oct. 2000
     <http://www.rottentomatoes.com/click/source-381/
     reviews.php?cats=&letter=c&sortby=movie&page=68&rid=
     775926>.

13. E-MAIL

Boothe, Jeanna. "Re: Top 100 Movies." E-mail to the author.
     16 Feb. 2001.

14. SINGLE-ISSUE CD-ROM, DISKETTE, OR MAGNETIC TAPE

"Pulp Fiction." Blockbuster Movie Trivia. 3rd ed. CD-ROM. New
     York: Random House, 1998.

15. WORK OF ART OR PHOTOGRAPH

Christenberry, William. Grave III. Hunter Museum of Art, Chat-
     tanooga, Tennessee.

16. INTERVIEW

Sanderson, Andrew. Telephone interview. 12 June 2002.

CBE Documentation

The Council of Science Editors recently changed their name from the Council of Biological Editors (CBE). The style book for this group, published in 1994, is still listed under this latter name and is called *Scientific Style and Format: The CBE Manual for Authors, Editors, and Publishers,* sixth edition (1994). The style described in that volume is most frequently used in the fields of biology and environmental science. Publishers and instructors who require the CBE style do so in two possible formats: a citation-sequence superscript format and a name-year format.

- If you use the citation-sequence superscript format, number and list the references in the sequence in which they are first cited in the speech (this system is the one usually used in speech classes).
- If you use the name-year format, list the references, unnumbered, in alphabetical order.

In the following examples, all of which refer to environmental issues, you will see that the citation-sequence format calls for listing the date after the publisher's name in references for books and after the name of the periodical in references for articles. The name-year format calls for listing the date immediately after the author's name in any kind of reference. Notice also the absence of a comma after the author's last name, the absence of a period after an initial, and the absence of underlining in titles of books or journals.

1. BOOK BY ONE AUTHOR   Be sure to list the total number of pages in the book.

Citation-Sequence Superscript

[1] Leggett JK. The carbon war: global warming and the end of the oil era. New York: Routledge; 2001. 341 p.

Name-Year

Leggett JK. 2001. The carbon war: global warming and the end of the oil era. New York: Routledge. 341 p.

2. BOOK BY TWO OR MORE AUTHORS

Citation-Sequence Superscript

[2] Goldstein IF, Goldstein M. How much risk?: a guide to understanding environmental health hazards. New York: Oxford University Press; 2002. 304 p.

Name-Year

Goldstein IF, Goldstein M. 2002. How much risk?: a guide to
understanding environmental health hazards. New York:
Oxford University Press. 304 p.

3. ARTICLE IN A JOURNAL

Citation-Sequence Superscript

[3] Stolzenberg W. Flocking together: Texas and Mexico team up to
conserve a hidden sanctuary. Nature 2001;51:20-21.

Name-Year

Stolzenberg W. 2001. Flocking together: Texas and Mexico team
up to conserve a hidden sanctuary. Nature 51:20-21.

4. ARTICLE IN A MAGAZINE

Citation-Sequence Superscript

[4] Wilcott B. Art for Earth's sake. Mother Jones 2000 June:16.

Name-Year

Wilcott B. 2000 June. Art for Earth's sake. Mother Jones:16.

5. ARTICLE IN A NEWSPAPER

Citation-Sequence Superscript

[5] Parson EA. Moving beyond the Kyoto impasse. New York Times
2001 July 1; Sect A:23(col 1).

Name-Year

Parson EA. 2001 July 1. Moving beyond the Kyoto impasse. New
York Times; Sect A:23(col 1).

6. WEB SITE Although the 1994 edition of *The CBE Manual*
includes a few examples for citing electronic sources, the
Council of Science Editors now recommends the guidelines
provided at the Web site of the National Library of Medicine
<www.nlm.nih.gov/pubs/formats/internet.pdf>. The follow-
ing formats are adapted from the advice on this site. The examples shown follow the citation-sequence format, but you
can easily adapt them to the name-year format. For a Web
site, include as many of the following as possible: the date of
publication (or, if this is not available, the copyright date);
the date of the most recent revision; and the date of access.

[6] Tennessee Department of Environment and Conservation. [Inter-
net]. Nashville, TN [cited 2003 Oct 3]. Available from:
http://www.state.tn.us/environment/

7. E-MAIL   List the author's name, the message's subject line, followed by the word "Internet" in square brackets. Next, include the words "Message to:" followed by the addressee's name, information about when the message was sent and when it was cited, and the length of the message.

[7] McGee E. Toxins in the Arkansas River [Internet]. Message to: Hannah Rubenstein. 2001 Sept 26, 3:35 pm [cited 2001 Sept 26]. [about 1 screen]

8. ELECTRONIC DISCUSSION LIST MESSAGE   Begin with the author's name, the subject line, the name of the discussion list, and include as much of the following information as possible.

[8] Affleck-Asch W. In: Colorado State Ecofem Mail Archive [Internet]. Boulder, CO: University of Colorado (US); 2002 Dec 2, 12:14:03 [cited 2003 Jan 2]. [about 4 paragraphs]. Available from: http://www.mail-archive.com/ecofem@csf.colorado.edu/.

IEEE Documentation

The Institute of Electrical and Electronic Engineers (IEEE) style requires that references appear at the end of the text, not in alphabetical order but in the order in which the references were cited in the text. A bracketed reference number beginning with *B* precedes each entry. For speakers, this means creating a bibliography of sources listed in the order in which they were cited in the speech (this is done in bibliographies for speeches in any format). For more information on IEEE documentation, check the IEEE Standards Style Manual online at <http://standards.ieee.org/guides/style>.

1. BOOK

[B1] Vorpérian, V., *Fast Analytical Techniques for Electrical and Electronic Circuits*. New York: Cambridge University Press, 2002, p. 462.

2. PERIODICAL

[B2] Brittain, J. C., "Charles F. Scott: A pioneer in electrical power engineering," *IEEE Industry Applications Magazine,* vol. 287, no. 6, pp. 6–8, Nov./Dec. 2000.

3. WEB PAGE

[B3] Harnack, A., and Kleppinger, E., "Beyond the MLA Handbook: Documenting Electronic Sources on the Internet" [Online style sheet] (June 1996), Available at: http://english.ttu.edu.kairos/1.2/

B Question-and-Answer Sessions

Deftly fielding questions is a final critical component of making a speech or a presentation. As the last step in preparing your speech, anticipate and prepare for questions the audience is likely to pose to you. Write these questions down, and practice answering them. Spend time preparing an answer to the most difficult question that you are likely to face. The confidence you will gain from smoothly handling a difficult question should spill over to other questions.[1]

Protocol during the Session

As a matter of courtesy, call on audience members in the order in which they raise their hands. Consider these guidelines:

- *Repeat or paraphrase the question* ("The question is 'Did the mayor really vote against . . . '"). This will ensure that you've heard it correctly, that others in the audience know what you are responding to, and that you have time to reflect upon and formulate an answer. Note that there are a few exceptions to repeating the question, especially when the question is hostile. One expert suggests that you should always repeat the question when speaking to a large group; when you're in a small group or a training seminar, however, doing so isn't necessary.[2]

- *Initially make eye contact with the questioner; then move your gaze to other audience members.* This makes all audience members feel as though you are responding not only to the questioner but to them as well.

- *Remember your listening skills.* Give questioners your full attention, and don't interrupt them.

- *Don't be afraid to pause while formulating an answer.*
  Many speakers feel they must feed the audience instanta-
  neous responses; this belief sometimes causes them to say
  things they later regret. This is especially the case in
  media interviews (see Appendix C). Pauses that seem
  long to you may not appear lengthy to listeners.

- *Keep answers concise.* The question-and-answer session is
  not the time to launch into a lengthy treatise on your
  favorite aspect of a topic.

Handling Hostile and Otherwise Troubling Questions

When handling hostile questions, do not get defensive.
Doing so will damage your credibility and only encourage
the other person. Maintain an attitude of respect, and stay
cool and in control. Attempt to defuse the hostile questioner
with respect and goodwill. Similarly, never give the impression that you think a question is stupid or irrelevant, even if
it clearly is.

- *Do not repeat or paraphrase a hostile question.* This
  only lends the question more credibility than it is
  worth. Instead, try to rephrase it more positively[3]
  (e.g., in response to the question "Didn't your department botch the handling of product X?" you might
  respond, "The question was 'Why did product X experience a difficult market entry?' To that I would say
  that . . . ").

- *If someone asks you a seemingly stupid question, do not
  point it out.* Instead, respond graciously.[4]

Ending the Session

Never end a question-and-answer session abruptly. As time
runs out, alert the audience that you will take one or two
more questions and then must end. The session represents
one final opportunity to reinforce your message, so take the
opportunity to do so. As you summarize your message,
thank your listeners for their time. Leave an air of goodwill
behind you.

C   Preparing for Mediated Communication

The underlying principles described throughout this guide will stand you in good stead as you prepare to communicate through an electronic medium such as television, radio, or the videoconference. These speaking engagements do present some unique challenges, however.

Speaking on Television

On television, you are at the mercy of reporters and producers who will edit your remarks to fit their time frame. As such, before your televised appearance, find out as much as you can about the speech situation, for example, how long you will be on camera and whether the show will be aired live or taped. You may need to convey your message in **sound bite** form — succinct statements that summarize your key points in twenty seconds or less.

Eye Contact, Body Movements, and Voice

The question of where to direct your gaze is critical on televised appearances, as is controlling body movement and voice. The following are some guidelines:

- Don't play to the camera. In a one-on-one interview, focus on the interviewer. Do not look up or down or tilt your head sideways; these movements will make you look uncertain or evasive.[1]

- If there is an audience, treat the camera as just another audience member, glancing at it only as often as you would at any other individual during your remarks.

- If there is only you and the camera, direct your gaze at it as you speak.

- Keep your posture erect.

- Exaggerate your gestures slightly more than normal.

- Project your voice, and avoid speaking in a monotone.

Dress and Makeup

To compensate for the glare of studio lights and distortions caused by the camera, give careful consideration to dress and grooming:

- Choose dark rather than light-colored clothing. Dark colors such as blue, gray, green, and brown photograph better than lighter shades.
- Avoid stark white, because it produces glare.
- Avoid plaids, dots, and other busy patterns, as they tend to jump around on the screen.
- Avoid glittering jewelry, including tie bars.
- Wear a little more makeup than usual because bright studio lights tend to make you look washed out.

Speaking on Radio: The Media Interview

Following are guidelines for preparing for media interviews on the radio. These same guidelines can also be applied to the television interview.

- Know the audience and the focus of the program. What subjects does the broadcast cover? How long will the interview be? Will it be taped or live?
- Brush up on background information, and have your facts ready. Assume that the audience knows little or nothing about the subject matter.
- Use the interviewer's name during the interview.
- Prepare a speaking outline on notecards for the interview. Remember that the microphone will pick up the sound of papers being shuffled.
- Remember that taped interviews may be edited. Make key points in short sentences, and repeat them using different words.[2] Think in terms of sound bites.
- Anticipate questions that might arise, and decide how you will answer them.
- Use transition points to acknowledge the interviewer's questions and to bridge your key message points, such as "I am not familiar with that, but what I can tell you is . . . "; "You raise an interesting question, but I think the more important matter is . . . "[3]
- Avoid the phrase "No comment." It will only exaggerate a point you are trying to minimize. Instead, say "I am not at liberty to comment/discuss. . . . "

> **QUICK TIP**
>
> ***Speaking in the Videoconference***
> ***Videoconferencing***, the live connection of two or more people
> via satellite or the Internet, typically takes place in conference
> rooms with participants assembled before cameras — one
> group in Alabama, for example, and another group in New
> York. Prepare as you would for on-site presentations, but
> pay particular attention to good diction, delivery, and
> dynamic body language.[4] Look into the camera; speak directly
> to the long-distance audience. Avoid sudden, abrupt, or
> sweeping movements. Speak and move a little more slowly
> and deliberately than normal to compensate for time lag
> between sites.

D Tips for Non-Native Speakers of English

In addition to the normal fear of being at center stage, non-native speakers of English face the burden of worrying about delivering a speech in a non-native language. If English is your first language, remind yourself of how difficult it would be for you to deliver a speech in another language. As you listen to a non-native speaker, place yourself in his or her shoes. If necessary, politely ask questions for clarification.

If you are a non-native speaker of English, think about public speaking as an opportunity to learn more about the English language and how to use it. As you listen to your classmates' speeches, for example, you will gain exposure to spoken English. Practicing your speech will give you time to work on any accent features you want to improve.[1] Research shows that thinking positively about preparing speeches actually reduces anxiety and helps you prepare a better speech. So tell yourself that by studying public speaking you will find many good opportunities to improve your English and become a better communicator of English. In addition, by spending time writing and outlining your speech, you will gain confidence in your written language skills.

Here are a few tips to get you started:

- *Take your time and speak slowly.* This will give your listeners time to get used to your voice and to focus on your message.

- *Identify English words that you have trouble saying.* Practice saying these words five times. Pause. Then say the words again five times. Progress slowly until the word becomes easier to pronounce.

- *Avoid using words that you don't really have to use, such as jargon* (see Chapter 16). Learn how to use a thesaurus to find synonyms, or words that mean the same thing, that are simpler and easier to pronounce.

- *Offer words from your native language to emphasize your points.* This will help the audience to better appreciate your native language and accent. For example, the Spanish word *corazón* has a lyrical quality that makes it sound much better than its English counterpart, "heart." Capitalize on the beauty of your native tongue.

Learn by Listening

Listening is the key to learning a language. Using textbooks to study usage and grammar is important, but it is through spoken language—hearing it and speaking it—that we gain fluency.

Listening to the speeches of colleagues or classmates, as well as those broadcast by television channels such as C-Span, can help you hone the skills you need to become a better speaker. Nearly all college libraries own many videocassettes and other recorded materials made specifically for ESL (English as a second language) speakers such as yourself, and the reference librarian will be happy to locate them for you. The Internet also offers many helpful listening resources. Among the many sites you can find is the *Talking Merriam Webster English Dictionary* (at <http://www.webster.com/>). This online dictionary allows you to hear the correct pronunciations of words.

Broaden Your Listeners' Perspectives

Consider sharing a personal experience with the audience. Stories from other lands and other ways of life often fascinate listeners. Unique cultural traditions, eyewitness accounts of newsworthy events, or tales passed down orally from one generation to the next are just some of the possibilities. Depending on the goal of your speech, you can use your experiences as supporting material for a related topic or as the topic itself.

One freshman public-speaking student from Poland related what life for her was like after the fall of communism in 1989. She described how goods she had never seen before suddenly flooded the country. A wondrous array of fruit and meat left the most vivid impression on the then-11-year-old, as both had been nearly impossible to find under the old regime. Her audience was fascinated with her firsthand account of historical events, and the speaker found that sharing her unique experiences boosted her confidence.

Practice with a Tape Recorder

Most experts recommend that you prepare for delivering your first speech (as well as for subsequent speeches) by practicing with a tape recorder.[2] Non-native speakers may wish to pay added attention to pronunciation and articulation as they listen. *Pronunciation* is the correct formation of word sounds. *Articulation* is the clarity or forcefulness with which the sounds are made, regardless of whether they are pronounced correctly. It is important to pay attention to and work on both areas.

Because languages vary tremendously in the specific sounds they use and the way these sounds are produced by the vocal chords, each of us will speak a non-native language a bit differently than do native speakers. That is, we speak with some sort of accent. This should not concern you in and of itself. What is important is identifying which specific features of your pronunciation, if any, seriously interfere with your ability to make yourself understandable. Listening to your speech with a tape recorder or videotape, perhaps in the presence of a native speaker, will allow you to identify trouble spots. Once you have identified which words you tend to mispronounce, you can work to correct the problem. If possible, try to arrange an appointment with an instructor to help you identify key linguistic issues in your speech practice tape. If instructors are unavailable, try asking a fellow student.

> **QUICK TIP**
>
> *Check for Correct Articulation*
> As you listen to your recording, watch also for your
> articulation of words. ESL students whose first languages don't
> differentiate between the /sh/ sound and its close cousin
> /ch/, for example, may say "share" when they mean "chair"
> or "shoes" when they mean "choose."[3] It is therefore
> important that you also check to make sure that you are
> using the correct meaning of the words you have selected
> for your speech.

Use Vocal Variety

In addition to having concerns about pronunciation and
articulation, the non-native speaker may also be accustomed
to patterns of vocal variety—volume, pitch, rate, and
pauses—that are different from a native English speaker.

The pronunciation of English depends on learning how
to combine a series of about forty basic sounds (fifteen
vowels and twenty-five consonants) that together serve to
distinguish English words from one another. Correct pronunciation also requires that the speaker learn proper word
stress, rhythm, and intonation or pitch.[4] As you practice your
speeches, pay particular attention to these facets of delivery.
Seek feedback from others, including your teacher, making
sure that your goal of shared meaning can be met when you
do deliver your speech.

Counteract Problems in Being Understood

With the exception of young children, virtually everyone
who learns to speak another language will speak that language with an accent. This issue is especially important in
business and professional settings where being understood
can have a direct impact on your career. What steps can you
take when your accent will make your oral presentation difficult for the audience to understand?

In the long term, interacting with native speakers in everyday life will help enormously. With immersion, non-native
speakers can begin to stop translating things word for word
and start thinking in English. Using a tape recorder and practicing your speech in front of others are also very important.

But what if your experience with English is limited but you must nonetheless give an oral presentation? Robert Anholt, a scientist and the author of *Dazzle 'Em with Style: The Art of Oral Scientific Presentation*, suggests the following:

- Practice the presentation often, preferably with a friend who is a native English speaker.
- Learn the presentation almost by heart.
- Create strong presentation aids that will convey most of the story by themselves, even if your voice is hard to understand.[5]

Glossary

abstract A brief summary of a study.

abstract language Language that is general or nonspecific.

acronym A word, usually a noun, formed from the first letter(s) of several words, such as WIN for *work, intensity,* and *no excuses.*

active listening A multistep, focused, and purposeful process of gathering and evaluating information.

after-dinner speech A speech that is likely to occur before, after, or during a formal dinner; a breakfast or lunch seminar; or other type of business, professional, or civic meeting.

agenda A document identifying the items to be accomplished during a meeting.

alliteration The repetition of the same sounds, usually initial consonants, in two or more neighboring words or syllables.

almanac A reference work that contains facts and statistics in many categories, including those that are related to historical, social, political, and religious subjects.

analogy An extended metaphor or simile that compares an unfamiliar concept or process with a more familiar one in order to help the listener understand the one that is unfamiliar.

anaphora A rhetorical device in which the speaker repeats a word or a phrase at the beginning of successive phrases, clauses, or sentences.

anecdote A brief story of an interesting, humorous, or real-life incident that links back to the speaker's theme.

antithesis Setting off two ideas in balanced (parallel) opposition to each other to create a powerful effect.

argument A stated position, with support, for or against an idea or issue; contains the core elements of claim, evidence, and warrants.

articulation The clarity or forcefulness with which sounds are made, regardless of whether they are pronounced correctly.

atlas A collection of maps, text, and accompanying charts and tables.

attitudes A predisposition to respond to people, ideas, objects, or events in evaluative ways.

audience analysis The process of gathering and analyzing demographic and psychological information about audience members.

audience perspective Stance taken by the speaker in which he or she adapts the speech to the needs, attitudes, and values of an audience.

beliefs The ways in which people perceive reality or determine the very existence or validity of something.

biased language Any language that relies on unfounded assumptions, negative descriptions, or stereotypes of a given group's age, class, gender, disability, and geographic, ethnic, racial, or religious characteristics.

body (of speech) The part of the speech in which the speaker develops the main points intended to fulfill the speech purpose.

body language The bodily activity of the speaker and the meaning the audience assigns to this activity.

brainstorming A problem-solving technique that involves the spontaneous generation of ideas. Among other techniques, you can brainstorm by making lists, using word association, and mapping topics.

brief example A single illustration of an idea, item, or event being described.

business and professional ethics Defines how individuals within a company or a profession integrate ethical ground rules into its policies, practices, and decision making.

call to action A challenge to audience members to act in response to a speech, see the problem in a new way, change their beliefs about the problem, or change both their actions and their beliefs with respect to the problem; placed at the conclusion of a speech.

canned speech A speech used repeatedly and without sufficient adaptation to the rhetorical speech situation.

canons of rhetoric A classical approach to speechmaking in which the speaker divides a speech into five parts: invention, arrangement, style, memory, and delivery.

case study A detailed illustration of a real or hypothetical business situation.

causal (cause-effect) pattern of arrangement A pattern of organizing speech points in order, first in order of causes and then in order of effects or vice versa; selected when the cause-effect relationship is well established.

central processing A mode of processing a persuasive message that involves thinking critically about the contents of the message and the strength and quality of the speaker's arguments. People who seriously consider what the speaker's message means to them are most likely to experience a relatively enduring change in thinking.

channel The medium through which the speaker sends a message, such as sound waves, air waves, and so forth.

chart A method of visually organizing complex information into compact form. Several different types of charts that are helpful for speakers include flowcharts, organization charts, and tabular charts or tables.

chronological pattern of arrangement A pattern of organizing speech points in a natural sequential order; used when describing a series of events in time or when the topic develops in line with a set pattern of actions or tasks.

circle organizational pattern A pattern of organizing speech points so that one idea leads to another, which leads to a third, and so forth until the speaker arrives back at the speech thesis.

claim The declaration of a state of affairs, often stated as a thesis statement, in which a speaker attempts to prove something.

claim of fact An argument that focuses on whether something is or is not true or whether something will or will not happen.

claim of policy A claim that recommends that a specific course of action be taken, or approved, by an audience.

claim of value A claim that addresses issues of judgment.

classroom discussion presentation A type of oral presentation in which the speaker presents a brief overview of the topic under discussion and introduces a series of questions to guide students through the topic.

closed-ended question A question designed to elicit a small range of specific answers supplied by the interviewer.

co-culture A community of people whose perceptions and beliefs differ significantly from those of other groups within the larger culture.

colleague within the field audience An audience of persons who share the speaker's knowledge of the general field under question but who may not be familiar with the specific topic under discussion.

common knowledge Information that is likely to be known by many people and is therefore in the public domain; the source of such information need not be cited in a speech.

comparative advantage pattern A pattern of organizing speech points so that the speaker's viewpoint or proposal is shown to be superior to one or more alternative viewpoints or proposals.

conclusion (of speech) The part of the speech in which the speaker reiterates the speech purpose, summarizes main points, and leaves the audience with something to think about or act upon.

connotative meaning The individual associations that different people bring to bear on a word.

coordinate points Ideas that are given the same weight in an outline and are aligned with one another; thus Main Point II is coordinate with Main Point I.

coordination and subordination The logical placement of ideas relative to their importance to one another. Ideas that are coordinate are given equal weight. An idea that is subordinate to another is given relatively less weight.

counterproductive roles Negative interpersonal roles or group members who focus on individual versus group needs. These individual needs are usually irrelevant to the task at hand and are not oriented toward maintenance of the group as a team.

crawler-based search engine A search engine that automatically scans and indexes documents containing the key words and phrases it has been commanded to search.

crisis-response presentation A type of oral presentation in which the speaker seeks to reassure an organization's various audiences ("publics") and restore its credibility in the face of potentially reputation-damaging situations.

cultural sensitivity A conscious attempt to be aware of and acknowledge beliefs, norms, and traditions that differ from one's own.

decoding The process of interpreting a message.

defamatory speech Speech that potentially harms an individual's reputation at work or in the community.

defensive listening A poor listening behavior in which the listener reacts defensively to a speaker's message.

definition by etymology Defining something by providing an account of a word's history.

definition by example Defining something by providing an example of it.

definition by negation Defining something by explaining what it is not.

definition by synonym Defining something by comparing it with another term that has an equivalent meaning. For example: A friend is a comrade or a buddy.

delivery The vocal and nonverbal behavior that a speaker uses in a public speech; one of the five canons of rhetoric.

demographics Statistical characteristics of a given population. Characteristics typically considered in the analysis of audience members include age, gender, ethnic or cultural background, socioeconomic status (including income, occupation, and education), and religious and political affiliation.

denotative meaning The literal or dictionary definition of a word.

design review presentation A type of oral presentation that provides information on the results of a design project; frequently delivered in technical fields such as engineering, computer science, and architecture.

devil's advocacy Arguing for the sake of raising issues or concerns about the idea under discussion.

diagram A schematic drawing that explains how something works or how it is constructed or operated; used to simplify and clarify complicated procedures, explanations, and operations.

dialectical inquiry Devil's advocacy (see above) that goes a step further by proposing a countersolution to an idea.

dignity The feeling that one is worthy, honored, or respected as a person.

direct quotations Statements made verbatim, or word for word, by someone else. Direct quotations should always be acknowledged in a speech.

disinformation The deliberate falsification of information.

domain The suffix at the end of a Web address that describes the nature of the Web site: business/commercial <.com>, educational <.edu>, government <.gov>, military <.mil>, network <.net>, or nonprofit organization <.org>. A tilde <~> in the address usually indicates that it is a personal page rather than part of an institutional Web site. Understanding the domain can help one assess the credibility of a site.

dyadic communication Communication between two people, as in a conversation.

eight by eight rule Rule of design according to which the speaker does not include more than eight words on a line or eight lines on one Microsoft PowerPoint slide or other kind of visual aid.

encoding The process of organizing a message, choosing words and sentence structure, and verbalizing the message.

encyclopedia A reference work that summarizes knowledge found in original form elsewhere and provides an overview of subjects.

ethical ground rules A code of ethical conduct in speechmaking; being trustworthy, respectful, responsible, and fair.

ethnocentrism The belief that the ways of one's own culture are superior to those of other cultures. Ethnocentric speakers act as though everyone shares their point of view and points of reference, whether or not this is in fact the case.

ethos The Greek word for "character." According to the ancient Greek rhetorician Aristotle, audiences listen to and trust speakers if they exhibit competence (as demonstrated by the speaker's grasp of the subject matter) and good moral character.

eulogy A speech whose purpose is to celebrate and commemorate the life of someone while consoling those who are left behind; typically delivered by close friends and family members.

evaluation research presentation A type of oral presentation reporting on the effectiveness of programs developed to address various issues; frequently delivered in social scientific fields.

evidence Supporting material that provides grounds for belief.

example (as form of support) An illustration whose purpose is to aid understanding by making ideas, items, or events more concrete and by clarifying and amplifying meaning.

expert or insider audience An audience of persons with an intimate knowledge of the topic, issue, product, or idea being discussed.

expert testimony Any findings, eyewitness accounts, or opinions by professionals who are trained to evaluate or report on a given topic; a form of supporting material.

explanatory research presentation A type of oral presentation focusing on studies that attempt to analyze and explain a phenomenon; frequently delivered in social scientific fields.

extended examples Multifaceted illustrations of the idea, item, or event being described, thereby getting the point across and reiterating it effectively.

extended research presentation See *field study presentation.*

fact book A reference work that includes key information on a given topic, such as facts about the geography, government, economy, and transportation of a given country.

facts Documented occurrences, including actual events, dates, times, places, and people involved.

fairness An ethical ground rule; making a genuine effort to see all sides of an issue; being open-minded.

feedback Audience response to a message, which can be conveyed both verbally and nonverbally through gestures. Feedback from the audience often indicates whether a speaker's message has been understood.

field study presentation A type of oral presentation typically delivered in context of science-related disciplines in which the speaker provides (1) an overview of the field research, (2) the methods used in the research, (3) an analysis of the results of the research, and (4) a timeline indicating how the research results will be used going forward.

figures of speech Expressions, such as metaphors, similes, analogies, and hyperbole, in which words are used in a nonliteral fashion.

First Amendment The amendment to the U.S. Constitution that guarantees freedom of speech. ("Congress shall make no law abridging the freedom of speech.")

fixed-alternative question A closed-ended question that contains a limited choice of answers, such as "Yes," "No," or "Sometimes."

fixed microphone A microphone that remains stationary.

flip chart A large (27–34 inches) pad of paper on which a speaker can illustrate speech points.

font A set of type of one size and face.

full-sentence transition A signal to listeners, in the form of a declarative sentence, that the speaker is turning to another topic.

gender stereotype Oversimplified and often severely distorted ideas about the innate nature of men or women.

general speech purpose A declarative statement of the broad speech purpose that answers the question "Why am I speaking on this topic for this particular audience and occasion?" Usually the general speech purpose is to inform, to persuade, or to celebrate or commemorate a special occasion.

graph A graphical representation of numerical data. Graphs neatly illustrate relationships among components or units and demonstrate trends. Four major types of graphs are line graphs, bar graphs, pie graphs, and pictograms.

group activity presentation An oral presentation that introduces students to an activity and provides them with clear directions for its completion.

groupthink The tendency of a group to accept information and ideas without subjecting them to critical analysis.

hand-held microphone A microphone that is attached to a source of electrical power by a cord.

handout A page-sized item that conveys information that is either impractical to give to the audience in another manner or is intended to be kept by audience members after a presentation.

hate speech Any offensive communication—verbal or nonverbal—directed against people's race, ethnicity, religion, gender, or other characteristics. Racist, sexist, or ageist slurs; gay bashing; and cross burnings are all forms of hate speech.

hierarchy of needs A model of human action based on the principle that people are motivated to act on the basis of their needs; developed by Abraham Maslow.

human directory Also called a "subject directory," a searchable database of Web sites that have been submitted to that directory and then assigned by an editor to an appropriate category or categories, such as "Reference," "Science," and "Arts and Humanities."

hybrid search engine A searchable database of Web sites that combines crawler-based search engine results with results from a human directory; Yahoo! is an example of such a search engine.

hypothetical example (as form of support) An illustration of something that could happen in the future if certain things occurred.

individual debate format A debate in which one person takes a side against another person.

individual search engine A search engine that compiles its own database of Web pages, such as Google and AltaVista.

information Data set in a context for relevance.

informative speech A speech whose general purpose is to increase the audience's understanding and awareness of a topic.

integrity The quality of being incorruptible, or able to avoid compromise for the sake of personal expediency.

internal preview An extended transition that alerts audience members to ensuing speech content.

internal summary An extended transition that draws together important ideas before proceeding to another speech point.

interpersonal roles Types of roles or styles of interacting in a group that facilitate group interaction.

interview A type of face-to-face communication conducted for the purpose of gathering information. Interviews can be conducted one-on-one or in a group.

introduction (of speech) The first part of a speech in which the speaker establishes the speech purpose and its relevance to the audience and previews the topic and the main points.

invisible web The portion of the World Wide Web that includes pass-protected sites, documents behind firewalls, and the contents of proprietary databases.

jargon Specialized terminology developed within a given endeavor or field of study.

key-word outline The briefest form of outline; uses the smallest possible units of understanding associated with a specific point to outline the main and supporting points.

lavaliere microphone A microphone that attaches to a lapel or a collar.

lay audience An audience of persons without any specialized knowledge of the general field related to the speaker's topic and of the topic itself.

lay testimony Firsthand findings, eyewitness accounts, or opinions from nonexperts such as eyewitnesses.

lazy speech A poor speech habit in which the speaker fails to properly articulate words.

LCD panel A device connected to a computer that is used to project slides stored in the computer.

LCD projector A projector designed for computer images that is equipped with an illumination, or light source, in its own case, thereby eliminating the need for an overhead projector.

lecture An informational speech to an audience of student learners.

library gateway An entry point into a large collection of research and reference information that has been selected and reviewed by librarians.

listening The conscious act of recognizing, understanding, and accurately interpreting the messages communicated by others.

listening distraction Anything that competes for a listener's attention; the source of the distraction may be internal or external.

logical fallacy A statement that is based on an invalid or deceptive line of reasoning.

logos The Greek rhetorician Aristotle used this term for appeals to reason and logic. Such appeals provide the justification for audience action.

main points Statements that express the key ideas and major themes of a speech. Their function is to make claims in support of the thesis statement.

malapropism The inadvertent use of a word or a phrase in place of one that sounds like it.

mass communication Communication that occurs between a speaker and a large audience of unknown people. The receivers of the message are not present with the speaker, or they are part of such an immense crowd that there can be little or no interaction between speaker and listener. Television, radio news broadcasts, and mass rallies are examples of mass communication.

message The content of the communication process—thoughts and ideas put into meaningful expressions. A message can be expressed both verbally (through the sentences and points of a speech) and nonverbally (through eye contact and gestures).

metaphor A figure of speech used to make implicit comparisons without the use of "like" or "as" (e.g., "Love is a rose").

meta-search engine A search engine that searches a variety of individual search engines simultaneously. Examples include MetaCrawler and Dogpile.

methods/procedure presentation An oral presentation describing and sometimes demonstrating an experimental or mathematical process, including the conditions under which it can be applied; frequently delivered in scientific and mathematics-related fields.

misinformation Information that is false.

mixed audience An audience composed of a combination of persons—some with expert knowledge of the field and topic and others with no specialized knowledge.

model A three-dimensional, scale-size representation of an object, such as a building.

motivated sequence A five-step process of persuasion; developed by Alan Monroe.

multimedia A single production that combines several media (stills, sound, video, text, and data).

mumbling Slurring words together at a very low level of volume and pitch so that they are barely audible.

narrative A story; can be based on personal experiences or imaginary incidents.

narrative organizational pattern A pattern of organizing speech points so that the speech unfolds as a story, with characters, plot, and setting.

noise Anything that interferes with the communication process between a speaker and an audience, so that the message cannot be understood; can derive from external sources in the environment or internally, from psychological factors.

open-ended question A question designed to allow respondents to elaborate as much as they wish; useful in probing beliefs and opinions.

operational definition Defining something by describing what it does. For example: A computer is something that processes information.

oral scientific presentation A type of oral presentation following the model used in scientific investigations, including an introduction, description of methods, results, and conclusion; commonly found in the disciplines of science and mathematics. Such a presentation can focus on original research or research conducted by others.

oratory In classical terms, the art of public speaking.

original research presentation See *oral scientific presentation.*

overhead transparency An image on a transparent background that can be viewed by transmitted light, either directly or through projection onto a screen or a wall. The images may be written or printed directly onto the transparency or handwritten during the presentation.

panel discussion A type of oral presentation in which a group of persons (at least three, and generally not more than nine) discusses a topic in the presence of an audience and by direction of a moderator.

parallelism The arrangement of words, phrases, or sentences in similar grammatical and stylistic form. Parallel structure can help the speaker emphasize important ideas in the speech.

paraphrase A restatement of someone else's statements or written work that alters the form or phrasing but not the substance of that person's ideas.

pathos The Greek rhetorician Aristotle used this term for appeals to emotion. Such appeals can get the audience's attention and stimulate a desire to act but must be used ethically.

pauses Strategic elements of a speech used to enhance meaning by providing a type of punctuation, emphasizing a point, drawing attention to a key thought, or just allowing listeners a moment to contemplate what is being said.

pay for placement A search engine that retrieves information paid for by commercial sponsors.

performance anxiety A feeling of anxiety that occurs the moment one begins to perform.

periodical A regularly published magazine or journal.

peripheral processing A mode of processing a persuasive message that does not consider the quality of the speaker's message but is influenced by such non-content issues as the speaker's appearance or reputation, certain slogans or one-liners, and obvious attempts to manipulate emotions. Peripheral processing of messages occurs when people lack the motivation or the ability to pay close attention to the issues.

perspective taking The identification of audience members' attitudes, values, beliefs, needs, and wants and the integration of this information into the speech context.

persuasion The process of influencing attitudes, beliefs, values, and behavior.

persuasive speech A speech whose goal is to influence the attitudes, beliefs, values, or acts of others in some way.

phrase outline A delivery outline that uses a partial construction of the sentence form of each point, instead of using complete sentences that present precise wording for each point.

pitch The range of sounds from high to low (or vice versa) determined by the number of vibrations per unit of time; the more vibrations per unit (also called *frequency*), the higher the pitch, and vice versa.

plagiarism The act of using other people's ideas or words without acknowledging the source.

policy recommendation report A type of oral presentation offering recommendations to solve a problem or address an issue.

poster A large (36" × 56"), bold, two-dimensional design incorporating words, shapes, and, if desired, color, placed on an opaque backing; used to convey a brief message or point forcefully and attractively.

poster session A format for the visual presentation of posters, arranged on freestanding boards, containing the concise display of a study or issue for viewing by participants at professional conferences. The speaker prepares brief remarks and remains on hand to answer questions as needed.

preparation anxiety A feeling of anxiety that arises when a speaker actually begins to prepare for a speech, at which point he or she might feel overwhelmed at the amount of time and planning required.

pre-performance anxiety A feeling of anxiety experienced when a speaker begins to rehearse a speech.

pre-preparation anxiety A feeling of anxiety experienced when a speaker learns he or she must give a speech.

presentation aid(s) Objects, models, pictures, graphs, charts, video, audio, and multimedia, used alone and in combination within the context of a speech; such aids help listeners to see relationships among concepts and elements, to store and remember material, and to critically examine key ideas.

presentational speaking A type of oral presentation in which individuals or groups deliver reports within a business or professional environment.

preview statement Statement included in the introduction of a speech in which the speaker identifies the main speech points.

primary research Original or firsthand research, such as interviews and surveys.

problem-cause-solution pattern of arrangement A pattern of organizing speech points so that they demonstrate (1) the nature of the problem, (2) reasons for the problem, (3) unsatisfactory solutions, and (4) proposed solution(s).

problem-solution pattern of arrangement A pattern of organizing speech points so that they demonstrate the nature and significance of a problem first, and then provide justification for a proposed solution.

progress report A report that updates clients or principals on developments in an ongoing project.

pronunciation The correct formation of word sounds.

prop Any live or inanimate object used by a speaker as a presentation aid.

propaganda Information represented in such a way as to provoke a desired response.

proposal A type of business or professional presentation in which the speaker provides information needed for decisions related to modifying or adopting a product, procedure, or policy.

prototype A model of a design.

public speaking A type of communication in which a speaker delivers a message with a specific purpose to an audience of people who are present during the delivery of the speech. Public speaking always includes a speaker who has a reason for speaking, an audience that gives the speaker its attention, and a message that is meant to accomplish a purpose.

public-speaking anxiety Fear or anxiety associated with a speaker's actual or anticipated communication to an audience.

qualitative research Research in which the emphasis is placed on observing, describing, and interpreting behavior.

quantitative research Research in which the emphasis is placed on statistical measurement.

questionnaire A written survey designed to gather information from a large pool of respondents. Questionnaires consist of a series of questions designed to elicit information and contain a mix of open- and closed-ended questions.

reasoning Logical explanation of a claim.

receiver The recipient of a source's message; may be an individual or a group of people.

reckless disregard for the truth A quality of defamatory speech that is legally liable.

reference librarian A librarian trained to help library users locate information resources.

refutation organizational pattern A pattern of organizing speech points in which each main point addresses and then refutes (disproves) an opposing claim to a speaker's position.

request for funding presentation A type of oral presentation providing evidence that a project, proposal, or design idea is worth funding; frequently delivered in technical fields such as engineering, computer science, and architecture.

research overview presentation A type of oral presentation in which the speaker provides context and background for a research question or hypothesis that will form the basis of an impending undertaking; typically delivered within the context of scientific and mathematical disciplines.

respect To feel or show deferential regard. For the ethical speaker, respect ranges from addressing audience members as unique human beings to refraining from rudeness and other forms of personal attack.

responsibility Evaluating a speech in light of its usefulness and appropriateness of the speech topic and purpose.

restate-forecast form A type of transition in which the speaker restates the point just covered and previews the point to be covered next.

review of academic article A type of oral presentation in which the speaker reports on an article or study published in an academic journal.

review of the literature presentation A type of oral presentation in which the speaker reviews the body of research related to a given topic or issue and offers conclusions about the topic based on this research; frequently delivered in social scientific fields.

rhetoric The practice of oratory, or public speaking.

rhetorical device A technique of language.

rhetorical question A question that does not invite actual responses but is used to make the listener or the audience think.

rhetorical situation Consideration of the audience, the occasion, and the overall speech situation when planning a speech.

roast A humorous tribute to a person; one in which a series of speakers jokingly poke fun at the individual being honored.

Roman numeral outline An outline format in which main points are enumerated with Roman numerals; supporting points with capital letters; third-level points with Arabic numerals; and fourth-level points with lowercase letters.

sales presentation A type of oral presentation that attempts to lead a potential buyer to purchase a service or product described by the presenter.

sans serif typeface A typeface that is blocklike and linear and is designed without tiny strokes or flourishes at the top and bottom of each letter.

scale question A closed-ended question that measures the respondent's level of agreement or disagreement with specific issues.

scanning A technique for creating eye contact with large audiences; the speaker moves his or her gaze across an audience from one listener to another and from one section to another, pausing to gaze briefly at each individual.

search engine Using powerful software programs, a search engine scans millions of documents that contain the keywords and phrases it has been commanded to search. A program then creates a huge index from the pages that have been read, compares it with the search request, and returns matching results, usually in order of relevance.

secondary research The vast world of information gathered by others.

selective perception A psychological principle that posits that listeners pay attention selectively to certain messages and ignore others.

sentence outline An outline in which each main and supporting point is stated in sentence form and in precisely the way the speaker wants to express the idea. Generally, sentence outlines are used for working outlines.

serif typeface A typeface that includes small flourishes, or strokes, at the top and bottom of each letter.

shared meaning The mutual understanding of a message between speaker and audience. Shared meaning occurs in varying degrees. The lowest level of shared meaning exists when the speaker has merely caught the audience's attention. As the message develops, depending on the encoding choices by the source, a higher degree of shared meaning is possible.

signposts Conjunctions and phrases used as transitions as the speech moves from one point to the next.

simile A figure of speech used to compare one thing with another by using the words "like" or "as" (e.g., "He works like a dog").

slander Defamatory speech.

small group A collection of between three and twenty people.

small group communication Communication involving a small number of people who can see and speak directly with one another, as in a business meeting.

socioeconomic status (SES) A demographic variable that includes income, occupation, and education.

sound bite A succinct statement that summarizes key points in twenty seconds or less.

source The person who creates a message, also called a *sender*. The speaker transforms ideas and thoughts into messages and sends them to a receiver, or an audience.

spatial pattern of arrangement A pattern of organizing main points in order of their physical proximity or direction relative to each other; used when the purpose of a speech is to describe or explain the physical arrangement of a place, a scene, or an object.

speaker credibility The quality that reveals that a speaker has a good grasp of the subject, displays sound reasoning skills, is honest and nonmanipulative, and is genuinely interested in the welfare of audience members; a modern version of *ethos*.

speaking extemporaneously A type of delivery that falls somewhere between impromptu and written or memorized deliveries. Speakers delivering an extemporaneous speech prepare well and practice in advance, giving full attention to all facets of the speech—content, arrangement, and delivery alike. Instead of memorizing or writing the speech word for word, they speak from an outline of key words and phrases.

speaking from manuscript A type of delivery in which the speaker reads the speech verbatim—that is, from prepared written text (either on paper or on a TelePrompTer) that contains the entire speech, word for word.

speaking from memory A type of delivery in which the speaker puts the entire speech, word for word, into writing and then commits it to memory.

speaking impromptu A type of delivery that is unpracticed, spontaneous, or improvised.

speaking outline A delivery outline to be used when practicing and actually presenting a speech.

speaking rate The pace at which a speech is delivered. The typical public speech occurs at a rate slightly less than 120 words per minute.

specialized search engine A search engine that searches for information only on specific topics.

special occasion speech A speech that is prepared for a specific occasion and for a purpose dictated by that occasion.

specific speech purpose A declarative statement expressing both the topic and the general speech purpose in action form and in terms of the specific objectives that a speaker seeks to fulfill in a speech.

speech of acceptance A speech made in response to receiving an award. Its purpose is to express gratitude for the honor bestowed on the speaker.

speech of inspiration A speech whose purpose is to inspire or motivate the audience to positively consider, reflect on, and sometimes even act on the speaker's words.

speech of introduction A short speech whose purpose is defined by two goals: to prepare or "warm up" audience members for the speaker and to motivate them to listen to what the speaker has to say.

speech of presentation A speech whose purpose is twofold: to communicate the meaning of the award and to explain why the recipient is receiving it.

staff report A report that informs managers and other employees of new developments relating to personnel that affect them and their work.

statistics Data that measure the size or magnitude of something, demonstrate trends, or show relationships with the purpose of summarizing information, demonstrating proof, and making points memorable.

style The specific word choices and rhetorical devices (techniques of language) speakers use to express their ideas.

subject directory See *human directory.*

subject-specific database An electronic database in which subject specialists, including but not limited to librarians, point to specialized databases created by other subject specialists.

subordinate points Ideas subordinate to others that are given relatively less weight. In an outline, they are indicated by their indentation below the more important points.

supporting material See *supporting points.*

supporting points The supporting material or evidence (examples, narratives, testimony, and facts and statistics) gathered to justify the main points and lead the audience to accept the purpose of a speech; used to substantiate or prove the thesis statement.

table A systematic grouping of data or numerical information in column form.

"talking head" A speaker who remains static, standing stiffly behind a podium, and so resembles a televised shot of a speaker's head and shoulders.

target audience Those individuals within the broader audience who are most likely to be influenced in the direction the speaker seeks.

task roles Types of roles that directly relate to the accomplishments of the objectives and missions of a group. Examples include "Recording secretary" and "Moderator."

team debate format A debate in which multiple people take sides against another team, with each person on the team assuming a speaking role.

team presentation A type of oral presentation prepared and delivered by a group of three or more people.

testimony Firsthand findings, eyewitness accounts, and opinions by people, both lay (nonexpert) and expert.

thesis statement The theme, or central idea, of a speech that serves to connect all the parts of the speech in a single line. The main points, the supporting material, and the conclusion all relate to the thesis.

toast A brief tribute to a person or an event being celebrated.

topical pattern of arrangement A pattern of organizing main points in random order, or any order relative to the other main points, without changing the message; used when the main points are of relatively equal importance.

transitions Words, phrases, or sentences that tie speech ideas together and enable a speaker to move smoothly from one point to the next.

trustworthiness The quality of displaying both honesty and dependability.

typeface A specific style of lettering, such as Arial, Times Roman, or Courier. Typefaces come in a variety of fonts, or sets of sizes (called the "point size"), and upper and lower cases.

values   Our most enduring judgments or standards of what's important to us (e.g., equal opportunity, democracy, change and progress, or perseverance).

virtual library   A collection of library holdings available online.

visualization   An exercise for building confidence in which the speaker, while preparing for the speech, closes his or her eyes and envisions a series of positive feelings and reactions that will occur on the day of the speech.

vocal fillers   Unnecessary and undesirable sounds or words used by a speaker to cover pauses in a speech or conversation. Examples include "uh," 'hmm," "you know," "I mean," and "it's like."

vocal variety   The variation of volume, pitch, rate, and pauses to create an effective delivery.

voice   A feature of verbs in written and spoken text that indicates the subject's relationship to the action; verbs can be either active or passive.

volume   The relative loudness of a speaker's voice while giving a speech.

vortal   The entry point to an online subject-specific database.

word association   A brainstorming technique in which one writes down ideas as they come to mind, beginning with a single word.

working outline   A preparation or rough outline in which the speaker refines and finalizes the specific purpose statement, firms up and organizes main points, and develops supporting points to substantiate them.

Notes

CHAPTER 1

1. D. Uchida, M. J. Cetron, and F. McKenzie, "What Students Must Know to Succeed in the 21st Century," special report (World Future Society) based on *Preparing Students for the 21st Century,* a report on a project by the American Association of School Administrators, 1966.

2. William Avram, "Public Speaking." *Compton's Online Encyclopedia.* Retrieved June 10, 2000, from the World Wide Web: <http://www.comptons.com/encyclopedia/>.

3. Robert Perrin, "The Speaking-Writing Connection: Enhancing the Symbiotic Relationship," *Contemporary Education* 65 (1994): 2.

CHAPTER 2

1. Merriam-Webster, *Merriam-Webster's Collegiate Dictionary*, 10th ed. (Springfield, MA: author, 2002), 995.

2. Susan Grogan Faller, Steven E. Gillen, and Maureen P. Haney, "Rights Clearance and Permissions Guidelines," paper prepared by law firm of Greenebaum Doll & McDonald, Cincinnati, Ohio, 2002.

3. W. Gudykunst, S. Ting-Toomey, S. Suweeks, and L. Stewart, *Building Bridges: Interpersonal Skills for a Changing World* (Boston: Houghton Mifflin, 1995), 92.

4. Ibid.

5. Michael Josephson, personal interview, May 10, 1996.

6. Ibid.

7. "How to Recognize Plagiarism," Indiana University Bloomington School of Education Web site. Retrieved June 16, 2002, from <http://www.indiana.edu/>.

8. Skyscraper Museum Web site. Retrieved June 26, 2002, from <http://www.skyscraper.org>.

9. Judy Hunter, "Lecture on Academic Honesty," presented to entering students at Grinnell College, Grinnell, Iowa. Retrieved December 10, 1996, from <http://ac.grin.edu/~hunterj/achon/lecture97.html>.

CHAPTER 3

1. Andrew Wolvin and C. Coakley, *Listening,* 4th ed. (Dubuque, IA: Wm. C. Brown, 1992), 28.

2. S. Golen, "A Factor Analysis of Barriers to Effective Listening," *Journal of Business Communication* 27 (1990): 25–36.

3. Thomas E. Anastasi Jr., *Listen! Techniques for Improving Communication Skills,* CBI series in Management Communication (Boston: CBI Publishing, 1982), 35.

4. Ibid.

CHAPTER 4

1. Edward P. J. Corbett, *Classical Rhetoric for the Modern Student*, 3rd ed. (New York: Oxford University Press, 1990).

2. Communication scholars Winston Brembeck and William Howell define the goal in this way: "Persuasion is communication intended to influence choice." See Winston L. Brembeck and William S. Howell, *Persuasion: A Means of Social Influence*, 2nd ed. (Englewood Cliffs, NJ: Prentice-Hall, 1976).

3. Annette Rottenberg, *Elements of Argument*, 4th ed. (Boston: Bedford/ St. Martin's, 1994), 10.

CHAPTER 6

1. James C. McCroskey, "Classroom Consequences of Communication Anxiety," *Communication Education* 26 (1977): 27–33; James C. McCroskey, "Oral Communication Apprehension: A Reconceptualization," in *Communication Yearbook* vol. 6, ed. M. Burgoon (Beverly Hills: Sage, 1982), 136–70; Virginia P. Richmond and James C. McCroskey, *Communication Apprehension, Avoidance, and Effectiveness*, 5th ed. (Boston: Allyn & Bacon, 1998).

2. Adapted from James C. McCroskey, "Oral Communication Apprehension: A Summary of Recent Theory and Research," *Human Communication Research* 4 (1977): 79–96.

3. Ibid.

4. Joe Ayres, "Coping with Speech Anxiety: The Power of Positive Thinking," *Communication Education* 37 (1988): 289–96; Joe Ayres, "An Examination of the Impact of Anticipated Communication and Communication Apprehension on Negative Thinking, Task-Relevant Thinking, and Recall," *Communication Research Reports* 9 (1992): 3–11.

5. S. Hu and Joung-Min Romans-Kroll, "Effects of Positive Attitude toward Giving a Speech on the Cardiovascular and Subjective Fear Responses during Speech in Speech Anxious Subjects," *Perceptual and Motor Skills* 81, no. 2 (1995): 609–10; S. Hu, T. R. Bostow, D. A. Lipman, S. K. Bell, and S. Klein, "Positive Thinking Reduces Heart Rate and Fear Responses to Speech-Phobic Imagery," *Perceptual and Motor Skills* 75, no. 3, pt. 2 (1992): 1067–76.

6. M. T. Motley, "Public Speaking Anxiety Qua Performance Anxiety: A Revised Model and Alternative Therapy," *Journal of Social Behavior and Personality* 5 (1990): 85–104.

7. Joe Ayres, C. S. Hsu, and Tim Hopf, "Does Exposure to Performance Visualization Alter Speech Preparation Processes?" *Communication Research Reports* 17, no. 4 (2000): 366–74.

8. Joe Ayres and Tim S. Hopf, "Visualization: Is It More than Extra-Attention?" *Communication Education* 38 (1989): 1–5.

9. Laurie Schloff and Marcia Yudkin, *Smart Speaking* (New York: Plume, 1991), 91–92.

CHAPTER 7

1. James C. McCroskey, Virginia P. Richmond, and Robert A. Stewart, *One on One: The Foundations of Interpersonal Communication* (Englewood Cliffs, NJ: Prentice-Hall, 1986).

2. Ibid.

3. Cited in Edward P. J. Corbett, *Classical Rhetoric for the Modern Student,* 3rd ed. (New York: Oxford University Press, 1990), 81.

4. Dominic A. Infante, Andrew S. Rancer, and Deanna F. Womack, *Building Communication Theory,* 3rd ed. (Prospect Heights, IL: Waveland Press, 1997), 158.

5. Michael Josephson, personal interview, May 10, 1996.

6. J. G. Melton, *Encyclopedia of American Religions,* 7th ed. (Detroit: Gale Research, 1999).

7. Disability Web site, <http://www.disabilityinfo.gov/>.

8. Geert Hofstede, *Culture's Consequences: International Differences in Work-Related Values* (Beverly Hills: Sage, 1980). Adapted from a discussion in Larry A. Samovar, Richard E. Porter, and Lisa A. Stefani, *Communication between Cultures* (Belmont, CA: Wadsworth, 1998).

9. Samovar, Porter, and Stefani, *Communication,* 68.

10. Disability Web site, 223–24.

CHAPTER 9

1. Richard F. Corlin, "The Coming Golden Age of Medicine," *Vital Speeches of the Day* 68, no. 18 (2002).

2. Pete Weissman, "Speechwriting Secrets from the Senate," *Vital Speeches of the Day* 69, no. 7 (2003).

3. K. Q. Seelye, "Congressman Offers Bill to Ban Cloning of Humans," *New York Times,* March 6, 1997, A3.

4. Bonnie Campbell, "Breaking the Silence on Domestic Violence," *Des Moines Register,* July 2, 1995, Op Ed. Retrieved from <http://www.ojp.usdoj.gov/vawo/speeches/bonoped.htm>.

5. Brock Evans, "A Gift for All of America" (address delivered to the Biennial Session, Wyoming Conservations Congress, Casper, WY, July 10, 1999). Retrieved May 1, 2000, from <http://www.votd.com/evans.htm>.

6. Ellen Greenlee, testimony before the U.S. House Committee on the Judiciary on the proposed victims-rights constitutional amendment, July 11, 1996. Retrieved April 28, 2000, from the World Wide Web: <http://gos.sbc.edu/c/chelian.html>.

7. J. C. Reinard, *Foundations of Argument* (Dubuque, IA: Wm. C. Brown, 1991).

8. Joseph A. Dear, "Work, Stress, and Health '95: Creating Healthier Workplaces," September 14, 1995. Retrieved May 23, 2000, from the World Wide Web: <http://www.osha-slc.gov/oshdoc/speechdata/sp19950914.html>.

9. Excerpted from S. R. Gawiser and G. E. Witt, *Twenty Questions a Journalist Should Ask about Poll Results,* 2nd ed. Retrieved July 2, 2002, from the National Council on Public Opinion Polls Web site: <http://www.ncpp.org/qajsa.htm>.

CHAPTER 10

1. Robert G. Torricelli, *Quotations for Public Speakers: A Historical, Literary, and Political Anthology* (New Brunswick, NJ: Rutgers University Press, 2002).

2. Robert J. Morgan, *Nelson's Complete Book of Stories, Illustrations, and Quotes: The Ultimate Contemporary Resource for Speakers* (Nashville: Thomas Nelson, 2000).

3. Robert Von Dassanowski, ed., *Gale Encyclopedia of Multicultural America,* 2nd ed. (Detroit: Gale Publications, 2000).

CHAPTER 11

1. Elizabeth Kirk, *Evaluating Information Found on the Internet.* The Sheridan Libraries of the Johns Hopkins University. Last modified

February 12, 2002. Retrieved May 4, 2002, from <http://www.library.jhu.edu/elp/useit/evaluate/counterfeit.html>.

2. Yelena Shapiro and Etelka Lehoczky, "Search engines," Searchengines.com Web site. Retrieved August 7, 2002, from <http://www.searchengines.com/search_engines_101.html>.

3. Ibid.

4. "Bare Bones 101. Lesson 4: Gateways and subject-specific databases." Page updated July 10, 2002. Board of Trustees of the University of South Carolina. Retrieved July 22, 2002, from <http://www.sc.edu/beaufort/library/lesson4.html>.

5. Ibid.

6. Ibid.

7. Andrew Harnack and Eugene Kleppinger, *Online! A Reference Guide to Using Internet Sources* (Boston: Bedford/St. Martin's, 2002), 3.

8. Ibid., 143.

CHAPTER 12

1. G. H. Bower, "Organizational Factors in Memory," *Cognitive Psychology* 1 (1970): 18–46.

2. Leonard J. Rosen and Laurence Behrens, *The Allyn & Bacon Handbook* (Needham, MA: Allyn & Bacon, 1992), 103.

CHAPTER 13

1. PBS, "Life on the Internet Timeline." Retrieved April 3, 2000, from <http://www.pbs.org/internet/timeline/index.html>.

2. Shadow Convention in Los Angeles Web site. Speech by Susan Sarandon and Tim Robbins on the war on drugs, August 15, 2000. Retrieved April 12, 2002, from <http://www.shadowconventions.com/speeches/robbinsspeech.htm>.

3. Sonja K. Foss and Karen A. Foss, *Inviting Transformation: Presentational Speaking for a Changing World* (Prospect Heights, IL: Waveland Press, 1994), 31.

CHAPTER 14

1. E. Thompson, "An Experimental Investigation of the Relative Effectiveness of Organization Structure in Oral Communication," *Southern Speech Journal* 26 (1960): 59–69; R. G. Smith, "Effects of Speech Organization upon Attitudes of College Students," *Speech Monographs* 18 (1951): 292–301; H. Sharp Jr. and T. McClung, "Effects of Organization on the Speaker's Ethos," *Speech Monographs* 33 (1966): 182ff.

2. Thomas J. Donahue, "Trucking's Agenda for Highway Safety," *Vital Speeches of the Day* 61, no. 15 (May 15, 1995): 477–80.

CHAPTER 15

1. Ron Hoff, *I Can See You Naked,* rev. ed. (Kansas City: Andrews McMeel, 1992), 41.

2. William Safire, *Lend Me Your Ears: Great Speeches in History* (New York: W. W. Norton, 1992), 676.

3. Edward P. J. Corbett, *Classical Rhetoric for the Modern Student,* 3rd ed. (New York: Oxford University Press, 1990).

4. W. Lee, "Communication about Humor as Procedural Competence in Intercultural Encounters," in *Intercultural Communication: A*

Reader, 7th ed., ed. L. A. Samovar and R. E. Porter (Belmont, CA: Wadsworth, 1994), 373.

5. Marvin Runyon, "No One Moves the Mail like the U.S. Postal Service," *Vital Speeches of the Day* 61, no. 2 (November 1, 1994): 52–55.

6. Robert L. Darbelnet, "U.S. Roads and Bridges," *Vital Speeches of the Day* 63, no. 12 (April 1, 1997): 379.

7. Bas Andeweg and Jap de Jong, "May I Have Your Attention?: Exordial Techniques in Informative Oral Presentations," *Technical Communication Quarterly* 7, no. 3 (Summer 1998): 271.

8. R. O. Skovgard, personal interview by author, June 10, 1995.

9. Holger Kluge, "Reflections on Diversity," *Vital Speeches of the Day* 63, no. 6 (January 1, 1997): 171–72.

10. William E. Kirwan, "Preventing School and Campus Violence," speech delivered to the SUNY Stony Brook Student–Community Wellness Leadership Symposium, Stony Brook, NY, February 15, 2000.

11. Hilary Rodham Clinton, "Women's Rights Are Human Rights," speech delivered to the United Nations Fourth World Conference on Women, Beijing, China, September 5, 1995.

CHAPTER 16

1. Robert Harris, "A Handbook of Rhetorical Devices," July 26, 2002, *Virtual Salt* Web site. Retrieved August 5, 2002, from <http://www.virtualsalt.com/rhetoric.htm>.

2. Peggy Noonan, *Simply Speaking: How to Communicate Your Ideas with Style, Substance, and Clarity* (New York: Regan Books, 1998), 51.

3. T. R. Horton, "That Old Management Magic," *Executive Speaker Newsletter* 9, no. 1 (October 5, 1987).

4. Andrea Lunsford and Robert Connors, *The St. Martin's Handbook,* 3rd ed. (New York: St. Martin's Press, 1995), 101.

5. L. Clemetson and J. Gordon-Thomas, "Our House Is on Fire," *Newsweek* 137 (June 11, 2001), 50.

6. *The Concise Oxford Dictionary of Linguistics* (Oxford University Press, 1997).

7. Gloria Anzaldúa, "Entering into the Serpent," in *The St. Martin's Handbook,* ed. Andrea Lunsford and Robert Conners (New York: St. Martin's Press, 1995), 25.

8. Howard K. Battles and Charles Packard, *Words and Sentences,* bk. 6 (Lexington, MA: Ginn & Company, 1984), 110.

9. Cited in William Safire, *Lend Me Your Ears: Great Speeches in History* (New York: W. W. Norton, 1992), 22.

10. Lunsford and Connors, *St. Martin's Handbook,* 345.

CHAPTER 17

1. James C. McCroskey, *An Introduction to Rhetorical Communication,* 8th ed. (Englewood Cliffs, NJ: Prentice-Hall, 2001), 273.

2. Robbin Crabtree and Robert Weissberg, *ESL Students in the Public Speaking Classroom: A Guide for Teachers* (Boston: Bedford/St. Martin's, 2000), 24.

CHAPTER 18

1. Susan Berkley, "Microphone Tips." *Great Speaking* ezine 4, no. 7 (2002). Retrieved September 1, 2002, from the Great Speaking Web site <http://www.antion.com>.

2. Kyle James Tusing and James Price Dillard, "The Sounds of Dominance: Vocal Precursors of Perceived Dominance during Interpersonal Influence," *Human Communication Research* 26 (2000): 148–71.

3. Lillian Wilder, *Seven Steps to Fearless Speaking* (New York: Wiley, 1999), 210–11. Reprinted with permission.

CHAPTER 19

1. Reid Buckley, *Strictly Speaking: Reid Buckley's Indispensable Handbook on Public Speaking* (New York: McGraw-Hill, 1999), 204.

2. Laurie Schloff and Marcia Yudkin, *Smart Speaking* (New York: Plume, 1991), 108.

3. Buckley, *Strictly Speaking,* 209.

4. J. P. Davidson, "Shaping an Image That Boosts Your Career," *Marketing Communications* 13 (1988): 55–56.

CHAPTER 20

1. Cheryl Currid, *Make Your Point: The Complete Guide to Successful Business Presentations Using Today's Technology* (Rocklin, CA: Prima Publishing, 1995), 117.

2. Robert Heinich, Michael Molenda, and James D. Russell, *Instructional Media and the New Technologies of Instruction,* 4th ed. (New York: Macmillan, 1993), 66.

3. Adapted from "Using Overhead Transparencies" by Lenny Laskowski. Retrieved December 2, 2002, from <http://www.ljlseminars.com/transp.htm>, and "Using Overhead Projectors" by Media Services, Robert A. L. Mortvedt Library, Pacific Lutheran University. Retrieved December 2, 2002, from <http://www.plu.edu/~librl/workshops/multimedia/overhead.html>.

CHAPTER 22

1. Ron Hoff, *I Can See You Naked,* rev. ed. (Kansas City: Andrews McMeel, 1992), 143.

CHAPTER 23

1. Howard K. Battles and Charles Packard, *Words and Sentences,* Bk. 6 (Lexington, MA: Ginn & Company, 1984), 459.

2. E. Thompson, "An Experimental Investigation of the Relative Effectiveness of Organization Structure in Oral Communication," *Southern Speech Journal* 26 (1966): 59–69.

3. Kenneth D. Frandsen and Donald A. Clement, "The Functions of Human Communication in Informing: Communicating and Processing Information," in *Handbook of Rhetorical and Communication Theory,* ed. Carroll C. Arnold and John Waite Bowers (Needham, MA: Allyn & Bacon, 1984), 334; R. E. Rowan, "A New Pedagogy for Explanatory Public Speaking: Why Arrangement Should Not Substitute for Invention," *Communication Education* 44 (1995): 236–50.

4. A. C. Nichols, "Effects of Three Aspects of Sentence Structure on Immediate Recall," *Speech Monographs* 32 (1965): 164–68.

CHAPTER 24

1. Richard E. Petty and John T. Cacioppo, *Communication and Persuasion: Central and Peripheral Routes to Attitude Change* (New York: Springer-Verlag, 1986).

2. Kathleen Reardon, *Persuasion in Practice* (Newbury Park, CA: Sage Publications, 1991), 210.

3. Russel H. Fazio, "How Do Attitudes Guide Behavior?" in *The Handbook of Motivation and Cognition: Foundations of Social Behavior,* ed. Richard M. Sorrentino and E. Tory Higgins (New York: Guilford, 1986).

4. Reprinted from Gregory R. Suriano, *Great American Speeches* (New York: Gramercy Books, 1993), 298–303.

5. Joseph R. Priester and Richard E. Petty, "Source Attributions and Persuasion: Perceived Honesty as a Determinant of Message Scrutiny," *Personality and Social Psychology Bulletin* 21 (1995): 637–54. See also Kenneth G. DeBono and Richard J. Harnish, "Source Expertise, Source Attractiveness, and the Processing of Persuasive Information: A Functional Approach," *Journal of Personality and Social Psychology* 55 (1987): 541.

6. Richard Petty and John T. Cacioppo, "The Elaboration Likelihood Model of Persuasion," in *Advances in Experimental Social Psychology* 19, ed. L. Berkowitz (San Diego: Academic Press, 1986), 123–205; Richard Petty and Duane T. Wegener, "Matching versus Mismatching Attitude Functions: Implications for Scrutiny of Persuasive Messages," *Personality and Social Psychology Bulletin* 24 (1998): 227–40.

7. Dennis S. Gouran, "Attitude Change and Listeners' Understanding of a Persuasive Communication," *Speech Teacher* 15 (1966): 289–94; J. P. Dillard, "Persuasion Past and Present: Attitudes Aren't What They Used to Be," *Communication Monographs* 60 (1966): 94.

8. Adapted from J. C. McCroskey, *An Introduction to Rhetorical Communication,* 6th ed. (Englewood Cliffs, NJ: Prentice-Hall, 1993).

9. Ibid.

10. Edward P. J. Corbett, *Classical Rhetoric for the Modern Student,* 3rd ed. (New York: Oxford University Press, 1990).

11. Herbert Simon, *Persuasion in Society* (Thousand Oaks, CA: Sage Publications, 2001), 385–87.

12. A. H. Monroe, *Principles and Types of Speeches* (Chicago: Scott, Foresman, 1935).

13. James R. DiSanza and Nancy J. Legge, *Business and Professional Communication: Plans, Processes, and Performance,* 2nd ed. (Boston: Allyn & Bacon, 2002), 236.

CHAPTER 25

1. Roger E. Axtell, *Do's and Taboos of Public Speaking: How to Get Those Butterflies Flying in Formation* (New York: Wiley, 1992), 150.

CHAPTER 26

1. For a review, see Priscilla S. Rogers, "Distinguishing Public and Presentational Speaking," *Management Communication Quarterly* 2 (1988): 102–15; Frank E. X. Dance, "What Do You Mean 'Presentational' Speaking?" *Management Communication Quarterly* 1 (1987): 270–81.

2. L. Kroeger, *The Complete Idiot's Guide to Successful Business Presentations* (New York: Alpha Books, 1997), 113.

3. Edward S. Inch and Barbara Warnick, *Critical Thinking and Communication: The Use of Reason in Argument,* 3rd ed. (Boston: Allyn & Bacon, 1998).

4. With thanks to Michal Dale of Southwest Missouri State University's Department of Communication.

5. Some points are derived from Robert Anholt, *Dazzle 'Em with Style: The Art of Oral Scientific Presentation* (New York: W. H. Freeman and Company, 1994); see also the Web site for Colorado State University's "Guides about Speeches and Presentations," section on poster sessions (August 28, 2000). Retrieved September 2, 2000, from <http://writing.colostate.edu/references/speaking.htm>.

CHAPTER 27

1. Robert Anholt, *Dazzle 'Em with Style: The Art of Oral Scientific Presentation* (New York: W. H. Freeman and Company, 1994).

CHAPTER 28

1. Deanna P. Daniels, "Communicating across the Curriculum and in the Disciplines: Speaking in Engineering," *Communication Education* 51 (July 2002): 3.

2. Ibid.

3. Ibid.

4. Office of Naval Research Web site. "Tips for Preparing and Delivering Scientific Talks and Using Visual Aids." Retrieved January 1, 2001, from <http://www.onr.navy.mil/onr/speak/>.

5. Frederick Gilbert Associates. "Power-Speaking Tips." Retrieved August 30, 2000, from <http://www.powerspeaking.com/powerspeaking/pstips.cfm>.

CHAPTER 29

1. James M. Henslin, *Sociology: A Down-to-Earth Approach,* 5th ed. (Boston: Allyn & Bacon, 2001), 139.

2. William E. Thompson and James V. Hickey, *Society in Focus: An Introduction to Sociology,* 2nd ed. (New York: HarperCollins, 1966), 39.

CHAPTER 33

1. H. Dan O'Hair, James S. O'Rourke, and Mary John O'Hair, *Business Communication: A Framework for Success* (Cincinnati: South-Western, 2001).

2. H. Dan O'Hair, Gustav Friedrich, and Lynda Dixon, *Strategic Communication for Business and the Professions,* 4th ed. (Boston: Houghton Mifflin, 2002).

3. K. D. Benne and P. Sheats, "Functional Roles of Group Members," *Journal of Social Issues* 4 (1948): 41–49.

4. Ibid.

5. M. Afzalur Rahim, *Managing Conflict in Organizations,* 3rd ed. (Westport, CT: Greenwood Publishing Group, 2001).

6. Dan O'Hair, Gustav Friedrich, John Wiemann, and Mary Wiemann, *Competent Communication,* 2nd ed. (New York: St. Martin's, 1997).

7. Geoffrey A. Cross, "Collective Form: An Exploration of Large-Group Writing," *Journal of Business Communication* 37 (2000): 77–101.

8. Irving Lester Janis, *Groupthink: Psychological Studies of Policy Decisions and Fiascoes* (Berkeley: University of California Press, 1982).

9. O'Hair, Friedrich, and Dixon, *Strategic Communication for Business and the Professions.*

10. Victor H. Vroom and Philip Yetton, *Leadership and Decision Making* (Pittsburgh: University of Pittsburgh Press, 1973); C. Pavitt, "Theorizing about the Group Communication-Leadership Relationship: Input-Process-Output and Functional Models," in *Handbook of Group Communication Theory and Research,* ed. Lawrence R. Frey, Dennis S. Gouran, and Marshall Scott Poole (Thousand Oaks, CA: Sage, 1999), 313–34.

11. L. Richard Hoffman and Norman R. F. Maier, "Valence in the Adoption of Solutions by Problem-Solving Groups: Concept, Method, and Results," *Journal of Abnormal and Social Psychology* 69 (1964): 264–71.

12. John Dewey, *How We Think* (Boston: D. C. Heath Co, 1950).

CHAPTER 34

1. Part of this classification of business presentations is adapted from Raymond V. Lesikar, John D. Pettit Jr., and Marie E. Flatley, *Lesikar's Basic Business Communication,* 8th ed. (New York: McGraw-Hill, 1999).

2. William L. Benoit, *Accounts, Excuses, and Apologies: A Theory of Image Restoration Strategies* (Albany: State University of New York Press, 1995).

3. Ibid.

4. Business for Social Responsibility Web site, "Business Ethics," copyright 2001–2002. Retrieved October 2, 2002, from <http://www.bsr.org/BSRResources/WhitePaperDetail.conf.>.

APPENDIX B

1. Patricia Nelson (Page revised Nov. 3, 1999). "Handling Questions and Answers." Toastmasters International, Edmonton and Area. Retrieved September 1, 2000, from <http://www.ecn.ab.ca/toast/qa.html>.

2. Diane DiResta, *Knockout Presentations: How to Deliver Your Message with Power, Punch, and Pizzazz* (Worcester, MA: Chandler House Press, 1998), 236.

3. Ibid., 237.

4. Lillian Wilder, *Talk Your Way to Success* (New York: Eastside Publishing, 1986), 279.

APPENDIX C

1. Lillian Wilder, *Talk Your Way to Success* (New York: Eastside Publishing, 1986), 281.

2. D. R. Bowman, *Presentations: Proven Techniques for Creating Presentations That Get Results* (Holbrook, MA: Adams Media), 177.

3. Oklahoma Society of CPAs (OSCPA). "Tips for successful media interviewing."

4. Adapted from Diane Howard, "Guidelines for Videoconference Presentations, Performances, and Teaching." Retrieved August 25, 2000, from <http://www.dianehoward.com>.

APPENDIX D

1. E. Flege, J. M. Munro, and I. R. A. MacKay, "Factors Affecting Strength of Perceived Foreign Accent in a Second Language," *Journal of the Acoustical Society of America* 97 (1995): 3125ff.

2. The content in this section is based on Robbin Crabtree and

Robert Weissberg, *ESL Students in the Public Speaking Classroom,* 2nd ed. (Boston: Bedford/St. Martin's, 2003), 23.

3. M. C. Florez, "Improving Adult ESL Learners' Pronunciation Skills." *National Clearinghouse for ESL Literacy Education,* 1998. Retrieved April 10, 2000, from <http://www.cal.org/NCLE/DIGESTS /Pronun.htm>.

4. Ibid.

5. Robert Anholt, *Dazzle 'Em with Style: The Art of Oral Scientific Presentation* (New York: W. H. Freeman & Co, 1994), 156.

Index

QUICK TIPS

CHECKLISTS

Getting Started

Development

Organization

Starting, Finishing, and Styling

Delivery

Presentation Aids

Types of Speeches

The Classroom and Beyond

CONTENTS